Becoming
Whole *and*
Holy

BECOMING WHOLE *and* HOLY

An Integrative Conversation about Christian Formation

JEANNINE K. BROWN, CARLA M. DAHL,
AND WYNDY CORBIN REUSCHLING

Baker Academic
a division of Baker Publishing Group
Grand Rapids, Michigan

© 2011 by Jeannine K. Brown, Carla M. Dahl, and Wyndy Corbin Reuschling

Published by Baker Academic
a division of Baker Publishing Group
P.O. Box 6287, Grand Rapids, MI 49516-6287
www.bakeracademic.com

Printed in the United States of America

Library of Congress Cataloging-in-Publication Data
Brown, Jeannine K., 1961–
  Becoming whole and holy : an integrative conversation about Christian formation / Jeannine K. Brown, Carla M. Dahl, and Wyndy Corbin Reuschling.
    p.   cm.
  Includes bibliographical references and index.
  ISBN 978-0-8010-3925-6
  1. Christian life. 2. Spiritual formation. I. Dahl, Carla M. II. Reuschling, Wyndy Corbin. III. Title.
  BV4511.B74 2011
  248.4—dc22   2010018159

11   12   13   14   15   16   17   7   6   5   4   3   2   1

To Robert Rakestraw

mentor, colleague, encourager, friend,
and most of all, exemplar of wholeness and holiness

Contents

ACKNOWLEDGMENTS

Where do we start? Our collaboration for this work has been supported and affirmed by many individuals and institutions. We are thankful that our collegial relationships and subsequent friendships were made possible by our affiliations with Bethel Theological Seminary. We are indebted to Provost Emeritus Leland Eliason, whose vision of integrative theological education both informed and energized our teaching and scholarship. Both Ashland Theological Seminary and Bethel are communities committed to an integrative approach to teaching and learning. We are grateful to be part of our respective institutions and appreciate the opportunities they afford for our own formation as teachers, scholars, activists, and colleagues.

This project was initially funded by a grant from the Bethel Seminary Alumni Council that made possible our initial face-to-face conversations in St. Paul. Jeannine took on the responsibility to secure funding (for which Carla and Wyndy say, "Thanks!"). We appreciate this early vote of confidence that helped us in the important formative stages of our project. The continuation of this work has been made possible through the Lilly Theological Research Grants program of the Association of Theological Schools, from which we are honored to have received a collaborative research grant for 2009–10.

We are appreciative of the many individuals who were interested in what we were doing, and why, and how our work was coming together in this collaborative project. We can't name them all, but we must name some because of the more direct interaction they offered with the manuscript at various stages. Our colleague and friend Steve Sandage read the manuscript in its entirety and offered thoughtful, integrative ideas and suggestions that we incorporated at many points. Likewise, colleague and friend Peter Vogt offered insights to Jeannine on her interaction with Old Testament themes of being, becoming, wholeness, and holiness.

For the initial spark and some refining flames, we are grateful to the students in three Bethel Seminary courses: Gospels and Formation (winter 2006), Hermeneutics and Human Development (winter 2009), and Becoming Whole and Holy (2010). Ross Jahnke and Tim Johnson, students at Bethel Seminary, provided close grammatical and literary readings of every section of the manuscript, as good graduate assistants in hermeneutics are apt to do. Their skills, good natures, and interest in this topic were invaluable and special thanks must go to them. The "formation guys" of Bethel's Center for Spiritual and Personal Formation—postgraduate teaching fellows Brian Majerus, Joel Jueckstock, and Shane Long—read with care, insight, and an amazing facility with short timelines. Kevin Himes, Tracy Kallio, Rob Sportsman, and Val Wysocki, all students from Ashland Seminary, read Wyndy's chapters and, in a grand act of role reversal, prodded with helpful suggestions and questions.

Our editor Rodney Clapp, executive editor at Baker Academic and Brazos Press, expressed enthusiasm in our early conversations that did not waver as we wrote on. Both Rodney and Lisa Ann Cockrel, editor at Baker Academic and Brazos Press, challenged our thinking about the dynamics of collaborative writing in ways that helped us hold in dynamic tension this one work in three voices. We would be remiss if we didn't publicly say thanks for the breakfasts, lunches, and coffee breaks with Rodney and Lisa while at AAR, SBL, or the Society of Christian Ethics. We are proud to be associated with the skilled, visionary editors and publishing community of Baker Academic and Brazos Press.

It will be obvious to our readers that we continue to be deeply formed by our relationships with each other and the others in our lives. This book was written in the context of the relationships between the three of us as we shared many conversations, lots of laughs, not a few tears, conference calls, flurries of email exchanges, and trips to and from airports in the midst of our nonwriting lives. These were not interruptions but rather great gifts for common reflection and formation. For us the very idea of wholeness means that the personal is public. A special note of gratitude is offered to those who continually make us who we are, the dogs with whom we walk (Heidi, Bella, Parker, and Trek) and the people who help us create home: Tim, Kate, Libby, Katie, and Mike.

One of our most memorable conversations occurred in the living room of our Bethel friend and colleague Robert Rakestraw (for Bob's Benediction Project, go to http://bobrakestraw.blogspot.com/). Carla made spontaneous arrangements at the end of one of Wyndy's early trips to St. Paul to spend time with Bob and his wife, Judy. Bob never fails to take us and our work seriously and is so eager to hear about this project. Even in the crucible of facing the end of his life, his openness to God and hospitality to others make Bob an inspiring expression of a whole and holy life. It is to Bob Rakestraw that we dedicate this book.

PROLOGUE
Introducing Ourselves

Fragmentation is a common experience at the beginning of this twenty-first century: the fracturing of families, cultures, organizations, and identities. While the problem of fragmentation is often laid at the feet of postmodernity, we posit that the modern paradigm, despite its apparent solidity, created false cohesion on a variety of levels. One significant example is the way the Western, modern idea of identity as self-sufficiency destabilizes relationships and thereby undermines an authentic self in relationship.

As scholars in three distinct disciplines, as colleagues engaged in the preparation of ministry leaders, and as friends negotiating the complexities of our social contexts, we find ourselves responding to this fragmentation with a plea for true cohesion. We believe the most promising path toward it emerges from a willingness to attend to formation in a holistic, integrative way.

The centerpiece of this book, therefore, is a conversation between three disciplines about the topic of Christian formation. Our goal is to explore the journey toward becoming whole and holy from the vantage points of social science, biblical hermeneutics, and Christian ethics. We do this with our students in mind, as well as the persons to whom they minister. We hope this conversation will also serve as a guide for faith communities as they journey from fragmentation toward integration.

To speak of these three disciplines apart from our professional and personal backgrounds would provide a less than complete and authentic introduction to this book. So we begin with an introduction to who we are individually and in relationship, our ongoing conversations with one another, and the emergence of the project that this book explores.

Our Selves and Contexts

Equipped with degrees in English literature, counseling psychology, and family sociology, I (Carla Dahl) found myself (somewhat to my surprise) in a seminary, with the privilege of developing a training program for marriage and family therapists. The accompanying privilege of joining a broad, interdisciplinary, integrative conversation quickly became a source of challenge, energy, and delight. As a member of a deeply collaborative formation team since 1995, I have had the opportunity to imagine and implement new ways of inviting students, as well as staff and faculty, into crucibles of formation in which their understandings of God, themselves, and others are refined. My grounding beliefs about formation are that God accomplishes it best in trustworthy community and that God's deep desire is to work through the person of the therapist, minister, or teacher more than through their techniques, theories, strategies, or interventions. The capacity for reflective practice therefore becomes a critical skill for those in the serving professions.

I (Jeannine Brown) teach New Testament and biblical hermeneutics, as I have since 1995, to seminary students. Since my doctoral work focused on a narrative reading of the Matthean disciples, I am particularly passionate about holistic readings of the Gospels that pay attention to the storied nature of each Gospel—the story it communicates within the stories it assumes and from which it arises. This kind of literary reading, with keen attention to historical moorings, leads naturally to a theological reading of the Gospels (and other biblical books as well). My interest in and writing on biblical hermeneutics attempt to take seriously these reading commitments while also engaging questions of contextualization, which ask how Scripture should and does form Christian communities and individuals in particular settings.

After graduating from college, I (Wyndy Corbin Reuschling) pursued the path of vocational Christian ministry in a variety of settings: parachurch, overseas missions, social services, and churches. I have always been intrigued with and committed to the social implications of Christian faith, perhaps due to growing up in the United Methodist Church and imbibing the Wesleyan spirit of social holiness. These sets of experiences provided the contexts for the questions and interests that would eventually result in my decision to pursue doctoral studies in Christian social ethics. I am fascinated with how Christians translate their faith claims into moral commitments and ethical practices, and how we respond to social issues with a distinctly Christian perspective. These commitments overflow into the vocational privilege of teaching ethics and theology in a seminary where women and men are training for and anticipating pastoral ministry.

Our Relationships and Intersections

Our three paths came together while teaching and leading at Bethel Seminary. Carla and Jeannine have been colleagues at Bethel Seminary–St. Paul for almost a decade. Wyndy spent five years at Bethel Seminary of the East, during which time faculty retreats provided opportunity for relationships to develop and for our scholarly conversations to begin. We were drawn together as colleagues, as women pursuing our vocations in the context of theological education, and as friends. These friendships have continued over the years and distances even as institutional locations have changed.

In 2006 we (Carla and Jeannine) taught a course together on the Gospels and spiritual and personal formation that sparked all kinds of intriguing conversations from the interaction of our disciplines both in and out of the classroom. The course intention was that, in the convergence of the disciplines of hermeneutics and social sciences, we all would find our perceived images of God illuminated, revealed, challenged, and brought more in line with truth. The directions pursued in these class sessions were delightfully surprising, both to students and to the two of us. It became clear that bringing two scholars from different disciplines into conversation with each other, and with eager and bright students, opens up a fertile space for dialogical learning. Such learning increases exponentially what a single discipline might offer for integrative learning.

The dialogue begun in that course has led to this book. Early on, we (Carla and Jeannine) recognized the value of bringing moral formation into our work on personal and spiritual formation and its relationship to Scripture. Without hesitation we invited Wyndy, our favorite ethicist, into the dialogue from which this book has emerged. As the three of us have interacted with one another in person and on the page, we have become deeply aware of this truth: offering fruits from our own disciplines to a collaborative endeavor challenges us and invites exploration of assumptions and convictions, thereby enriching our own understandings and work. In the end, beyond the production of this book the three of us have been and continue to be formed by our dialogue. Formation is not just our topic of discussion; it has been the fruit of the discussion for our own lives and work. And for this we are grateful.

LOCATION

Our Selves, Our Disciplines, Our Process

Our overarching goal in this book is to propose ways of conceiving of human formation (becoming), wholeness, and holiness informed by the insights of the social sciences, biblical hermeneutics, and ethics. In this chapter we begin by speaking to the promise and challenge of collaboration. We locate ourselves within our disciplines and identify some of our assumptions. We then explain why questions of becoming, wholeness, and holiness are important for each of us personally and for this conversation. We conclude by describing our integrative method.

Collaboration as a Pathway to Integration

Collaborative work is a gift and a challenge, as are the attempts to integrate the insights and contributions of our respective disciplines in the social sciences, hermeneutics, and Christian ethics. We embrace this gift and challenge in order to present an integrated understanding of formation and to offer an expanded conception of human wholeness and holiness in the context of Christian faith. Collaboration is a gift in that it expands our understandings, exposes our limitations, energizes our imaginations, and prods us to see beyond the narrow confines of our disciplines. Collaborative work is challenging for the same reasons. It is hard work to wrestle with our assumptions, to own our limitations, and to risk putting ourselves and our ideas "out there" in conversation with other people. This risk is heightened by the tendency to view others as competitors instead of dialogue partners. It is certainly much more convenient and simple to work within the confines of our own disciplines, and to converse with people and ideas that are more accessible and likely more agreeable to our preexisting convictions.

Yet we believe collaborative and integrated thinking is essential for addressing the questions we are posing about human becoming, wholeness, and holiness. Why?

First, these three areas—the social sciences, hermeneutics, and ethics—are important avenues for understanding what it means to be human. They are crucial for answering complex questions about becoming, wholeness, and holiness. No one discipline is omnicompetent to address the "thick" questions related to our humanity.[1] Social sciences, hermeneutics, and ethics each say something about wholeness, holiness, and becoming. The questions that inspire thinking, research, and debate in each discipline come from different theoretical and methodical standpoints, offering the possibility of enriching the conversation. This is especially the case given the methodological angles of our disciplines. While hermeneutics and ethics tend to locate themselves primarily in prescription (What should be?), social sciences offer methods for description (What is?). Together these disciplines can expand our access to truth about what it means to be human.

Second, questions about our humanity are communal and not just personal concerns. Both our sense of the self and our image of the whole and holy person are shaped and supported—or subverted and suppressed—by the social contexts in which we are located and in which we become. We are particularly concerned with exploring the various social contexts and sources that aid us in understanding what it means to become and be more human. For us these focus on formation, scriptural interpretation, and morality. The three of us are located as white, Western (American), middle-class, highly educated professional women who first met as colleagues in an evangelical seminary. We are aware of the ways in which our own contexts have offered us images and perceptions of what it means to be human,

2

white, female, Christian, and American privileged professionals, identities that are often in competition with one another and send mixed messages for what it means to be whole and holy. We recognize these influences, yet in no way do we claim them as normative criteria for understanding becoming, wholeness, and holiness. Instead, we will attempt, by bringing together insights from the social sciences, hermeneutics, and ethics, to offer an integrative conception of becoming that is more faithful to the purposes of God and reflective of actual human experience. We hope the result will be more dynamic understandings of wholeness and holiness.

Finally, we believe this kind of integrated narrative of wholeness and holiness is essential for ministry formation. In other words, the social sciences, hermeneutics, and ethics are crucial for the practices of ministry. How one engages with Scripture is both a formative and a moral act. What we do with what we believe is a matter of ethics. What we do, in turn, forms us in very particular ways and directs us to desired ends. Those wanting to take more seriously the ways in which persons and communities can be formed in ongoing patterns of dynamic faithfulness will find engaged (and we hope engaging!) conversation partners in this book. Those interested in richer ways of interpreting and allowing Scripture to set our moral agendas will discover a deeper appreciation for the myriad ways that Scripture speaks about becoming, wholeness, and holiness. Those wanting a more socially engaged, holistic morality that pays attention to the becoming and well-being of other selves may find expanded ideas of what wholeness and holiness mean for how we actually live together. By bringing our respective disciplines together we offer a proposal for becoming whole and holy persons. This project is intended for people of faith who want to open themselves to the formative work of God in their lives, who care about reading and understanding Scripture well, and who want to do justice and love mercy. We also believe these are important concerns for Christian leaders who desire what is good, right, and true for faith communities.

The Social Sciences and Formation (Carla)

Before I knew sciences as natural or social, before I knew formation as a discipline, I was drawn to notions of being and becoming

3

not as conceptual categories but as realities experienced primarily through story. When I was a child, reading provided companionship, adventure, respite, safety—all the things that make that activity pleasurable. Also, stories began to build a template for noticing and appreciating process (those wonderful beginnings, middles, and endings) and development (characters, plot, and subtext). Those early notions of being and becoming laid a foundation for academic and professional experiences with qualitative research and narrative therapies. These have become an integrating motif in my teaching, research, and therapy.

I have found significant contributions to being and becoming in the social sciences, particularly as they are in conversation with other disciplines. My primary assumption about social sciences is that they are human endeavors to understand truth God offers through both special and general revelation. As human endeavors they are fallible (as are all human attempts to understand the triune God, whether through avenues of social science, natural science, formal science, or the humanities). However, they are not inherently more fallible than other human endeavors conducted with curiosity, integrity, and skill. In their attempts to apprehend and understand the whole of truth present in Scripture and the created world, they inform and are informed by the work of other disciplines. Dennis Hiebert, in his exceedingly helpful discussion of dialogue between sociology and theology, describes this mutuality.

> For biblical scholars and theologians, worldview and scholastic methods often are undifferentiated; their methods employ their entire worldview and their worldview is represented entirely in their methods. For Christian social scientists, worldview and scholastic methods are strongly differentiated; their methods do not employ their entire worldview and their worldview is not represented entirely in their methods. . . . However, worldview does not necessarily dictate method or vice versa.[2]

I also hold some foundational assumptions about formation. First, I see formation, like faith, as a human universal.[3] Psychology and neurobiology provide compelling evidence that humans are created for development, relationship, and integration—all of which are dimensions

4

of formation.[4] Not only are those needs and desires hardwired in our bodies, but they were also evident in Jesus's body as God incarnate.

My personal and professional experiences have also led me to assume that formation is inherently invitational. Most of us have learned—whether through teaching, parenting, gardening, or wishing for change in our own lives—that growth cannot be produced upon demand. Well, one can demand it, but it isn't likely that such a demand will result in authentic development. Even scriptural commands for holy living are framed in the context of a relationship that begins with God's invitation.

In addition to being invitational, formation is multidimensional. We enter through many portals, relative to all of life's dimensions: spiritual, emotional, relational, physical, financial, sexual, and so on. Formation incorporates a broad range of contextual factors that persons bring to their formation: social location, culture, ethnicity, gender, disability, age, family of origin, temperament, physical health, faith journey, and theological commitments. When God works in us nothing is useless, and nothing is spared.

I expect that this energizing conversation with Wyndy and Jeannine will continue to be an avenue through which God further forms me. As I listen more deeply to their insights, questions, the contributions of their disciplines, and the experiences that have shaped their perspectives—in other words, as our stories are shaped by one another's—I will be enjoying again the excitement that comes with new understandings of being and becoming.

Hermeneutics and Biblical Interpretation (Jeannine)

My journey with the Bible was initially shaped by a deeply held conviction that it was written to me and my world. As a teenager I was captivated by a close reading of Bible passages and their immediate applicability to my life. In my college years I became increasingly aware that there was a historical distance between my world and the world in which the Bible was written. As a seminarian I was thrown into the biblical worlds of the ancient Near East and the Greco-Roman and Jewish convictions and practices of the first century.

My assumptions about the Bible changed significantly and profoundly in the ensuing years. My first naiveté, Paul Ricoeur's term for the assumption that the Bible speaks directly and immediately to me, was supplanted by a keen awareness of the reality of the gap between my location and that of the Bible. Out of this set of experiences came a healthy respect for the otherness of the Bible and a conviction of the necessity of reading it on its own terms. Doing so fostered a commitment to knowing what type of literature I was reading (genre analysis), the setting of any particular biblical book (historical analysis), the full scope of that biblical book (literary analysis), as well as attention to the book's placement and role in the Bible more broadly (canonical analysis).

As I became increasingly aware of the gap between my world and that of the Bible, a second assumption soon developed within me. This was the fundamental conviction that I, along with all interpreters, am finite and located. I cannot attain or possess a pure, objective reading of the Bible. This means that hermeneutics is unavoidable. Biblical hermeneutics—intentional reflection on oneself and one's community in the reading of the Bible, with constant attention to the contexts of both the reader and the Bible—is a necessary part of responsible theological engagement with the Bible.[5] As I put it in an earlier book,

> We [listen well to the Bible] by knowing ourselves and what we bring to our reading of the Bible, as well as what might get in the way of hearing the message of the Bible. We listen well by reading the Bible on its own terms, not assuming that we have always understood its message, not imposing our own messages on it.[6]

Gratefully, what Paul Ricoeur calls the second naiveté has been a reality in my ongoing interaction with the Bible.[7] Even as I honor it as from another time and place, I regain the experience of the Bible as addressed to me (a second naiveté). This brings me to another related assumption: that the Bible still speaks. The Bible is Scripture, a word from God for our world and for God's people in particular. The assumption that the Bible continues to speak long after its inception is not to say that it always speaks simply or directly to contemporary life and issues. While the Bible speaks and guides, we must discern its messages in other than simplistic ways. We do this by taking seriously the differences between the original and our contemporary contexts. Yet this serious historical engagement does not dilute the ways in which the Bible continues to speak powerfully, and with a claim on me and my world. Recontextualization of Scripture's original messages is the work of all Christians and a crucial task of biblical hermeneutics practiced from a confessional vantage point.[8]

Another, final, assumption about the Bible is particularly relevant to this project. Scripture not only teaches the Christian community; it also (and maybe more importantly) *forms* individuals and communities of faith. As Joel Green affirms, "We come [to Scripture] not so much to retrieve facts or to gain information, but to be formed."[9] Scripture shapes whole persons, not only minds. It certainly communicates at a cognitive level, but to limit its role and influence to this level is to cut off a primary means of our own personal, moral, and spiritual formation. As we acknowledge and live into the reality of Scripture's role in forming us into wholeness and holiness, we will not only study and analyze Scripture, but we will allow it to analyze us. We will entrust ourselves to the clarifying and shaping gaze of the Scriptures and the God who communicates with us through them.[10]

How does Scripture guide its readers toward becoming whole and holy—toward spiritual formation? That question will frame my contribution to this conversation.[11] The disciplines of biblical studies and hermeneutics hold a monopoly neither on this question nor on the answers that emerge from reading Scripture for formation. The reading I offer is my own reading, informed by my study and my academic discipline. I offer my reading since I am located in a particular context, which effectively opens some avenues of exploration while hiding others. So I welcome the opportunity to join Wyndy and Carla in reflection on their reading of Scripture, their thinking about and practice of spiritual formation, and their own moral discernment.

Christian Ethics and Morality (Wyndy)

Early in my graduate studies in Christian social ethics at Drew University, my advisor, Dr. Traci West, offered a powerful and poignant piece of advice that has stuck with me: "If this work doesn't matter for somebody, then it doesn't matter." This initial conversation set the stage for how I came to understand what I was doing in graduate studies. More importantly, it helped me keep clear why I was pursuing teaching and research, and how I was to go about my vocation as a Christian social ethicist. Dr. West's words of wisdom became part of the assumptions that now inform some fundamental commitments I have made about Christian ethics, the moral life, and ideas about human wholeness and holiness.

First, I understand the adjective "Christian" to be an important qualifier for how we conceive of the shape, content, and purpose of the moral life.[12] Christian ethics is foremost about discerning the normativity of Jesus Christ for our moral vision. I mean "moral vision" broadly: our conception of what is good and fitting, our interpretation of duties and obligations, and our images and descriptions of what whole and holy persons and communities look like (or should look like). Christian ethics asks, What difference does being a Christian make for how I conceive of the moral life and for how I ethically deliberate and discern who I am, who I am becoming, and what I am to do? It is here that Christian ethics is linked with my understanding of discipleship. Discipleship is the lifelong task of learning to follow Jesus, being formed into his image, and discerning "what is fitting to, or worthy of, the *gospel*" in order to live faithfully in our varied social contexts.[13] It is from Jesus that we take our clues about what is good and holy, about who we are, and about what we are to do.

The adjective "Christian" also means we draw on the sources of Christian faith, including Scripture, tradition, reason, and experience. Most Christian ethicists agree on the authority and normativity of Scripture in Christian ethics while not always agreeing on how we bring scriptural claims, ideas, and paradigms to bear on real-world issues. This disagreement arises from the hermeneutical necessities and complexities of working with Scripture and its implications for our lives.[14] One of my fundamental assumptions is that Scripture shapes the Christian moral life and informs our ethical deliberations in surprising, complex, and rich ways. Scripture offers us a compelling moral vision, a narrative context of understanding our duties and obligations to God and others, and paths of wisdom and virtue necessary for becoming whole and holy moral agents.

Second, I understand the Christian moral life to be essentially social. It is formed, shaped, and exercised in community and relies on the capacity of humans to think and care about others. Christian ethics is not (just or only) about my personal sense of piety, my personal ethical code of conduct, or the guarantee that I will act rightly in the world if I claim to be right with God. It is not the tight-fisted adherence to ungrounded or overly simplistic principles and absolutes lobbed from some pulpits and podiums. The social dynamics of Christian morality mean that the moral life is concrete, embodied, and dynamic. It involves an acknowledgment of interdependence—what Robert Roberts calls "the tissue of mutual dependencies"—as crucial for ethical deliberation.[15] The fact that we exist, are created in God's image, and share space with others means we bear responsibilities for them to various degrees. Our lives impinge upon theirs and theirs on ours. Christian ethics takes seriously our shared social contexts as moral spaces, acknowledging their power to construct our ideas about wholeness and holiness in ways that may actually truncate human becoming or legitimate the harming of some people.

Third, Christian morality is more than casuistry or quandary ethics. While decisions are important and ethical conundrums require thoughtful analysis, the Christian moral life also encompasses who we are and who we are becoming as fundamentally important. Christian ethics provides us the tools and ways of asking questions about who we are and what we believe for how we should live and make decisions. Therefore, Christian ethics involves the shaping of our character, affections, and dispositions. It is also about learning and practicing the skills to think about the moral life from the perspective of Christian faith and discerning how to bring these claims to bear on actual issues.

I have much to learn from Carla and Jeannine. I am eager to hear, receive, and integrate their insights. Given the interdependence of our lives, questions about humanity are central to Christian morality. Theology and ethics can provide some insights into these often neglected questions; so can social sciences and hermeneutics.

Our Motivating Questions

In this section the three of us explore the questions that brought us to this interdisciplinary, integrative conversation. Subsequent chapters will suggest answers to some of those questions, as well as more questions emerging from some of those answers. Our intention is not to arrive at a hypothetical end point at which integration is finished and we (or the reader) are through "becoming." Rather, we intend to describe a model for this kind of conversation and demonstrate that model through the structure and content of this book. We do so not because we want to institute a normative pattern for all interdisciplinary study of humanity and becoming human, but because we want to engage in a transparent process, one in which we show our work so that others might discover the integrative possibilities in their own contexts.

The central question for our project has been, What does it mean to be human? The importance of this question comes from its centrality to Christian faith and practice. In turn, the question of human meaning generates other questions. What do we believe about wholeness and holiness? How are they embodied and developed in the experience of an individual and a community?

Our title implies our primary answer to our central question: "being fully human means becoming whole and holy." But this is where the integrative conversation begins. In our respective disciplines we have each seen this question addressed narrowly, simplistically, or in isolation. Sometimes the answer is assumed, as though we would all "just know" and agree on a definition of holiness. At other times wholeness is limited to the spiritual in contradistinction to the physical. Sometimes formation is approached as if becoming or formation is automatic.

Given these tendencies we believe that the topic of formation— or becoming whole and holy—deserves a robust interdisciplinary conversation. The importance of the question of human being and becoming requires us to entertain it as a complex question, connected to other categories. For this reason we have developed the following process. Each of us, in two chapters, offers perspectives on dimensions of this central question from her discipline, trying to maintain nuance and connection through the use of "thick" description that allows each discipline its full voice (chaps. 2–3, 5–6, and 8–9). Complexity and connection are developed further in response chapters that allow the other two of us listening in to discuss, validate, raise questions, and define points of convergence and divergence (chaps. 4, 7, and 10).

Once we have wondered, speculated, resisted, welcomed—in short, integrated—we conclude with a chapter of conversation (chap. 11) between the three of us on an ethical issue (immigration), a specific biblical text (Acts 10:1–11:18), and a spiritual practice (prayerful listening). We intend this final turn to enact and illustrate the complexities and benefits of integrative conversation. We also provide in that final chapter an integrative summary of our work on wholeness, holiness, and becoming.

A Thicker Description of Our Integrative Method

We wrestled in initial phases of this conversation to define a structure for this intended activity and outcome and eventually arrived at a process we call *offering, reception,* and *integration*. One author offers, the other two receive, then we all integrate. Of course, the responses also become offerings, which the initial author receives, with the intention that we all engage in ongoing integration within and across disciplines in ways that make a difference in life and practice.[16] In the writing of this book, in the past year of being and becoming, we have attempted to *offer* with humility, *receive* with curiosity, and *integrate* with creativity. As we explored and described integrative concepts such as differentiation and reciprocity, we found that these concepts became more than conceptual categories for us. They became deeper lived realities.

We recognize that there is more than one way to pursue interdisciplinary integration. How we go about the integration between our discrete areas of study speaks volumes about what we perceive integration to be. Method, of course, influences outcomes. The integrative approach we pursue in this book is a relational one, first of all because it has emerged out of the prior relationships shared by the three of us; our history of connections and conversations informs the shape of this book. Also, our method is relational because of a basic conviction that human knowledge is relational. As LeRon Shults astutely observes, "Knowledge emerges out of relationality inherent in reality. . . . It appears that we are made for relational knowing and that the world is made for being known relationally."[17] Or as Paul wrote, "Whoever loves truly knows."[18]

One important facet of this relational methodology is that we assume that who we are as scholars and persons makes a difference

11

for our integrative work. We have chosen to introduce ourselves and our relationships with our disciplines, in part, to live out this truth. We do not, therefore, offer the *definitive* conversation between social science, ethics, and hermeneutics around the topic of human formation. Instead, we invite our readers into our conversations as a social scientist, an ethicist, and a biblical scholar on this topic. In other words, we want to acknowledge and capitalize on "the irreducible influence of the method-*ist*" in the process of constructing an interdisciplinary method.[19] With this guiding assumption the integrative approach of this book can be described by the three movements of offering, reception, and integration. These movements are not singular, nor are they precisely linear. They resemble a conversation more than a to-do list.

The relational, dialogical basis of our work also means that the primary impetus for integration is not the question, How can *I* discover what is relevant from *your* field for *my* own work? Instead, each of us offers what is significant from our own work to our conversation partners. In response those receiving this offering look for connections to their own disciplines, listening for points of deep and authentic integration. They bring the strength of their own disciplines to the listening process, since from that point of strength they are best equipped to hear resonance between their own discipline and those of their conversation partners. We hope it is clear that the two movements just described are both conversational and complex, what Al Wolters has described as an "intricate interplay."[20] The aim is to bring distinct disciplines "into the desegregation of mutual influence."[21]

In the latter stages of the conversation we are most ready to discern integrative connections. In the third movement (integration) we listen for points of significant connection between the offerings of one discipline as received by the others. For example, in co-teaching a course, Jeannine offered some insights from narrative criticism about characterization and reader identification with a story's characters. Carla heard a certain resonance between these ideas and the psychological category of transference. This offering and response led to further conversation about the authenticity and depth of these integrative connections. In pursuing integration it is particularly important to look beyond linguistic and even conceptual connections, since these are often discipline-specific. It is helpful to assess possible integrative connections at the level of judgments (that which is affirmed in context and how it is affirmed).[22] The judgments of a particular discipline are brought into interaction with the judgments of another discipline to assess their level of coherence with each other.[23]

It is also the case that this third movement of integrative method will uncover areas of discontinuity between disciplines. Interaction may even reveal significant points of dissonance between our disciplines. By attending to what fits and what does not, we are better able to foster truly integrative work that allows each discipline to speak from its own standpoint without sacrificing its distinctives or attempting to trump another discipline. Also, when we acknowledge points of dissonance along with true connections, we achieve a kind of relational, differentiated integration. Differentiation—the capacity to maintain both healthy, non-anxious connectedness and healthy, non-anxious autonomy—is essential for sustaining any real conversation.[24]

Implicit in this brief methodological description is the equal value of each discipline for integration. In this conversation the three of us maintain an egalitarian view of our disciplines. God's truth is the ultimate authority, not any particular area of human endeavor. So social science will not trump hermeneutics, ethics will not trump social science, and so on; no single discipline will hold a place of ultimate primacy in the conversation.[25] We offer to each discipline a version of what family therapists describe as "multidirectional partiality": a place of authority for its *particular* questions and an assumption of ethical relating to the other disciplines.[26]

This is not a universal assumption in interdisciplinary work within all Christian theological contexts. In some circles biblical studies and theology are understood to have an authoritative role over all other disciplines. Yet every discipline, including biblical studies and theology, is based on "a number of foundational assumptions that shape its theoretical work. . . . It is impossible to do scholarship, to engage in the business of academic inquiry, without basing oneself to a significant extent on pre-theoretical commitments which cannot themselves be justified on theoretical grounds."[27] As a result, while we can rightly claim Scripture as normative for our work, none of us can claim objective or final understandings of it. It is crucial to acknowledge that "when we do access textual meaning, we do so in partial ways. This condition provides great encouragement to read carefully, with an awareness of what we bring to the hermeneutical process, and to read in community."[28] Our own communal work of integration arises from a healthy respect for the integrity of each of our disciplines and their right to an equal voice at the interdisciplinary table.[29]

Conclusion: Writing as Formation

Formation is relational and social and occurs even in the midst of the writing process. In fact, we write out of our need and desire to be formed. We choose to be formed and shaped by disciplines, practices, and insights other than those in which we are already trained and comfortable. This goes beyond the mere appropriation of ideas to the expansion of our cognitive and experiential categories.

We have attempted in this project to live in a relational formation context. As we have already indicated, we committed at the beginning of the work to avoid cherry-picking ideas from one another's disciplines in an effort to prove our particular discipline's point or affirm its validity. **It is not just the Other's ideas that shape us; it is the "Other" herself.**[30] The worldview of the Other is part of the Other, to be sure, but it is not the whole of the Other. The point of this interdisciplinary and integrative experiment is not just that we think differently or even more expansively, but that our conversation will move each of us toward a greater degree of wholeness and holiness, and our three-person authorial "community" will reflect similar growth or movement.

BEING AND BECOMING

A Journey toward Love (Carla)

I n this chapter I will offer some social-science perspectives on the nature of our becoming and constraints on that becoming, and suggest love as a primary formation strategy.[1] Why social-science perspectives? The recent history of mutual suspicion between theology and social science belies their earlier, more harmonious relationship. In fact, theology is "historically an immediate ancestor of psychology. At the time of psychologist William James (1902) these were still closely related fields, making it only natural for him to study spiritual experience. It was later that a great chasm opened between them, leaving only two relatively isolated fields, pastoral counseling and the psychology of religion, with any family resemblance. It appears that the twenty-first century will witness some reconciliation of psychology and spirituality."[2] My hope is that our integrative conversation may serve the reestablishment of this historic disciplinary collaboration.

The reconciliation of theology with the social sciences will depend in part on the confidence and humility with which the conversation partners approach the dialogue. I have noted the presence of a significant "hermeneutic of suspicion" on the part of each discipline in a variety of interdisciplinary endeavors. Dennis Hiebert offers this matter-of-fact observation that might structure a rapprochement between wary interdisciplinary explorers.

> If indeed God created and continually sustains nature, He is already inherent and operative in both the subject and the method of scientific inquiry, whether the scientist acknowledges His transcendent, superempirical existence or not. . . . This, for example, means that God's truth is already present in the central sociological insight of the social construction of reality, including the social construction of religious faith, and the method by which sociology continually finds it to be true. Yet for the Christian sociologist, methodological naturalism, while valid and useful as a method of knowing significant aspects of reality, is incapable of being totalizing. Humans can never be "nothing but" socially constructed, even while sociology reveals the extent to which they are socially constructed, something theology would be foolish and arrogant to deny.[3]

We hope our interdisciplinary project may serve as a model for gracious, challenging, collaborative dialogue.

The Nature of Becoming

A particular contribution of social science to this conversation is its long-standing interest in how people change. I will not attempt to summarize this body of knowledge in this chapter. However, I would like to offer a brief discussion of one question that I believe has particular relevance for our understanding of becoming: Do we change bit by bit, or does transformation occur like a bolt from the blue?

I am curious about what Jeannine and Wyndy will suggest in their chapters with regard to this question. After all, in Scripture we see Moses standing barefoot in front of a burning bush, and Paul blinded by a literal bolt from the blue. Are we to assume, then, that the best kind of becoming is that which interrupts our experience in sensational ways and disrupts every aspect of our lives? Or, since we also see in Scripture disciples who changed incrementally, in fits and starts, along the way doubting, denying, and asking impertinent questions, is gradual change that emerges organically out of everyday life preferable?

Scriptural evidence and social science suggest that both instantaneous and incremental change happen, both produce lasting results, and neither is somehow better than the other. Perhaps, however, people trust or desire one more than the other. William James speculated in *The Varieties of Religious Experience* in 1902 about both kinds of change;[4] and gradual, incremental change has been formally studied by hundreds of scholars. But in the hundred years since James, few researchers have sought to understand the discontinuous, abrupt change experienced by Moses, Paul, and many others. William Miller and Janet C'de Baca call this kind of becoming "quantum change" and define it as "a vivid, surprising, benevolent, and enduring personal transformation."[5]

Quantum change may be *insightful* or *mystical*.[6] Insightful quantum change is an accumulation of insights that resonate with the changer in ways that invite relinquishing control and seeing oneself in a new identity. Mystical quantum change is much more sudden and transient and is felt to be beyond words, full of deep truth, and resulting in awe, peace, and joy. Although the two sound quite similar, Miller and C'de Baca found some significant differences:

> Those with mystical epiphanies were twice as likely to remember the exact time of day it occurred, even though the insightful quantum changes had occurred much more recently on average (two and a half years versus fourteen years ago). Those who had the epiphany type of quantum change were twice as likely to say that they had felt completely loved, that they had a "vision," and that they felt themselves to be in the hands of a Higher Power during the event. They were four times more likely to report "hearing" a voice and five times more likely to say that someone had been praying for them at the time of their quantum change.[7]

As a Christian social scientist curious about the nature of becoming, I find Miller and C'de Baca's work fascinating. I also find fascinating, however, the personal stories I hear about change that happened over years, with stretches of despair along the way. Transformation, no matter how it happens, is an amazing human phenomenon. We should also take note that no matter what the nature of change might

17

be, it cannot happen without community and, indeed, it sometimes happens *to* a community. When we examine the story of Peter and Cornelius in chapter 11, we will notice the impact of Peter's mystical quantum change on the Jewish Christians back home. Communities can support, resist, ignore, inspire, and shape the becoming of their members, and vice versa. It is worthwhile to dwell for a moment on this communal, relational nature of becoming.

Creating Trustworthy Contexts for Becoming

Christ's willingness to experience the developmental nature of human experience by becoming incarnate as an infant is one of the significant examples of development in Scripture. Narratives of the disciples' less-than-linear formation processes encourage us in our own formation in "fits and starts" as we pursue the goal of "attaining to the whole measure of the fullness of Christ" (Eph. 4:13). The author of 2 Peter also offers an example of spiritual growth and development (2 Pet. 1:3–11), and Paul's letters are full of encouragements and admonishments related to formation successes and challenges.

A conceptual shift regarding the notion of development has occurred in the social sciences in the last several decades. In the past there was a focus on the stages of cognitive development (Erikson, Piaget, Kohlberg, or Fowler); however, scholarly focus has shifted to a more relational and less linear development of consciousness and capacity.[8] The current conversation is reflective more of the work of Kegan and Loder, as well as the contributions of interpersonal neurobiologists such as Daniel Siegel and Louis Cozolino.[9] The most helpful formation metaphors are no longer linear and sequential. They are now metaphors—such as the chambered nautilus—suggesting spiraling growth that allows for revisiting, reworking, and finding deeper healing for earlier unresolved challenges.

Even in the aspects of becoming that seem individual and intrapersonal, it is important not to miss the essential relational nature of formation. Marital therapist David Schnarch says, "Stop working on your marriage. Realize that your marriage is working on you."[10] It's a contemporary version of Proverbs 27:17: "As iron sharpens iron, so one person sharpens another." It is not the existence of the relationships alone that provides the context for formation, but also

18

the challenges arising within them. Outside of intimate relationships, where else in life is one offered (too eagerly, it sometimes seems) such direct feedback about the desire others have that we become something different from what we are at present? Although some avoid intimacy in order to maintain illusions about their wholeness and holiness, even the most superficial of relationships has the potential to dismantle or at least challenge those illusions.

This relational challenge can be visualized as a crucible, the container for a refining flame.[11] The relational challenge itself is not the fire that transforms, but rather a holder for that fire. Within that holder we encounter anxiety, anger, sadness, questions, risk, shame, regret, chaos, and truth. We encounter ourselves and God and become aware of the impact—both for good and for harm—that others have on us and we on them.

Although we sometimes find ourselves unexpectedly in one, crucibles that nurture formation and becoming are sometimes deliberately constructed. That is, we can intentionally shape a context or an experience in ways that invite others into the encounter with self, other, and God, and then conscientiously provide support and presence to those who enter these crucibles. Because of the risks involved, it is of utmost importance that the container be trustworthy. Trustworthiness is a more complex concept than it may initially appear to be. It is more a synonym for faithfulness and reliability than for comfort, relief, or ease. Because others do not typically expect us to do things intentionally that make them anxious, the honest and truthful encounters necessary for authentic trustworthiness can initially create disequilibrium. Yet without such potentially anxiety-producing experiences, transformation is less likely. Therefore, a trustworthy relational container maintains the transforming fire at an effective but "nonlethal" temperature by balancing a number of paradoxical "both/ands."

Social scientists in various disciplines describe these both/ands in similar ways. Educator and activist Parker Palmer refers to this as constructing an environment that is both safe and charged.[12] Learners feel free to tell the truth about where they are so that they can take the risk of moving to a new place. Leadership theorists Martin Linsky and Ron Heifetz describe finding the right mix of anxiety and support.[13] In their account both leaders and followers are challenged to move beyond what they know, but with enough support that they aren't paralyzed by the anxiety. To take another example, hypnotherapist Milton Erickson defines this both/and quality of formation clinically and therapeutically as "pacing and leading."[14] He sees becoming as a dance that involves joining clients "where they are" and being able to intuit when to step out ahead and invite the clients to follow.

Maintaining these both/ands is essential to providing a trustworthy crucible and creating a context that sees "truth as troth," or living in relationships of both understanding and accountability.[15] It can be challenging work, but as Wellesley College president Diana Chapman Walsh says, "When we are resolute and lucky, I think we do create a container in which [others] can safely and genuinely experience confusion and conflict in all its complexity and can grow through and with it to greater wisdom and maturity."[16]

What Formation Is Not

Delineating what becoming is *not* can also help clarify the concept. Becoming is not:

Solely our responsibility. Despite the plethora of self-help books available, our desire to improve ourselves and our performance, reputation, or income is often a poorly disguised attempt to control our environment. Such attempts at control and self-improvement can quickly become exhausting and discouraging. It is heartening that the apostle Paul assures us that the one "who began a good work in you will carry it on to completion until the day of Christ Jesus" (Phil. 1:6).

Solely God's responsibility. The previous disclaimer is not intended to lull us into passivity, however. For centuries Christ followers have employed spiritual practices that are not ends in themselves but rather means of orienting oneself to God in a receptive posture— turning toward God in order to receive the healing, equipping, challenging, comforting, nurturing, illuminating, sanctifying work of God. Although spiritual practice can devolve into obligatory or self-congratulatory activity, its intent is reorientation.[17]

Inevitable. Developmental theories are sometimes misinterpreted to imply deterministic, unidirectional movement toward a single, monolithic goal. Although there are some kinds of development that do unfold without (and at times in spite of) human intervention—adding inches to one's height, for example—"becoming" as we are using the term does not suggest that desired changes will occur simply because time passes.

Linear. A related qualification in defining becoming has to do with the nature of the process. Metaphors for development sometimes include steps, arrows, or the most desirable Wall Street profit charts—perhaps growth stutters now and then, or temporarily plateaus, but it generally follows a forward and upward direction. My contention is that formation is much more accurately reflected by metaphors of transformation (butterflies, for example), or of recapitulation (such as musical themes), or of the growth spiral of a chambered nautilus.

Unrelated to its context. Becoming is not a-contextual, ahistorical or asocial. To the contrary, the goals and processes of formation are shaped by the context of the one being formed. Attempts to make formation "one-size-fits-all" will result in "one-size-fits-none."

Five Helpful Dispositions for Becoming

Responsiveness to this God-initiated, reorienting, variable, nonlinear, contextual process of becoming is enhanced by several attitudes and capacities that can be deepened through awareness, reflection, and practice. Chief among these are:

1. *The willingness to hear God's invitations in the voices of others.* We may sometimes find ourselves impatient with our spiritual practices. We may disagree with observations and developmental recommendations others make about us. We may be tempted to be dismissive of spiritual disciplines and ways of being with God that are different from our own. Such experiences are often veiled invitations from God to look more deeply into the impatience, disagreement, and judgmentalism in order to allow God to work in new ways. Invitations are easiest to accept when they make sense to us, but when the disciples denied knowing the destination, much less the route, Jesus assured them that he was the Way (John 14:1–6). The one who is the Way is also the one who invites us on the way of becoming.

2. *A tolerance for ambiguity.* Between where we are and where we are going lie turbulence, confusion, and lack of clarity. New informa-

tion collides with old, the end is not always clear from the beginning, and paradoxes abound. Formation work can be unsettling, but being able to function in the midst of ambiguity requires more faith in the God of our beliefs than in the beliefs themselves.

3. *A spirit of exploration.* In an ideal world of becoming, we would expect and value encounters with challenging ideas and would be energized by learning to integrate them into an ever-deepening understanding of God. Unfortunately, not all of us do. Some operate from a standpoint of rigid certitude.[18] Yet it *is* possible to hold convictions deeply and still be willing to examine them critically. Respect for differences and humility about our human limitations enable us to live in authentic, transforming community.

4. *The capacity to live in the moment.* Too often we view times of growth and transition as life in a holding pattern. Students often say, "Things will be different when I'm through with school." Parents say, "Things will be different when the kids are out of the house." Young adults say, "Things will be different when I'm out of my parents' house." In all cases, things undoubtedly *will* be different, but unfortunately not less complicated, stressful, or busy. Putting off personal formation work, ignoring relational difficulties, or assuming God will seem closer at some arbitrary future point means we may miss a unique formation opportunity.

5. *The ability to manage anxiety.* Anxiety is an inevitable—but not necessarily bad—aspect of human existence. It can be a helpful early warning system for us, preparing us for action (particularly fighting or fleeing) and alerting us to threat and danger. However, it can also inhibit rational thought and responses, causing us to default instead to reactivity and instinct. Our ability to notice when our anxiety is escalating, to interrupt that escalation, and to calm ourselves is an indispensable resource when we enter the unknown terrain of becoming.

Constraints on Becoming

The great gift of the one who forms us is the promise that when we seek, we will find. Experience sometimes seems at odds with that promise. How do we understand the obstacles to formation, the constraints on becoming? Perhaps ironically, the constraints are often relational and contextual, as is the becoming, meaning they do not block formation as much as they shape it.

For example, our anxiety about the unknown in becoming can activate previous relational learnings. Our first encounters with being and becoming tend to take one of four forms. Attunement, the sense of "feeling felt" by another, is an important kind of resonance for a child to experience with his or her caregiver.[19] When that occurs continuously with a caregiver who is able to notice and respond to the child, a *secure* attachment is said to exist. Such an attachment enables the child to explore his or her world with the knowledge that there is a haven to which to return. Of course, no caregiver can be perfectly attuned to a child. Some social scientists have posited that the caregiver simply needs to be "good enough" or, at some point, has offered repair work to the child so that there develops what can be called "earned security."[20]

If attunement does not occur, and caregivers are emotionally unavailable, the child develops an *avoidant* attachment style, which becomes a dismissive style in adulthood. In this style, a worldview develops that excludes any conceptualization of the significance of emotions and interpersonal relationships.[21] If attunement is inconsistent, the resulting unpredictability (in which the caregiver is sometimes intrusively present and sometimes unexpectedly absent) results in an *anxious/ambivalent* attachment style for the child. This style represents a fear that one's needs will not be met and may persist into adulthood as preoccupation with the desire for closeness and the fear of losing it. And fourth, if the caregiver is actually a source of inescapable terror for the child, the child develops a *disorganized* attachment style, which can appear in adulthood as dissociation—disconnecting from one's present experience in an effort to avoid the danger and pain of the "now." This style is often connected to unresolved trauma or grief.

As mentioned earlier, it would be incorrect to think that any of the three kinds of insecure attachment prohibit or prevent growth and development. However, they do shape the nature of one's formation challenges, including faith formation. Since our representations of God flow at least initially from our conceptions of our parents, one can hypothesize about the challenges of attaching to God if there was an insecure attachment to one's parents.[22] "With the cohesive states

23

of insecure attachment, the mind is 'holding on' to old patterns in an outdated effort to just survive. This inflexible cohesiveness puts the person at risk for chaotic or rigid states."[23] Later in the chapter we will explore some particular implications for formation given such inflexibility and rigidity.

The effect of the brokenness and sins of others relates to the nature of childhood and adult attachment styles on our path to becoming. If we have experienced relational betrayal or physical trauma in either childhood or adulthood, our areas of challenge and growth in formation will be shaped by that part of our narrative, at least for a season.[24] The same would be true of one's experiences under oppressive or unjust social structures.[25] Suffering is an integral part of formation and remains part of individual and communal narratives, even after the painful events have passed.

Genetic realities will also shape the nature of one's becoming. Cognitive deficits, physical disabilities, aging, predisposition to certain mental and/or physical illnesses, and so on in no way prevent formation or becoming. They do, however, shape the direction and expectations of formation, as do all our experiences. Again, this serves as an important caution against developing universal formation strategies.

These factors are all constraints on formation. But I want to focus in greater detail on a relational dynamic that I believe is one of the biggest constraints on formation for individuals and communities: a meaning-making process that is characterized by rigidity, fear, and exclusion. I identify this as a *fundamentalist relational process*, which is quite different from using the word "fundamentalism" to describe a set of beliefs or the content of a worldview.[26] Though both fundamentalist content and process would inhibit formation, I contend that fundamentalist processes within communities and systems are both more widespread and insidious than is fundamentalist content.

Fundamentalism as Relational Process

The capacity to self-soothe appears to be present in humans by about the age of three months. Skill in noticing and calming our own anxiety is an invaluable ally in the formation process, which by definition involves encountering the new, the challenging, and the anxiety pro-

24

voking. For some, "as the need to defend against anxiety increases, the need to know diminishes, and one's mind becomes incrementally closed to different views—all in the unarticulated hope that rigid adherence to beliefs or a cause will secure connection, respect, and dignity."[27] This diminished curiosity and receptivity compromises one's ability to respond to invitations to become.

The ongoing process of constructing meaning is enhanced by a person or group's ability to tolerate change, manage stressful events, and remain in conversation with one another. These abilities enable members of a group to construct, deconstruct, and reconstruct meanings as needed throughout the life cycle. At points of transition or crisis one's underlying plausibility structures about the world are challenged, so it is necessary to continue the meaning-making process as part of a communal conversation. Also, applying one's faith commitments and interpretations of Scripture to unfamiliar experiences and situations requires one to engage in the construction of meaning—not the invention of truth, but the contextualization of what we know to be true.

For some communities, however—including congregations, families, or organizations—conversations about definitions, interpretations, and expressions of spirituality are difficult. Some members' voices are stifled, some subjects are off-limits, and some terms simply cannot be defined in any shared way. In these communities there is only *one* possible interpretation of events, *one* group story, *one* valid perception of truth. Such a system is characterized by an attachment to a simplistic code of morality based more on rules than on principles, a refusal to value individual thinking, and an inability to allow any member to write his or her own story or to reinterpret or re-author family stories.

Such systems typically are anxious and undifferentiated, often experiencing significant pain but unable to move toward reconciliation. The movement of a member away from the one past, familiar story means that that member is threatened with exclusion from the family, either emotionally or physically. Those who go against a distorted family story and refuse to behave as if the image were actually the reality are often ostracized, scapegoated, believed to be bad, or treated as though they were defective and perhaps sick. In some way the family worldview takes precedence over the relationship. This intensity, rigidity, and lack of emotional safety are what I mean by fundamentalism as a relational process.

Again, I am not talking here about fundamentalism as the content of an individual or group's religious or political beliefs, but about fundamentalism as *process*, as an ongoing approach to making sense of life. This distinction between process and content is important. This kind of process can be seen in congregations, families, and institutions—any place where a group of people is involved in constructing and interpreting meaning. In this regard, we could identify fundamentalism as a system process in groups of therapists, clergy, journalists, educators, postmodernists, modernists, egalitarians, complementarians, even dog or cat owners—because it is not a set of beliefs, but the approach a relational system takes toward constructing, maintaining, and passing on those beliefs.

Also, I am not talking about systems that hold strong moral and religious values and then use those values as guidelines for life together. Holding passionate convictions is not synonymous with engaging in fundamentalist relational process. If we are able to hold our convictions in a nonanxious way, then we are able to allow others with whom we are in relationship to explore, challenge, or disagree—to write their own stories, even when those stories differ dramatically from those we would have imagined or desired.

One final clarification: it is important to see this characteristic on a continuum. Some individuals and groups demonstrate little or none of this kind of approach to life, while others are characterized by little else. Perhaps most of us are somewhere in the middle. And even those who usually maintain a respectful posture may sometimes exhibit a greater degree of fundamentalist process in times of stress, ambiguity, and transition.

For example, I believe I was a paragon of parental empowerment during the year my daughter explored college options. I did research, paid for campus visits, and mostly kept my opinions to myself. The official candidate-reply deadline approached, and I became even more exemplary in my serenity. But as I finished writing the enrollment deposit check to the school my daughter chose, she asked for feedback about some information on her roommate preference form. When I noticed she had already checked yes with regard to being assigned to a coed floor, my immediate response revealed my inability to let her write her own story: "*What are you thinking?!*" Looking back on the conversation that followed, I have to acknowledge this as evidence that sometimes our own fundamentalism surprises us. Perhaps it provides a defense against the anxiety inherent in the uncertainty and ambiguity of the meaning-making process, particularly at times when meanings must be renegotiated and life stories begin new chapters.

Characteristics and Implications of Fundamentalism as Relational Process: Case Examples from the Larsons

Fundamentalism as a relational process is important to examine because of its potential for rupturing and cutting off relationships, particularly those most important in our formation. Any time we make agreement with our viewpoint or conformity to our systemic rules the primary basis for inclusion in an emotional system, we run the risk of moving away from God's expectation that we love our neighbors as ourselves. Some of the most painful moments I experience in teaching or doing therapy are those in which I hear a person's story of having been excluded from a group for being themselves, for challenging the system's dominant story, or for speaking the truth about their experience.

My favorite shorthand definition of fundamentalism as a relational process comes from a phrase used by Thomas Moore in *Care of the Soul*: he describes a certain kind of thinking as "the tendency to freeze life into a solid cube of meaning."[28] I have come to think of individuals, families, congregations, or communities who live with fundamentalism as an integral part of their process as "frozen." In order to understand this kind of process in action, let me introduce a family (I'll call them the Larsons) who can serve as a case study in frozen relationships.[29]

Three generations of this family include an elderly woman, her middle-aged son, and his young adult daughter. The content and practice of religious beliefs have differed substantially from one generation to the next. The grandmother, Berit, was raised in a family that practiced religion fairly haphazardly until she was twelve. Then her father and brother died in the same week, and all religious involvement ended. Her son Clifford has viewed himself as the spiritual leader of the home since age three, when he accepted a neighbor's invitation to attend a summer vacation Bible school program. He is extremely active in a conservative evangelical church, so much so that his wife accuses him of neglecting her. His daughter Beth, who lives with her fiancé, practices a very individualistic religious life in which she reports feeling a personal connection with God.

These three members of the same family represent quite a varied set of religious beliefs and practices. But it seems with some families that, even though some of the content of religious belief changes from one generation to the next, the underlying story about God, life, and themselves often remains the same. In excerpts from interviews with these individuals, notice the consistent view of God as punitive, harsh, and arbitrary:

- Berit: "I guess I think about God, especially if TV is lousy. Especially I think that he's not helping me enough with these cigarettes. I've asked the Lord to take it [smoking] away, and I'd give him the money. I know it's me; he can't just do it. But he should be able to put it in my mind. Maybe he's punishing me for something I did. I'm sure he's going to punish me some more. . . . I never asked why [when her husband died, leaving her with three adolescents]. But I did wonder why for the kids, why did they have to go through it? I guess to punish the parents."

- Clifford: "I especially like songs about God having his way; one of my favorites is 'Whatever will be, will be.' God can do whatever he wants. If I'm not being chastised, then maybe I'm not being loved." According to Clifford, anger at such chastisement or tests of obedience is "a sign of immaturity."

- Beth: When a relationship ended that she had thought would lead to marriage, she said, "It's like God threw a steak at a dog and didn't let him eat it." The Old Testament story of the exodus has been a favorite of hers, but not because of the powerful, liberating force of God displayed there. Rather, the cruelty of the plagues God was willing to send demonstrates that "he will *make* you understand, no matter what it takes. You don't cross God. If you do, you'll get it. I never dare talk back [to God]. I know in my head that anger isn't bad, but I *feel* that it is. Telling God I don't like what he did to me would be dangerous. If I did, it might get worse. Ever hear of Job?"

In phenomenological terms, it seems as though this family's stock of knowledge about the character of God contains diverse bits of wisdom and interpretation that, taken together, are not necessarily coherent or logical. But they constitute a multigenerationally frozen family narrative about God, and in this particular family deviating from that narrative—internally inconsistent though it may be—is not acceptable.

Persons and systems characterized by fundamentalist process fight for the narrative or worldview they have adopted. It requires constant reinforcement, relies on adherence to rules, and is fairly narrow in the range of allowable behaviors and attitudes.[30] Again, I am talking not about a set of beliefs but about a mandated perspective: "Good families always agree with one another," "Christians should never be angry," "Questions are dangerous." Fundamentalism as a relational process means that those who have the power to determine the "shoulds" also have the power to control the system's worldview.

It's not that rules are inherently bad. Healthy systems do provide structure for their members, but when fundamentalism is part of the process of determining and enforcing those rules it becomes problematic. As Miroslav Volf writes:

> Obsession with the rules—not bad rules, but salutary rules!—encourages self-righteousness and the demonization of others. To make the rules stick, one must reduce moral ambiguity and the complexity of social agents and their interaction. Insistence on observance of the rules fosters polarities where none actually are and heightens them where they do exist. As a result, one is either completely "in" (if no rule was broken) or completely "out" (if a rule has been broken).[31]

Thus, this obsession with rules can result in an artificial dichotomy between being right or being in relationship.

Beth describes having experienced a significant amount of criticism and exclusion from both her religious community and her father for having broken rules related to lifestyle choices, such as smoking, cohabitation, and lack of church involvement. Partly in response to being frozen out of community, Beth has constructed an interpretation of love that also includes acceptance: "You can't have a relationship with someone you judge. That's not doing God's will. I thought we are taught to love everybody. Live and let live, that's my theme."

There is a poignancy in Beth's desire to rejoin her family of origin and participate in the community ritual possible there: "At some point I'd like to come back to the church. . . . I'm no longer a core person here, and so I don't get included in things, and then [I] get my feelings hurt. . . . There will be pettiness anywhere, but why should I put up with that with strangers? This is where I grew up. It's a family to me. . . . This is my church, even though it really hasn't been for the last ten years."

For the Larsons, discrepancies between Clifford's and Beth's interpretations of spirituality have emerged at several key points. Unfortunately, these discrepancies have made the family conversation into a stilted process in which Beth's stories have been ignored, reframed, or squeezed into a more acceptable format by her father:

> We're a close family; my parents were fairly strict in how you should act and how you should think. Dad always says, "Do what I say, think this way." . . . Questioning anything would be like questioning God. . . . I believe two people can have two opinions and both of them can be OK. To my dad, one has to be wrong. . . . If I had kids, I would want their spirituality to be personal. My parents think I am so unspiritual because I don't go to church. But I pray, I read the Bible, I have God-like feelings. Curt [her cohabiting partner] and I find ways to bring God into our relationship. God is important to me but not in a religious sense.

Her father offers his interpretation of the family conversation:

> I'm very disappointed in all three of my kids spiritually. I've asked others to pray for them. . . . They've been religious but not spiritual. They're not vibrant or alive in their faith. Church isn't important, and they don't have time for God in their lives. . . . [The Bible says] we will be known by our fruits. It makes me wonder where they stand with God.

Asked what he means by "fruits," Clifford responds:

Knowing what God means to them, that they attend church, the kinds of people they're friends with. . . . I feel pretty cheated by [Prov. 22:6] and that formula. We did all the sports, the activities, summer musical ministry as a family, vacations—we were *there* for them. Any bitterness I have in my life might come in that area. . . . I'm disappointed with where they are spiritually. . . . Giving them a good example didn't work. I don't see active faith in any of my three kids. And I just don't understand this.

In some frozen families the agenda they espouse and the rules they enforce are often linked to a purportedly noble cause: "being an example" to other families, perhaps, can justify an emphasis on appearance over against substance. Unfortunately, in some systems characterized by fundamentalism God's primary role is defined as being a cause under which they fight. Disrespect, coercion, and even violence are reframed as means of obedience to God's expectations. Clifford, in discussing his disapproval of his daughter's cohabiting relationship, says:

I'm still the parent, I'm still the role model. There's kind of a dual role. You know, she's happier than I've seen her in years. But you've gotta stay true to your convictions. . . . I have to play the role of the disapproving father. . . . I want to do what's right for God, not for my daughter.

Why Attend to Fundamentalist Process in Our Becoming?

In relational systems fundamentalist processes shape interaction, producing contagion (because other fundamentalists then feel more free to exclude) and/or oppression (because more-moderate voices are stifled). There is also the danger of what I would call "reciprocal fundamentalism." If I, as a member of the system, perceive your emphases as invasive and dogmatic, I may become equally so in insisting on the rightness of my own views. In these ways fundamentalism becomes more and more entrenched in the life of the system, recreating itself in future generations.

So how might we help frozen individuals or systems thaw? Since there's no formation microwave on which we can push the programmed "defrost" button, helping frozen relationships thaw out is perhaps more analogous to treating hypothermia in winter survival camping. Without blankets, hot drinks, or fire, the most effective way to prevent the victim from freezing to death is skin-to-skin contact. Frozen relationships need the warmth of human connection, and such connection derives most basically from our ability to acknowledge that lives can be more difficult than they sometimes appear and, whenever possible, to offer grace and compassion rather than criticism and judgment. Our ability to humbly join individuals or a system on the journey, rather than stand apart and direct that journey, enables us to expand and enrich a story rather than manipulate it.

Of course, to return to our winter metaphor, it's most helpful if the person providing emergency treatment for hypothermia is not also freezing to death. So our own ability to model intellectual flexibility, nonanxious presence, and respectful empowerment (even of fundamentalist members of the system) becomes important. This may mean monitoring our own tendencies toward reciprocal fundamentalism and toward the desire to exclude. It may mean that we develop skills for dialogue, which starts with questions that are at least as finely honed as our skills for debate, which starts with answers. Those of us who prefer argument might do well to keep in mind the colloquial definition of a fanatic: one who will change neither his mind nor the subject.

This task of thawing frozen systems also has a macro-level component. As effective formation companions, we need to challenge systemic arrangements based on inclusion and exclusion, and recognize that using conformity to determine insider and outsider status actually creates outsiders, aliens, and strangers. We need to welcome the stranger and the outsider, those who have been excluded by their families of origin or their families of faith, even if it unsettles the norms and power arrangements that we're used to. We need to continue to be what Walter Brueggemann calls the "abrasive prophetic voice of criticism and possibility."[32]

Portrait of a Thawed-Out System

What might a thawed-out system look like? Jesus's parable of the prodigal son in Luke 15 provides a foundation for Miroslav Volf's fascinating discussion of a system refusing to buckle to fundamentalism as a relational process. Volf offers a clear example of a father who refuses, even in a time of stress and ambiguity, to succumb to fundamentalist family process. Volf reminds us that "the father who lets the son depart does not let go of the relationship between them."[33] As a result, upon his return the son's identity shifts from the "son-not-worthy-to-be-called-a-son" to the father's claim of him *as* son. Volf says that "the secret of the son's transformation is the same as the secret of his unconditional acceptance: the father would not let his son . . . out of his heart's embrace."[34]

In the older brother's mind, and even in that of the younger brother, the younger son clearly had broken the rules and was "out." The older brother evaluated his brother in categorical terms of good or bad. The younger brother had behaved badly, and consequently he should have been excluded from relationship. But Volf says that

> what is so profoundly different about the "new order" of the father is that it is not built around the alternatives as defined by the older brother: either strict adherence to the rules or disorder and disintegration; either you are "in" or you are "out," depending on whether you have or have not broken a rule. The father rejected this alternative because his behavior was governed by the one fundamental "rule": relationship has priority over all rules. Before any rule can apply, he *is* a father to his sons and his sons *are* brothers to one another.[35]

Rather than using his oldest son's fundamentalist categories of good or bad behavior, the father uses a relational emphasis to construct meaning about his son's departure through categories of "lost and found," "dead and alive." Volf summarizes the father's decision this way:

> Relationship is prior to moral rules; moral performance may do something to the relationship, but relationship is not grounded in moral performance. Hence the will to embrace is independent of the quality of behavior, though at the same time "repentance," "confession," and the "consequences of one's actions" all have their own proper place. The profound wisdom about the priority of the relationship, and not some sentimental insanity, explains the father's kind of "prodigality" to both of his sons.[36]

In this family's story there was the potential to live by a fundamentalist process that would include fighting for and against and under, but the father refused to allow that potential to determine the quality of relationships within the family. I don't know if that melted the heart of the older brother. But I do know that at the end of the story the father said to him, "I really want you inside. Please come."

May we who have experienced God's refusal to exclude us or to leave us outside be people who imitate God's faithfulness and creativity, who welcome strangers, who free persons and systems from fundamentalist processes that stifle and exclude, and who allow God to write a much bigger story than we could ask or imagine. In other words, may we be people who love.

Love as a Formation Strategy

One might notice that in Scripture God only provides commandments for things we might otherwise forget to do or try to avoid. We find no directives such as "Thou shalt breathe" or "Thou shalt eat" or "Thou shalt try to rationalize thine own behavior." The greatest command is one that apparently doesn't come naturally: "Love the Lord your God with all your passion and prayer and intelligence. . . . Love others as well as you love yourself" (Matt. 22:37, 39 *Message*). This is challenging enough that we find ourselves wandering into some unusual ways of thinking, perhaps not unlike one of Dostoevsky's characters:

> "I heard exactly the same thing, a long time ago to be sure, from a doctor," the elder remarked. "He was then an old man, and unquestionably intelligent. He spoke just as frankly as you, humorously, but with a sorrowful humor. 'I love mankind,' he said, 'but I am amazed at myself: the more I love mankind in general, the less I love people in particular, that is, individually, as separate persons. In my dreams,' he said, 'I often went so far as to think passionately of serving mankind, and, it may be, would really have gone to the cross for people if it were somehow suddenly necessary, and yet I am incapable of living in the same room with anyone even for two days, this I know from experience. As soon as someone is there, close to me, his personality oppresses my self-esteem and restricts my freedom. In twenty-four

hours I can begin to hate even the best of men: one because he takes too long eating his dinner, another because he has a cold and keeps blowing his nose. I become the enemy of people the moment they touch me,' he said. 'On the other hand, it has always happened that the more I hate people individually, the more ardent becomes my love for humanity as a whole.' "[37]

Although it may seem simple to reduce the process of human becoming to loving God and others, determining what it means to be loving is a challenge. Loving as we have been loved by God—with abandon—may collide with our fundamentalist tendencies and our attachment injuries. We may find ourselves afraid (of the unfamiliar, of being taken advantage of, of being hurt), arrogant (if we disagree, clearly they are wrong and will not listen, so why bother?), insecure (if we disagree, I must be wrong), weary (too tired to do the work of understanding a different culture or worldview), or guided by false information (stereotypes that are so ingrained that we do not notice them or pause to question their accuracy). These can be daunting impediments to love. It is difficult to love when one is anxious or fearful.

Here, however, interpersonal neurobiology offers us an exciting perspective on the teaching in 1 John 4:18, that perfect love casts out fear. Daniel Siegel cites Steven Porges's concept of "love without fear": "When we come to 'feel felt' by another person, we feel not only aligned with the other, but our brain likely establishes a state of what Steven Porges has called a 'neuroception' of safety." Porges "proposes that our nervous system evaluates the state of threat or safety of a situation and activates the brainstem's vagal and autonomic nervous systems to respond with either a sense of open receptivity with 'safety' or with . . . 'threat.' "[38] With threat we either take action (fight or flight) or we collapse (freeze). With safety we become receptive. Even though an Other (God, a loved one, a stranger) may be unpredictable and out of our control, we may still perceive them as safe in the sense of being trustworthy, as we discussed earlier in this chapter. C. S. Lewis captures this in *The Lion, The Witch, and the Wardrobe* when the beavers tell the children that Aslan is a lion:

"Ooh!" said Susan, "I'd thought he was a man. Is he—quite safe? I shall feel rather nervous about meeting a lion."

"That you will, dearie, and no mistake," said Mrs. Beaver, "if there's anyone who can appear before Aslan without their knees knocking, they're either braver than most or else just silly."

"Then he isn't safe?" said Lucy.

"Safe?" said Mr. Beaver. "Don't you hear what Mrs. Beaver tells you? Who said anything about safe? 'Course he isn't safe. But he's good. He's the King, I tell you."[39]

Early followers of Christ were famous for their love. They were what we might call "strange attractors." Their unusual, countercultural behavior created enough intrigue that others noticed. Before we turn this invitation to live in love relationships with God and others into an oppressive formation burden, we might do well to notice that when love appears in Scripture the reference is most often to how much we are loved *by* God. Perhaps becoming whole and holy is most likely, most possible, and most joyful when that awareness becomes most real to us.

Having introduced and discussed the process of becoming from the perspective of the social sciences, I now turn toward the deeply desired product of our becoming—wholeness and holiness.

3

WHOLENESS AND HOLINESS

Selves in Community with God and Others (Carla)

Human curiosity about change, discussed in the last chapter, is perhaps surpassed by human interest in the desired outcomes or results of change. In this chapter I will offer social-science perspectives on those outcomes. One challenge, of course, is that social science has historically been more concerned with wholeness than with holiness, although recent efforts to incorporate spiritual well-being and maturity into conceptualizations of health represent an interesting expansion in that dimension.

Until recently, the social sciences (particularly psychology) have typically focused on human pathologies, deficits, and challenges. The current wave of positive psychology, strengths-based leadership theory, and resilience research has added an important complement to our understanding of humans and their relationships. Among these contributions are significant new findings from interpersonal neurobiologists—those scientists who integrate natural science understandings of the brain and nervous system with psychological and sociological observations.[1]

As we begin this exploration, three caveats are in order with regard to wholeness and holiness. First, even as one articulates optimal or deeply desired outcomes, one must necessarily accept that humans will only understand and achieve a greater or lesser degree of wholeness and holiness. At least in this lifetime, no one will achieve perfect wholeness or holiness, so it will be important to avoid either/or categories in this discussion.

Second, common usage of these terms tends to evoke the idea of individual wholeness and holiness, but the terms also have implications for community. Conceptions of wholeness and holiness are determined by the contexts and narratives in which one is located, and the effects of communities on the formation of individuals, and vice versa, can be detrimental or salutary. Indeed, oppressive social structures can inflict harm rather than engender wholeness or holiness, and unregulated, unhealthy individuals can wreak havoc within communities.

Third, a focus on wholeness and holiness should not be misread as an acceptance of them as an appropriate end. They do not constitute an ultimate goal. Rather, growing evidence of individual and communal wholeness and holiness would be evidence of the actual ultimate goal: those individuals' and communities' authentic intimacy with, obedience to, and partnership with God.

Toward What End?

Formation is about God's work in us and about our capacity for orienting ourselves toward God and our receptivity to that work. It is the process of opening oneself to the work of God in one's life "so that the body of Christ may be built up until we all reach unity in the faith and in the knowledge of the Son of God and become mature, attaining to the whole measure of the fullness of Christ" (Eph. 4:12–13). We are invited toward and equipped for growing up into the image and likeness of Christ. This is normative for Christians. Even though we address issues that are of concern and interest to persons in every culture and generation, we do so with a unique sense of motivation and capacity.

The process leading to this end is characterized by at least three important features. First, *formation is multidimensional*. Distinctions between spiritual formation and other kinds of formation are largely semantic. As an example, a personal formation goal may be to better manage personal finances, a worthy goal for anyone, believer or nonbeliever. Yet this goal may also have spiritual implications, such as learning to live with generosity and trust. Likewise, moral concerns may emerge out of a failure to use wealth on behalf of those in need. Each aspect of this formation goal informs the others. What makes it Christian formation is that the motivation to act on this invitation is to become more Christlike in this area—to allow God to reveal ways in which money has become an idol and an impediment to seeing and following Christ. I may find help toward this goal in a variety of places, but Christian formation suggests that this work is initiated, sustained, and completed by God, and that openness to such work derives from a desire to glorify God and exemplify Christlikeness in every domain of life.

Second, *becoming incorporates both process and event*—developmental milestones, life transitions, and traumatic experiences, as well as the time and experiences between those. It involves cognitive, intellectual work and growth as well as emotional and psychological healing and development. Relational integrity and differentiation are essential elements of formation, as are spiritual understanding and practice. Formation is about both ontology (being) and epistemology (knowing), and it inspires vocational imagination and passion.

Finally, *formation is essentially invitational*. Invitations are most clear when they make sense to us. If, however, we really believe we follow a God who is always doing something new (Isa. 42:9; 43:19), then it is likely that invitations will sometimes seem confusing. Some invitations come in the area of work, vocation, and calling. Some come in the area of relationships: family, friends, and colleagues. Some center on physical health and wholeness, and others on spiritual and emotional healing. Accepting God's invitation to "the next step" requires a listening posture and a willingness to notice invitations in unexpected places.

I have described formation as a multifaceted invitational process with many points of entry. Individual and communal responses to God's call to wholeness and holiness are informed through reflection on the biblical and theological foundations of faith, the theoretical and practical dimensions of life and practice, and personal experiences of God in the past and present. This reflection serves as the basis for the ongoing process of integration that is essential for Christian maturity.

As we engage in formation processes, identified through individual and community reflection, we will demonstrate in increasing measure:

- A desire for and commitment to living in a covenant love relationship with God that is marked by a passion for the Word of God, personal obedience and discipleship, spiritual hunger, and a lifestyle of holiness and spiritual maturity;
- A desire for and commitment to living with others in covenant love relationships that are marked by integrity, respect, justice, service, reconciliation, and the ability to build bridges across the potential barriers of difference, including race, culture, gender, socioeconomics, and theological perspective;
- An ability to develop a biblically grounded theology of spiritual and personal formation, to recognize historical instances of the movement of the Holy Spirit, and to critically examine the practice of formation as understood by a variety of Christian traditions;
- An awareness of our own brokenness, call, and gifting that enables us to maintain healthy personal and professional boundaries, appropriately use authority and power, and respond sensitively to the pain of others; and
- An ability to respond to God's call in our lives with proactive, lifelong personal and professional development strategies that are characterized by honesty, accountability, and a commitment to justice and wholeness—spiritually, emotionally, physically, financially, and relationally.

The Goal of Becoming

Articulating a conceptualization of wholeness and holiness must start with a sense of the *imago Dei*, one of the givens of creation: that humans bear the image of the triune God. I will leave most of that discussion to the biblical scholar and ethicist, but would like to introduce the helpful integrative work of social scientists Jack Balswick, Pamela Ebstyne King, and Kevin Reimer, with their concise summary of this aspect of the goal of human becoming:

The doctrine of the Trinity reveals that God exists as Father, Son and Holy Spirit. The three divine persons of the Godhead live in unity as one, yet remain three distinct persons. The communion of the Godhead does not compromise the distinctiveness of the three.

40

In this way, *particularity* and *relatedness* co-occur because their relatedness is characterized by perfect *reciprocity* where the three live with and for each other. . . . [T]o live as beings made in the image of God is to exist as reciprocating selves, as unique individuals living in relationship with others. We then assert that developmental teleology, the goal of human development as God intends, is the reciprocating self. To live according to God's design is to glorify God [by living and acting] as a distinct human being in communion with God and others in mutually giving and receiving relationships.[2]

This "developmental teleology" has the potential for resolving the existential dilemma defined by Robert Kegan as the "lifelong tension [humans hold] between the yearning for inclusion and distinctness."[3] This dual yearning is what draws us into the crucible described in chapter 2. As humans confront themselves by facing both the truth of intimacy and the reality of otherness, by welcoming both connection and separateness, by engaging in both internal and interpersonal attunement,[4] they are transformed and that yearning for both/and is resolved.

I find myself wondering how that yearning is experienced differently across cultures. In a more individualistic context, such as the United States, perhaps the experience is truly a tension that must be held. But perhaps in a more collectivist culture it is different. Notice the contrasting starting point in this observation from Archbishop Desmond Tutu of South Africa:

We Africans speak about a concept difficult to render in English. We speak of *ubuntu*. . . . You know when it is there and it is obvious when it is absent. It has to do with what it means to be truly human, it refers to gentleness, to compassion, to hospitality, to openness to others, to vulnerability, to be available for others and to know that you are bound up with them in the bundle of life, *for a person is only a person through other persons.*[5]

A Thicker Description of Components of Particularity and Relatedness

These conceptualizations of our goal of becoming offer a context within which I will articulate some aspects of particularity and relatedness informed by the social sciences. The curriculum of the

41

seminary where Jeannine and I (Carla) teach was reconfigured in 1995 around three centers, each of which was intended to contribute to an interdisciplinary, integrative conversation: centers for biblical and theological foundations, transformational leadership, and spiritual and personal formation. Since this reordering, faculty members in each center have attempted to identify a limited number of distinctive characteristics their center would be best positioned to emphasize in the development of students. Of course, each center's characteristics rely partly on those of the other two in order to be fully realized in the life of any student.

The Center for Spiritual Formation identified the following five characteristics to which we intended to pay special attention: authentic piety, differentiation of self, emotional intelligence, humility, and generativity. These five characteristics (described more fully in fig. 1) provide one typology of wholeness and holiness that incorporates attitudes and dispositions. For our purposes these attitudes and dispositions both inform and are informed by the contributions of hermeneutics and ethics.

Table 1. Five Key Components of Wholeness and Holiness

Quality	Indicators
Authentic piety	An awareness of and desire for the holy
	Capacity for both joy and lament
	Ability to tolerate the wilderness and to encounter doubt
	Engagement in spiritual practice
	Evidence of experience of grace
	Ability to offer grace and forgiveness
	Stance that embraces both listening and action
	Concern for and action to promote justice
	Gratitude
	Evidence of having acknowledged one's representations of God and submitted them to the Spirit's illumination
Differentiation of self	Appropriate boundary maintenance
	Management of anxiety
	Ability to develop and sustain a self-directed plan for growth and health
	Comfort with both intimacy and autonomy
	Ability to live in healthy community
	Celebration and appropriate expression of sexuality, holistically understood
	Ability to regulate one's behavior
	Intellectual and emotional flexibility

Quality	Indicators
Emotional intelligence	Empathy
	Compassion that moves one to action
	Ability to use personal authority appropriately
	Appropriate use of humor and playfulness
	Ability to refrain from objectifying people
	Refusal to exploit or manipulate others
	Awareness of one's limitations and vulnerabilities
	Ability to contextualize
Humility	Openness to differences
	Responsiveness to authority
	Ability to dialogue as well as persuade
	Willingness to offer authentic hospitality
	Willingness and ability to empower others
	Ability to be passionate about convictions *and* open to possibility of error
	Ability to acknowledge one's biases and assumptions
	Ability to receive influence
	Ability to tolerate ambiguity
Generativity	Willingness to nurture others, especially marginalized populations and future generations
	Vocational imagination, seeing oneself as partnering with God in the world
	Personal and professional creativity
	Desire to "pay it forward"
	Concern for and action to create social justice

These five components, when demonstrated by the presence of the indicators listed in table 1, and in combination with similar prime components from disciplines in the other two centers, represent wholeness and holiness from the perspective of the social scientists in the Center for Spiritual and Personal Formation. As indicated earlier in this chapter, these components will be present to a degree in the life of a Christ follower, and as they are evident in greater measure, the follower may be considered to be more whole and holy.[6]

In addition to maintaining an awareness of the degree of wholeness and holiness, it is also important to distinguish between well-being and maturity with regard to wholeness and holiness. A common mistake is to assume that comfort is synonymous with some notion of having arrived, of having completed the formation process. Although there are certainly seasons and places of rest in the formation process, it would be incorrect to equate tranquility or self-satisfaction with wholeness or holiness. Immature persons sometimes have a fairly impervious sense of well-being.

An equally inaccurate corollary would be to assume that soul distress, intellectual unease, relational upset, or poor physical health represents immature or inadequate formation. Indeed, the process of being formed is often disruptive, disorienting, and painful on the way to maturity. To complicate matters, the process of resisting formation can also be discomfiting. Thus, neither tranquility nor turbulence can be used to determine well-being or maturity. As a tree is known by its fruit, so perhaps a journey can be identified by its end point. Although assessment is especially tricky with something that often invites resistance, is a largely internal process, and is a lifetime venture that sometimes entails what can look, on an inventory, like backward movement.

From the Cellular to the Transcendent: Nine Domains of Integration

In chapter 1 we described our integrative method and noted that this book is partially an effort to "do" interdisciplinary integration. However, it is also a call for faith-praxis integration and an explication of the invitation to experiential integration—to *be* integrated persons who do integrative work. This is another dimension of the goal of our becoming. Interpersonal neurobiologist Daniel Siegel describes a kind of experiential integration when he notes, "The flexible, adaptive, coherent, energized, and stable (FACES) flow of mental well-being can be seen to appear as integrated systems emerge across time. *FACES* is the term we can use to refer to this integrated state, a state that may underlie well-being."[7] For Siegel this integrated state is constituted of three separate, equally necessary and irreducible aspects: neural integration, mental coherence, and empathic relationships.[8]

Siegel proposes an expansive model of nine domains of integration, from the cellular level to the transcendent, with enthusiastic encouragement that "[i]f we focus on the domains of integration within our neural systems, we can see the simultaneous creation of empathy with others and coherence within." I will briefly summarize these nine domains in order to highlight the potential for integration that is "hard-wired" into us.

The first domain of neural integration is that of consciousness: intentionally placing our attention. Siegel writes, "Sharing attention initiates attunement."[9] As I mentioned earlier, attunement to self and other helps us resolve that existential dilemma of belonging and distinctness. The second domain is vertical integration, which relates information shared within our embodied selves. Vertical integration allows us to receive important information from our bodies, perhaps about unresolved states of trauma, loss, or adaptive dissociation. "Bringing somatic input into the focus of our attention changes what we can do with this information: *Consciousness permits choice and change.*"[10]

This intentional reflection on experience, including physical experience, is also an important starting point for theological reflection.[11] This is not, as is sometimes feared, so that experience and subjectivity become our guides and final arbiters of truth. Rather, we can bring everything into the light of God's Spirit so that all may be healed, redeemed, corrected, and brought into conformity with God's intentions for us.

The third domain of integration proposed by Siegel is horizontal. The two hemispheres of our brains specialize in different activities and do not easily communicate. When they are not attuned to each other, "it's easy to feel bereft. . . . What people don't realize is that our attachment history [which I discussed in chap. 2] can create modes of adaptation . . . which can be seen to prevent bilateral integration and leave one hemisphere dominant over the other."[12] Thus, attending to relational wounds and allowing God to heal them may have the effect of nurturing a more balanced capacity for intellectual and emotional flexibility.

Memory integration, the fourth domain, allows humans to understand what is in the present and what is from the past. For example, we may react to an event in the present (say, the loss of a job) in ways that echo previous experiences of loss or rejection. The more traumatic the earlier experiences, the more likely it is that they will intrude on and perhaps complicate our response to what is happening in the present moment. Memory integration allows us to discriminate between which aspects of our current disequilibrium are part of our present experience and which are echoes of the past.

This is related to narrative integration, the fifth domain, in which we "story" and "re-story" our lives.[13] As Siegel discusses this narrative integration, he proposes that "the mindful telling of our tale can be greatly healing of unresolved issues in our life."[14] Louis Cozolino agrees and adds the importance of storytelling for the attainment and sharing of wisdom—something we see throughout Scripture.[15]

The sixth domain of integration is state integration, which involves becoming aware and accepting of the coexisting, and sometimes conflicting, states of mind within ourselves, because that awareness also allows for the possibility of choice and change. This is the kind of integration that allows us to hold paradoxes in tension: How do we understand that in losing our lives, we find them (Matt. 16:25)? Or that the last shall be first (Mark 10:43-44)? How do we feel both relief and grief when a loved one dies after a painful, debilitating illness? State integration helps us avoid the kind of "splitting" behavior that says persons and events (and the self) are either all good or all bad.

The seventh domain, temporal integration, has as its focus "learning to live with our awareness of the transience of time," particularly as that transience incorporates uncertainty, impermanence, and death.[16] For some, this activates a strong desire to control as many aspects of life as possible—clearly a challenge in our being and becoming.

The final two domains of integration suggested by Siegel—interpersonal and transpirational—return us to the essential nature of wholeness and holiness proposed earlier: differentiated individuals living in authentic encounter with God and others. Interpersonal attunement, according to Siegel (and consistent with the social scientists we discussed earlier), "is not a luxury; it is a requirement of the individual to survive and to thrive." Our created, hard-wired desire for relationship draws us toward others as well as into the formation crucible discussed in chapter 2. And transpirational integration draws us toward the transcendent—toward God.

> With transpirational integration our sense of ourselves is transformed. . . . The sacred suffuses each breath, our essence, each step through this journey of life. . . . Seeing transpiration as part of the spectrum of integration can help us to understand the convergence of its appearance within contemplative and religious practice, and its presence in the nonsectarian studies of happiness and mental health.[17]

Again, integration itself is not the end goal. Rather, the parallel processes of integration that are present in our created, embodied selves suggest that it may be a means to a goal. As we attend to the levels of integration Siegel describes—intrapersonally and interpersonally—the process of becoming whole and holy, of being willing and capable to live in covenant love relationships with God and others, is supported. This willingness and capacity form a foundation for experiencing and offering deep authentic welcome. I conclude this chapter with a discussion of this marker of formation that is particularly relevant for our interdisciplinary conversation.

Hospitality: A Marker of Wholeness and Holiness

When Jesus joined two disciples on the road to Emmaus following his resurrection, the disciples did something that apparently came very naturally to them and was very appropriate in that context. Although they didn't recognize Jesus, they invited him in for a meal (Luke 24:13–35). I can imagine that this might have been like many situations in which a host asks a guest to offer thanks for a meal. When Jesus did so, the disciples recognized him in the ordinariness of praying together, of sharing a meal together. What an extraordinary experience to happen in the middle of their ordinary hospitality.

A significant marker of wholeness and holiness is one's ability to create a hospitable space in which others can recognize and experience the presence of God.

Hospitality? Really? To some of us that sounds more like the work of a cruise director or a hotel concierge than the important work we had hoped God would entrust to us. Eugene Peterson challenges this categorization: "Hospitality is daily practice in keeping sacrifice local and immediate. . . . When we are talking about the salvation of the world, a bowl of rice seems like an insignificant launching pad. But it wasn't too insignificant for Jesus. Will we replace Jesus' humility with our grandiosity?"[18]

Actually, hospitality is at the heart of the Christian life. God first extended hospitality to us—joined us when we were strangers, welcomed us into the trinitarian community, loved us first. And our appropriate response, if we really understand God's hospitality, is to turn around and do the same.

Most of the syllabi in the Center for Spiritual and Personal Formation at Bethel Seminary lay out guidelines for course interaction, one of which is that students will presume and extend welcome. We commit not to allow differences of any kind—gender, cultural, socioeconomic, denominational, or theological—to supersede our willingness to know and receive one another as if we were receiving Christ himself. We want students to have enough of an experience of authentic hospitality that they will be able and willing to offer it to others in their present and future ministries, whether they partner with God as children's ministers, therapists, preaching pastors, leaders of parachurch ministries, well-informed laypersons, or academic scholars.

In order to do this it is necessary to learn from Jesus, who was so good at creating a welcoming space for authentic encounter with him that would lead to transformation. Sometimes he did that with questions, not always easy ones, and never ones that coddled others. Deceptively simple questions, like: What do you want me to do for you? Who do you say that I am? Do you believe that I am able to do this? What does it matter to you how I deal with someone else?

Sometimes he did it with stories—stories that connected with his listeners' lives even as they tipped expectations upside down. Whether you were more familiar with sheep, messy houses, or problem kids, Jesus had a story that would welcome you into reflection and learning and that would locate you in the larger story authored by God. This is the hospitality not of cozy friendliness but of authentic welcome.

And sometimes Jesus did it with invitations: Follow me. Come and eat. Push out into deeper water.

Whole and holy Christ followers are able and willing to create hospitable space that allows for transformation through direct encounter with God, with others, and with self—through asking and answering questions, through telling and hearing stories, and through receiving and offering invitations. In these direct encounters both inviters and invited may experience what those disciples in Emmaus did: the ability to recognize Jesus. In many ways this is formation: learning to recognize the presence of God; being open to that presence when it's least expected; and growing up into Christ's image and likeness, individually and communally.

One challenge for us is that we must accurately understand that image and likeness. Do we understand God accurately? Are we willing to examine our most cherished preconceptions and let God change them when necessary? This is significant not only for our intellectual constructs about God, but perhaps even more so for our unconscious representations of God.[19]

This matters because we serve the God we imagine, and we invite others into the presence of that same God. As C. S. Lewis says in *A Grief Observed*, "My idea of God is not a divine idea. It has to be shattered time after time. He shatters it Himself. He is the great iconoclast. Could we not say that this shattering is one of the marks of His presence?"[20]

Although shattering doesn't sound particularly hospitable—and we certainly hope it happens through encounter with God and not with hurtful others—it reminds us of the risks inherent in hospitality. The Emmaus disciples had noticed that their hearts burned within them. When we experience the intense excitement that comes with new insight, new awareness of God, and a deeper, more complex understanding of truth, it does feel like our heart is on fire. Physiologically speaking, excitement and anxiety are not far apart in our emotional experience, and examples of people like Moses and Job remind us that encountering God can be a terrible thing, in the best sense of that word.

So this particular signifier of wholeness and holiness involves taking the risk of encountering God and inviting others into God's presence. Paul encourages Timothy and Titus to be sure that leaders are hospitable (1 Tim. 3:2; Titus 1:8). Christian wholeness and holiness are never about exerting power; rather, they are about extending welcome—especially to those who are on the margins. As Walter Brueggemann notes in *Interpretation and Obedience*: "To welcome the stranger is to challenge the social arrangements that exclude and include. Thus any serious welcome of a stranger is a gesture that 'unsettles' the power arrangements to which we have become accustomed."[21]

This echoes the definition of hospitality and its motivation in Matthew 25:

When he finally arrives . . . the King will say to those on his right, "Enter, you who are blessed by my Father! Take what's coming to you in this kingdom. It's been ready for you since the world's foundation. And here's why: I was hungry and you fed me. I was thirsty and you gave me a drink. I was homeless and you gave me a room. I was shivering and you gave me clothes. I was sick and you stopped to visit. I was in prison and you came to me." Then those "sheep" are going to say, "Master, what are you talking about? When did we ever see you hungry and feed you, thirsty and give you a drink? And when did we ever see you sick or in prison and come to you?" Then the King will say, "I'm telling the solemn truth: Whenever you did one of these things to someone overlooked or ignored, that was me—you did it for me." (Matt 25:31, 34–40 *Message*)

Love and hospitality are often linked in Scripture: "[God] defends the cause of the fatherless and the widow, and loves the foreigners residing among you, giving them food and clothing. And you are to love those who are foreigners, for you yourselves were foreigners in Egypt" (Deut. 10:18–19). "Let love be genuine. . . . Love one another with mutual affection . . . extend hospitality to strangers" (Rom. 12:9–13 NRSV). "Let mutual love continue. Do not neglect to show hospitality to strangers, for by doing that some have entertained angels without knowing it" (Heb. 13:1–2 NRSV). "Above all, love each other deeply, because love covers over a multitude of sins. Offer hospitality to one another without grumbling" (1 Pet. 4:8–9). Perhaps they are linked so often because both involve sacrifice.

The sacrifice of authentic hospitality means opening our hearts to make room for strangers, foreigners, and people on the margins whom we would prefer to ignore—or who are so invisible to us that we do not even know we are ignoring them. Sometimes our task is to follow Christ's example as he rebuked those who put barriers up to prevent others from experiencing welcome, whether children, tax collectors, prostitutes, or partiers. Speaking truth to power instead of smothering truth with power is the goal, because of the hospitality we ourselves experienced from God when we were still on the margins.

We do not and cannot extend hospitality perfectly. Sometimes our space gets messy. We try to keep it neat, but the realities of life mean sometimes there are dishes in the sink. This is all right, because hospitality is not about entertaining. We had a lot of guests in our home when I was young, and I probably confused hospitality with vacuuming. Maybe we should vacuum before people come into our space—but then we would be able to use *not* vacuuming as a way to avoid the anxiety of being hospitable. And that would be unfortunate. If I had been on the road to Emmaus, before my eyes were opened, before I recognized that God was present, would I *not* have invited Jesus in because I hadn't vacuumed? Let us take the risk. Let us encounter God. Let our desire for wholeness and holiness lead us into the margins.

Reception and Integration of Offerings from Social Science

A Response (Jeannine and Wyndy)

As we indicated in chapter 1, the method that centers our work is an interplay of offering, reception, and integration. Carla has provided offerings from social science in the previous two chapters. In this chapter we (Jeannine and Wyndy) respond to her work, exploring areas of resonance and dissonance between our disciplines and areas of study. By our reflective reception of Carla's work we hope to move further toward integrative understandings of human formation, wholeness, and holiness.

Reception and Integration from Hermeneutics (Jeannine)

Carla,

You begin your chapters by acknowledging that our interdisciplinary conversation could really begin with any of our disciplines. There is no magic starting place. As you note, it's simply important to start the conversation. I want to acknowledge that there might be a presumption by some that the right place to start is with my chapters, since the Bible ought to set the tone and undergird the rest of our work. While I affirm with great conviction the authority of Scripture for understanding human formation, we very intentionally chose to begin with formation and your field of social science, for at least two reasons. The first is that we wanted to acknowledge in the ordering of our conversation that each of us offers her own perspectives on God and the ways God has wired human individuals and communities. No one of us approaches this endeavor to understand from an objective, bird's-eye perspective. I do not provide *the* biblical viewpoint in my chapters, for instance. So our ordering is intended not to prioritize disciplines but to equalize them. Our belief is that we come to the interdisciplinary conversation as equal, though not at all identical, partners. Second, and more simply, in a book about human formation it makes great sense to hear from you first, since you live and breathe these issues on a daily basis in your teaching and scholarship. Yours is the voice I wanted to hear first!

The first set of observations I want to make revolves around areas of convergence between your contributions and what I will offer from a reading of Scripture in the next two chapters. We intentionally did not interact with each other's core contributions until after we had written our own. Given this, I am impressed and pleased by the significant resonance between your work and mine. I heard your affirmations related to the image of God as an important resource for understanding human identity and vocation. This will be thematic in my chapters as well. A common emphasis also emerged regarding the communal nature of wholeness and holiness; these are not only or primarily individual concerns.

Your discussion of the daunting task of love as a means of formation coheres with the New Testament call to *cruciformity*, the willingness to take up our cross for others, as a pattern of Christian living that I will explore. Again, this is not surprising. Yet the connections you draw between our attachment history and neurobiology and the risk of love (which might be able to hold both safety and unpredictability!) provide a real-life connection to what might easily be an idealized vision of conforming to Christ's image in his death (Phil. 3:10).

In fact, your contribution on the nature of love is one example of an overarching contribution social science can make to a biblical theology of formation. Social science can infuse theology with a dose of reality, since the latter tends to emphasize the ideal goals for and behaviors of humanity. I noticed this tendency as I was writing my chapters. Even while accounting for the role of sin in the biblical story, in those chapters I tend to emphasize God's intention for humanity, leaning toward an idealization of God's people as model humanity (in both Old and New Testaments). Social science offers a needed reality check. Your reminder that persons will only achieve a greater or lesser degree of wholeness and holiness was a good balance to idealized readings of a biblical vision for human holiness and wholeness.[1]

I was also reminded of this potential corrective when reading your insights on the importance of a trustworthy environment for formation. Given that I will refer to trust as a crucial human response to God and to others, your emphasis on the trustworthiness of the formation intermediary, or "container," is an important balance to my emphasis. Any unqualified exhortation to trust situations, systems, or even other Christians without the corresponding emphasis that the formation crucible be trustworthy could lead at least to stagnation rather than formation and, at worst, to trauma and violence.

I heard both convergence and divergence in your descriptions of holiness and wholeness as not ends but means to "authentic intimacy with, obedience to, and partnership with God" (chap. 3). This fits quite nicely with my affirmation that holiness is penultimate to wholeness and authentic life lived in covenant with God. Yet in chapters 5 and 6 I will frame that final goal to include wholeness. So I wondered about the tension between wholeness as process toward life with God (as you've expressed it) and wholeness conceived as part of the final goal for humanity (as I will express it). How much does the concept of wholeness, as defined by social science, cohere with a scriptural conception of wholeness? This seems to be a crucial question for navigating the discontinuity I'm hearing. I will describe wholeness as completeness, or integrity, primarily viewed communally and eschatologically. I heard you describing wholeness, at least initially, as a (possible) current experience of an individual embedded in community. Our disciplines seem to attend to different facets of this concept; consequently, we use the term in somewhat distinct ways.[2] So a conversation around the nature of wholeness psychologically and biblically could prove particularly fruitful.

Another of your contributions that pushed me to move beyond my typical ways of thinking was your attention to the nonlinear and nonintuitive nature of formation. You have emphasized that formation is not always, or even usually, forward moving. Your suggestions of alternate formation metaphors (metamorphosis, musical recapitulation, and growth spiral) were thought provoking. I will offer a sketch of the biblical story of humanity in relation to becoming (chap. 5) that could be read to imply a fairly linear process of formation (although I do not intend such a conception). Your offering reminded me that some of the stories in Scripture are about formation that happens in fits and starts. For instance, Peter's denial of Jesus (John 18:15–18, 25–27) provides what you have called a "crucible" experience in Peter's relationship with his master. Although it might look like Peter's denial is the end of their relationship, there is restoration on the horizon for him and an opportunity to reaffirm his loyalties (John 21:15–19). From Acts we hear of a metamorphosis experience in Peter's life. He receives a divine vision of clean and unclean animals (Acts 10:9–16) that revolutionizes his understanding of God (10:34) and his understanding of how Gentiles are welcomed fully into the messianic community without conversion to Judaism (10:44–45; 11:1–18).

The nonintuitive nature of formation also resonated with me. Specifically, you describe the inaccurate, though common, perception that distress indicates immaturity and a lack of formation. This false assumption is particularly captivating in the comfort-driven context of twenty-first-century America. Yet, resonating with your assertion, whole books in the Old Testament attest to the opposite: when we are in distress God is at work, though often in ways hidden from us. This is what Walter Brueggemann refers to as "Israel's countertestimony," which he finds in Job, Ecclesiastes, and the lament psalms.[3] It is precisely these more neglected parts of Scripture in my tradition that offer a holistic and realistic picture of formation. Job certainly does not experience well-being in the first forty-one chapters of that book. Yet at the end of his crucible experience Job finds that God was present to him in profound yet unimaginable ways (Job 42:1–6). Now I'd very much prefer not to experience Job's distress in my lifetime, but to assume that his distress signals a lack of maturity (as Job's friends did) is wrongheaded and destructive to all who experience suffering

(Job 42:7). I appreciate that you sketch a picture of formation that is complex enough to account for these ambiguities and realities.

My final responses to your chapter concern areas that seemed particularly fertile for future integrative conversations, in part because of their great personal interest: hermeneutics and identity. I resonated with the dialectic of particularity and relatedness you introduce for understanding human development (or "intimacy and alterity," as in Sandage, Jensen, and Jass).[4] I hear something like this dialectic in the biblical mandates for humanity to image God without falling into the sin of presuming to be like God, as well as the commands to be distinctive from culture while living within it (chaps. 5 and 6). Your offering suggests how important it is to hold an individual's autonomy in tension with his or her connectedness (differentiation). You indicate that this tension offers great potential for formation. Balancing that tension—rather than ignoring either pole or attempting to dissipate the tension—seems to be the key.

Living with a similar dialectic is important to biblical hermeneutics. Teaching hermeneutics to Bethel students in their first quarters of seminary requires introducing this dialectic. Most of our students come to seminary with a strong sense of connection (their relatedness) to Scripture—something like the Bible as friend and companion. As a result, I emphasize the Bible as Other (its alterity), helping students to wrestle with its particularity that arises from the various sociocultural settings in which and to which it was written.[5] Early on, students often rush to generalize or abstract the messages of a particular passage or book from its original historical context. I intentionally bring them back to the particularities of the text that push us to acknowledge its otherness.[6] Yet my goal in emphasizing the pole of particularity in my courses is to bring students to a place where they can live in the tension between Scripture's particularity and its relatedness to contemporary believers and believing communities. I would be very interested in further exploring this dialectic with you and Wyndy.

Another of your offerings that intersects with hermeneutics is your discussion of fundamentalist systems, in which the process of making sense of life is characterized by anxiety, defensiveness, and exclusion, and where "the worldview takes precedence over the relationship." As I read your description and case study of a fundamentalist system, I thought to myself, "that's why hermeneutics is important." Hermeneutics is a second-order task. When applied to the Bible, it is the study of what we are doing when we read and interpret. One problem with fundamentalism as a process (as a hermeneutic—a way of making sense of life), it seems to me, is that it doesn't distinguish reality from the act of interpreting it. Hermeneutics, properly understood as an interpretive process that is not coterminous with the realities it attempts to interpret, offers a way through the anxiety of being the holder and protector of all truth. It offers a way to metaphorically step back from my engagement with people and ideas and ask the very important question, How and why am I interpreting this person or this idea in this way? While we may not be able to answer this question fully or even accurately at every turn, recognizing that the question can and should be asked is a necessary starting point.

Exploring this connection between fundamentalist process and hermeneutics led me to wonder if the distinction you made between fundamentalism as content and fundamentalism as process might not be so clear and sharp. I appreciate your clarification that any group of people (religious or not, conservative or not) can be typified by a fundamentalist process. What I am left wondering is if fundamentalism in one's faith content virtually necessitates fundamentalism in systemic process. Christian fundamentalist belief in the necessity of "a 'naked' reading of Scripture" would seem to make virtually impossible a process that acknowledges, let alone assesses, the gap between the interpreter and her interpretation.[7] I am interested in exploring this further with you.

Finally, throughout our project together questions about human identity have surfaced for me. If humans are always becoming, that is, never arriving, what does this mean for the basis of human identity? As we noted in our prologue, the experience of fragmentation in our contemporary contexts is significant and real. What do our disciplines offer for such fragmentation of identity? I hear a glimmer of hope for this issue in your chapters. You note that love as a formation strategy can best emerge from an awareness of the subject of love in Scripture. You comment that the Bible speaks more of how we are loved than of how we are to love. I remember asking a question of the two of you in a past conversation: What might be a solid foundation for human identity? Carla, I remember vividly your suggestion that being God's beloved might be at that human core. Our identity might best be understood not in light of something inherent in us but in light of God's covenantal relationship and loving commitment to us—I can live with that.

Reception and Integration from Ethics (Wyndy)

Carla,

Thanks for these perspectives on becoming, wholeness, and holiness from the social sciences. You provide a helpful starting point for our conversation by offering these insights about formation that contribute to and prod my own thinking about it from the perspective of Christian ethics. Your insights from social science are helpful for starting us on this journey to more integrative approaches to fundamental questions about human life. This leads me to ask further questions, as good conversations should.

Your contributions have important points of coherence with means and ends in Christian moral thought. It does not just matter *that* we become and *what* we become; it matters *how* and *why* we become. One interesting theme that keeps coming up in our work is the importance of story and the deeply communal dimensions of formation, critical for the whats, whys, and hows of the process. I found fascinating your contributions on the domains of integration, especially memory integration, story, and "re-story" in chapter 3. I have been wondering for some time if it is possible to see conversion as the acceptance of and socialization into a new narrative or story; and if so, how do salvation and conversion contribute to healing brokenness by "re-storying" our lives? We certainly see evangelism as telling a story, but it is usually one's personal story of conversion to Christ. And it is almost always relayed verbally. I think for many, conversion is perceived as a one-time event of "getting saved" as the beginning and end of Christian experience and the goal of Christian life.[8] From a theological perspective, your insights can expand our conceptions of conversion as that which is ongoing without the danger of destabilizing ourselves (e.g., change out of boredom or Paul's illustration of being "tossed back and forth by the waves and blown here and there," Eph. 4:14–16). It seems necessary to keep processes and means of formation focused on the end of the story, which is complete restoration of ourselves and perfect wholeness and holiness in Christ. Your insights help us address some fragmentations and bifurcations: event from process; self from community; intellectual growth from praxis; personal differences from communal integrity; and spiritual understanding from practices. It also addresses the bifurcations between salvation and morality, and faith and ethics, which I consider crucial not just to bridge but to integrate at many levels.

Your discussion in chapter 2 on fundamentalism as relational process and approach to life was really interesting; I found many points of connection with dynamics of moral formation. As we were writing the book and reading each other's chapters, a series was airing on PBS's *The American Experience* called "We Shall Remain."[9] It is a fabulous but convicting five-part series on the history, presence, and subsequent removal of American Indians from their lands, often justified by the beliefs of certain groups of Christians who came to colonize and evangelize this "new" land. I have been watching this series on Monday evenings, writing our book, and teaching a Christian ethics class all at the same time (ah, yes, integration everywhere we turn). I find an important link between your insights on fundamentalism as a relational process, as opposed to a set of beliefs, and assurances of our own moral goodness, which I hear fairly regularly in such grand statements as " 'we' are a Christian nation" and "our lives would be much better if 'we' just returned to our biblical roots" (often phrased as a moral mandate).[10] I was drawn, therefore, to your insights on fundamentalism as an approach to life that insists on one story, excluding the stories of others, and fails to recognize the historiographies of all stories, including our own. I am reminded of how important it is to "remember rightly" as a moral practice.[11] The story of American Indians is also our story and must be told and remembered rightly in the quest for healing, restoration, and *shalom*.

I see fundamentalism as an approach to life appropriated in some forms of ethical thinking where defending right belief becomes the moral thing to do; or it appears in a tight-fisted adherence to rules and principles as the sum total of our moral obligations. I have often wondered if this was one of Jesus's concerns with the Pharisees. Were they more concerned with being right than with being righteous? There is an overwhelming fear of relativism that robs us of vital skills in moral discernment, wonder, and imagination, necessary for bringing our moral claims to bear in contested and complex moral spaces.[12] There is a difference between relativism (the belief that all things are relative with no morally stable reference points) and contextualism (taking our lived realities seriously for discerning how to live more faithfully) that seems pertinent to identifying how fundamentalism as an approach to life functions in morality and ethics. It is easy to claim moral absolutes. It is much more difficult to faithfully and coherently live out our moral claims in diverse and complex social contexts. I think your offerings on fundamentalism also have interesting implications for the moral qualities of our communities, where our becoming more whole and holy does or does not happen. You mention how important trustworthiness, openness, and inclusion of various voices are to the overall health and vitality of our communities. It's an odd thing how much our lives are impacted by the communities in which we live and the social structures that determine so many aspects of our lives (and yes, the church and the seminary are social structures). Yet we are so individualistic in confronting the problems that befall us.[13] There seems to be an operating assumption that conflicts are personal (i.e., people who do not get along with each other) and are solved by certain persons (usually the perceived "agitators") making amends and learning to do things the right way. I am still left in this conundrum when it comes to the social dimensions of formation: Can we really live the Christian story without a community that is committed to becoming more whole and holy, one that pays attention to means and ends? How do we become more whole and holy communities? Where does it start and who is responsible?

I have been thinking about your insights on a multidimensional approach to formation that challenges the adjectives we place in front of "formation" to qualify, and even minimize, our conception of it. Your reminders in chapter 2 of what formation is not clearly identify some of the ways in which our formation is short-circuited and how unformed our ideas of formation often are. I think this is important in light of the renewed interest in spiritual formation, a renewal that often amuses me given that formation has been central to Christian faith and practice throughout the history of the church. It's interesting to me that there is no absence of spirituality in our contemporary rhetoric. Just look at the presence of the paranormal on television programs today. It is not difficult to talk with people about spirituality broadly conceived, because many people would identify themselves as spiritual though not religious. This reflects what Gregory Jones calls "consumer spirituality."[14] It is individual, selective, a-contextual, ahistorical, non-storied, and essentially non-formative.[15] I fear that, in practice, this is what is referred to in contemporary articulations of spiritual formation that are co-opted by the ideologies of individualism and consumerism.[16] You offer a broadly conceived paradigm of formation that encompasses all aspects of our lives: the material, economic, social, psychological, moral, and spiritual. This helps me to rethink my interests in the relationships between spiritual and moral formation, wondering if these adjectives are even helpful. I am pressed to think again of formation as multifaceted so that a particular kind of formation, such as moral or spiritual formation, is not privileged as an ultimate means or ends of formation since, as you note, formation occurs in many ways and on many levels. Alternately, your work helps me to make tighter connections between multidimensional formations that, as you describe them, are processes of being always formed into the divine image. This has enormous moral implications.

I wonder how to best integrate these insights on formation from the perspective of the social sciences into theology classes. I teach in a seminary with a large contingent of counseling students, working on the degree track that prepares them for licensure as professional counselors. The integration of theology and social sciences becomes very tricky from both perspectives. We (at Ashland Seminary) are committed to integration in theory, but tend to practice what has been identified in our first chapter as a less than helpful process of integration—*my* discovery of what is relevant from *your* field for *my* own work. This is what I'm still pondering as a person who teaches Theology 1 to first-year students from all degree programs at Ashland. What relationship does the image of wholeness and holiness from a trinitarian perspective have to do with psycholog-ical theories of the self?[17] How are wholeness and holiness related to mental health?[18]

I am interested in further exploring these questions with you and Jeannine. So, while we (the three of us) believe that no discipline should be privileged over another, I have found this egalitarian approach we are proposing a bit more difficult to put into practice where I teach. I am sure there are a host of reasons for this. I have typically heard from counseling students their dread of taking courses in theology and biblical studies, because these courses are perceived as either too hard or arcane to their proposed course of study. My sense is that it is the latter, with an unintended result that unexamined theories of the self come from a variety of places and experiences. Of course students are not alone in this. I am sure part of the fault lies with theologians, for whom theology is nothing but a tried and true (re)articulation of belief without the openness to new possibilities and perspectives that may actually move us to take God more seriously in all domains of human life, and who avoid social science insights into important questions about what it means to be human. I'm interested in exploring more how the study and teaching of theology and the practice of beliefs may contribute to understandings of healing, human wholeness, recovery, and "restorying" one's life. I wonder what you think of this and what way forward you would offer to those of us who teach foundational theology courses in a seminary.

I will end by expressing my appreciation for your contributions on hospitality as a marker of wholeness and holiness as a powerful ending to your chapters. These cohere with how I see generosity and justice not just as related to our becoming more whole and holy, but also as social virtues crucial for the well-being of other persons. I thought of using hospitality in my chapter but instead opted for generosity as having a stronger tie to justice.[19] The insights you offer about hospitality are so important for Christian ethics. The moral life is grounded in God's hospitality to us and propelled forward by Jesus's command to "go and do likewise" (Luke 14:37) by extending generous hospitality to others. You express how our openness and attention to others is a way of becoming more whole and holy in visible and concrete ways, reaffirming formation as both personal and public. I so appreciate this proposal and possibility you offer.

BEING AND BECOMING

The Scriptural Story of Formation (Jeannine)

In our work together we are exploring the idea of becoming whole and holy. In the next chapter I will sketch some of the contours of wholeness and holiness from Scripture. The prior question, which I attend to in this chapter, is the issue of becoming. What does it mean to be "becoming"—to be in process? How do humans "become"— that is, how do we change and develop? How are we formed and what are the means and agency of that formation? Of the two sets of questions (What is wholeness/holiness? How do humans become?), I believe the latter is more difficult to answer, in part because it is the one asked less often, and its answer is more often assumed. By arriving at a good definition of wholeness and holiness we might be prone to think that we have covered essential ground in the conversation on spiritual and moral formation. Yet if we don't take the time to reflect upon the prior question of what it means to be becoming, we will leave unexamined fundamental issues about the divine goals for human formation and whether and how human growth happens.

A brief comment about hermeneutics is in order before I begin my own look at the biblical witness on the themes Carla, Wyndy, and I are addressing. I strive throughout this chapter and the next to address these themes without resorting to proof-texting. It is my conviction and that of my discipline to interpret individual biblical books well in their original contexts. Thus, I am more comfortable studying a single New Testament book than gathering together biblical material on a single topic or theme. Yet the nature of this project repeatedly does not allow me this luxury. I have had to bring together themes from across the whole Bible to address becoming, wholeness, and holiness.

This constraint (or freedom?) has led me to frame this chapter, in large part, as a retelling of the biblical story line. Interpretively, I have tried to attend to the key themes and movements of the story of God and God's people that emerge for me from a reading of Scripture (this is why, for example, certain passages like Gen. 12:1–3 and Exod. 19:3–6 come up more than once in these chapters). While I certainly accept that this is *my* understanding of the canonical story line, I would claim that all of us interpret the Bible all of the time with one or another rendering of the biblical story in view. All readers of the Bible assume and assert a telling of the biblical story whenever they interpret any particular text. My hermeneutical assumptions and commitments lead me to affirm that the Bible tells a coherent story of God's work in this world, one we can draw theological and ethical insights from when understood in context.[1] It is from this rendering of the biblical story that I find crucial resources for what it means to become, and what it means to become whole and holy.

The Biblical Story: Implications for Human Becoming

The greatest scriptural resource I know for addressing this set of fundamental human questions is the broad framework of the biblical story itself. "For the biblical writers . . . , 'what is it to be human?' is ultimately a narrative-ethical . . . question. It cannot be named apart from the drama of creation, fall, redemption, and consummation."[2] With creation on one side and the renewal of all things on the other, the biblical story of God's relationship with humanity provides a number of crucial affirmations for understanding how human formation occurs.

The early chapters of Genesis signal two central themes for understanding human becoming: God's intentions for humankind, and the role of sin in circumscribing human potential.

Creational Purposes and Becoming

God's creational intention for human beings, expressed in Genesis 1:26–27, is that they be bearers of the divine image. Whether the particularities of imaging God are grounded in the task of caring for and ruling the earth on God's behalf (Gen. 1:26; Ps. 8), in humanity's relational nature (created as male and female to image God; Gen. 1:27), or in the human vocation of carrying on God's creative work,[3] the Old Testament motif of imaging God finds its ongoing narrative focus in Israel's call to be like Yahweh, its God. "Be holy because I, the LORD your God, am holy" (Lev. 19:2). God's intentions for humanity (Gen. 1:26) and for Israel form the same kind of "covenantal commission."[4] The refrain of reflective holiness defines and compels Israel toward its calling to image God to those nations that do not yet know Yahweh as the true God (Exod. 19:5–6). To be holy is not simply about Israel looking different from its neighbors. Israel is to look *like* Yahweh—to image God. According to the New Testament, which picks up the divine image motif, Jesus the Messiah displays the glory and image of God (2 Cor. 4:1–6; Col. 1:15–20; Heb. 1:1–4). Utterly faithful to humanity's and Israel's mission, Jesus makes possible the re-creation of humanity and the full restoration of God's image (Rom. 8:18–23; Col. 3:9–10).

Corresponding to imaging God, God's intention for humanity is also discernible in humanity's nature as *created beings*. Dependent on its creator, humanity is finite, finitude being a fundamental creational quality. "Creation in the image of God both assigns a certain likeness to God and at the same time makes clear that this is precisely a likeness in created form."[5] Humanity as created—and thus finite—grounds human becoming in God's intention at creation, rather than in the fall and its consequences. Built into human being is human becoming. Terence Fretheim emphasizes the ongoing creational activity of God into which humanity is invited to participate as God-imagers. Even before the fall, "there is an element of incompleteness that is integral to the very structures of created existence . . . ('subdue' the earth, Gen. 1:28)."[6] This incompleteness, rooted in finitude, sets humanity on a trajectory of growth and formation and invites human participation in the work of God through imaging God. Human finitude is no barrier to human imaging of God;

67

instead it would seem that God intentionally paired finitude and divine imaging in humanity.

Ironically, it is the attempt to transgress finitude that defines the story of sin in the garden. It is the temptation to become godlike that precipitates the fall of humanity (Gen. 3:5). In the specific narrative context it is the desire to "be like God, knowing good and evil" that poses a threat to human wholeness.[7] We glimpse here an implication for human spiritual formation. Thinking that we can achieve godlike knowledge is an attempt to shed our God-given creatureliness, our finitude. Yet the biblical witness affirms time and again the finite nature of humanity.

> As for mortals, their days are like grass,
>   they flourish like a flower of the field. (Ps. 103:15 NRSV;
>   see 13–19; also Ps. 102)

> Then Job replied to the LORD:
>   "I know that you can do all things;
>   no purpose of yours can be thwarted.
>   You asked, 'Who is this that obscures my plans without
>   knowledge?'
>   Surely I spoke of things I did not understand,
>   things too wonderful for me to know." (Job 42:1–3)

Supposing that we can see from God's vantage point contradicts our finite perspective. We are located, as we were created to be. We see and understand from a limited point of view, and so we were created to be.

Yet the claim that we possess God's perspective seems easily made in at least some contemporary Christian circles. Our desire for right theology can lead us to overemphasize our ability to acquire full knowledge of God. This may be understandable given Christianity's focus on God's revelation in Jesus the Messiah, in Scripture, and through the particularities of human history and experience. This is, however, a line that must be walked with care. While affirming God's revelation to humanity, we must never lose sight of our own finitude. While God's revelation is truly accessible, it is not something we can know outside of our particular human locations. The infinite God cannot be fully understood by finite persons. As Martin Buber starkly claims, "God . . . the eternal presence, cannot be had. Woe unto the possessed who fancy that they possess God."[8] Any claims to absolute knowledge ironically and inevitably mirror the fall.

Alternately, human knowledge is most possible within a set of commitments that do not place knowledge as the only or highest goal. John Goldingay characterizes the quest for knowledge in the Old Testament wisdom literature as "not objective and cautious [in modern fashion] but . . . based on commitment, trusting in the world and life and experience and the order that it expresses, and behind that, trusting in YHWH."[9] As Paul affirms to the knowledge-obsessed Corinthian church, true knowing comes to those who have taken the prior ethical stance of love toward others.

> Those who think they have something do not yet know as they ought to know.
> But whoever loves truly knows. (1 Cor. 8:2–3)[10]

Relational knowledge ("knowledge emerg[ing] out of relationality inherent in reality")[11] is the only knowledge available to finite human persons. Yet relational knowledge is precisely the kind of knowledge needed, according to Paul—not knowledge abstracted from relationships with God, others, and the world, but knowledge that has love as both foundation and goal. In the context of a relational knowledge, we can join in the Eastern Orthodox affirmation that, though we cannot know God fully, we may know God truly.

Idolatry as a Factor in Becoming

So far we have explored the biblical story and its creational themes of divine image-bearing and finitude that ground human becoming. And it is precisely this divine purpose for humankind to image God and to live as finite creatures in relationship to an infinite God that propels humanity onto the path of becoming, of formation. Yet a biblical theology of human becoming is also significantly shaped by the second act of the human drama: the fall. The human propensity to turn from allegiance to God and God's ways defines human existence throughout the scriptural narrative. As we have already noted, the initial sinful turn is defined by a presumption to shed finite constraints and "be like God." This movement to idolatry, which we might define as putting anything, including self, in God's place, impacts all subsequent biblical testimony about human formation. While the inevitability of human formation is rooted in creation, the need for spiritual *re*-formation and *re*-orientation is necessitated by the fall.

While worshipping other gods is the primary way the nations of the ancient Near East, and sometimes Israel, turned their back on the true God, human attempts toward autonomy from God also appear in biblical warnings.

> You have trusted in your wickedness and have said, "No one sees me."
> Your wisdom and knowledge mislead you when you say to yourself,
> *"I am, and there is none besides me."* (Isa. 47:10, emphasis mine)

This indictment of Babylon plays on a refrain from Isaiah's description of Yahweh ("I am the LORD, and there is no other," 45:6; see 45:14, 18, 21, 22; 46:9) and exposes this autonomous claim from the lips of finite people as idolatrous. Idolatry is Israel's nemesis, from the inception of God's covenant with Israel where God commands full loyalty ("you shall have no other gods before me," Exod. 20:1–6) to the prophets' critique of Israel that they have turned away to idols (e.g., "[My people] consult a wooden idol," Hosea 4:12–19; see also Isa. 2:5–8; Jer. 2:11–12, 26–28; Amos 5:25–27; Mic. 5:10–15; Zeph. 1:4–6; Zech. 13:2). The New Testament also depicts loyalty to Israel's God as antithetical to idolatrous practices, which extend to immorality and greed (1 Cor. 10:7–8; Eph. 5:5; Col. 3:5).[12] "Dear children, keep yourselves from idols" (1 John 5:21; see also 1 Cor. 10:7, 14; 1 Thess. 1:9–10; 1 Pet. 4:1–3).

God's Initiating of Relationship for Redemption

The solution to the problem of human sin and idolatry comes in the form of covenant faithfulness and loyalty. And it is God's loyalty to humanity that begins and grounds covenantal redemption. In faithfulness to all creation, God reinitiates relationship with fallen humanity through saving and covenanting with Noah's family (Gen.

8:20–9:17). In faithfulness God chooses Abraham and his family for blessing so that they will be a means of blessing to all nations (Gen. 12:1–3). The human side of the equation comes through responsive covenant loyalty. Those who respond with trust in and loyalty to God's covenanting work become interwoven in God's plan to bring restoration to all peoples (Gen. 4:26; 5:22; 6:9; 15:6). When God redeems Israel from Egypt for covenantal relationship, it is called in mission to the nations. "The Sinai covenant . . . is a formalization of Israel's role in the world—to be a holy nation and a kingdom of priests (Exod. 19:3–6). The giving of the law to an already redeemed people is in the service of this vocation."[13]

This intermingling of God's faithful covenanting and Israel's vocation of responsive loyalty and mission forms the backdrop for Jesus's vocation. Matthew (along with other New Testament writers) highlights Jesus as the faithful representative of Israel who demonstrates complete loyalty in the face of his people's historical struggle to remain faithful to the covenant (see 2 Kings 24:20–25:21; Jer. 31:32). Matthew shows the parallel lives of Israel and Jesus in Matthew 2–4. The evangelist compares Jesus to Israel: both are forced into Egyptian exile before returning to the land (2:13–23, esp. 2:15). Matthew portrays Jesus as the faithful Son (3:17) who demonstrates his covenant loyalty to God in the same wilderness setting where Israel proved disobedient (4:1–11, with Jesus's citations from Deut. 6–8, reflecting Israel's wilderness disloyalties). Jesus lives out the life of faithful humanity that God intended all Israel to live. And he does so on behalf of Israel and in mission to all nations (Matt. 1:21; 28:18–20).

On the other hand, Matthew also shows Jesus embodying Yahweh, Israel's God, in mission and identity. This is communicated most clearly, though implicitly, through a number of narrative motifs. First, Matthew highlights various characters who worship Jesus, including the magi at the beginning of the narrative (2:2, 11) and Jesus's followers at its climactic, post-resurrection moments (28:7, 17). Matthew also connects Jesus's mission with Yahweh's at key points by showing Jesus to be the one who enacts Old Testament expectations for Yahweh's return to Israel (e.g., Matt. 3:3; cf. Isa. 40:1–5). Finally, Matthew portrays Jesus as universal lord and judge after his resurrection, a role reserved in the Hebrew scriptures for God alone (Matt. 28:18; cf. Dan. 7:13–14). According to Richard

Bauckham, Jesus's universal lordship implicitly affirms his inclusion in the "unique divine identity."[14] In his willing obedience, even to the point of his missional death, Jesus faithfully enacts both the divine and the human sides of the covenant, making human faithfulness possible for all those who trust in his faithful work. God overcomes human sin and idolatry in Jesus, the locus of both divine forgiveness and human faithfulness (Rom. 3:21–26; 2 Cor. 5:19).

Implications for Human Formation

What are the formation implications of the biblical story of redemption to the nations, first through Israel and then through Jesus as Israel's faithful representative? The first implication is for returning to God. If idolatry is at the center of the human dilemma, then turning back to God is required. Yahweh's covenant with Israel provides the opportunity to return and the relational context that empowers return. The exhortation in the prophets to repent from idolatry fits this returning theme (e.g., Isa. 31:6–7; Ezek. 14:6; Hosea 14:1–3). In fact, Zechariah's God-given message is framed by returning language: "Therefore tell the people: This is what the LORD Almighty says: 'Return to me,' declares the LORD Almighty, 'and I will return to you,' says the LORD Almighty" (Zech. 1:3). John the Baptist and Jesus also issue this prophetic call for repentance in preparation for receiving God's saving work (e.g., Mark 1:4, 15). Paul describes the believers in Thessalonica as those who "turned to God from idols to serve the living and true God" (1 Thess. 1:9).

This returning or repentance is not solely or even primarily of human initiation, however. It comes as a response to divine offering and empowering, according to various Scriptures.

> I have swept away your offenses like a cloud,
>   your sins like the morning mist.
> Return to me,
>   for I have redeemed you. (Isa. 44:22)

I will give you a new heart and put a new spirit in you; I will remove from you your heart of stone and give you a heart of flesh. And I will put my Spirit in you and move you to follow my decrees and be careful to keep my laws. (Ezek. 36:26–27)

And so goes the pattern across Scripture of God's repeated covenantal initiative and call for human response.

Returning as response to God's restoration leads to a second formation implication of the biblical story sketched here: participation. By returning to God in response to God's restoring work, humanity has the opportunity to once again participate in the divine intention of imaging God. We see this at the moment of God's covenantal affirmation with Israel in the call to be a holy nation (Exod. 19:3–6). In the New Testament Paul frequently draws on language evoking participation to explain the relationship between the believing community and the work and person of Messiah Jesus.

We could look at 1 Corinthians 1:4–9 as an example of how Paul envisions believers participating in what Jesus has accomplished.

> I always thank my God for you because of his grace given you *in Christ Jesus*. For *in him* you have been enriched in every way—with all kinds of speech and with all knowledge—God thus confirming our testimony about Christ among you. Therefore you do not lack any spiritual gift as you eagerly wait for our Lord Jesus Christ to be revealed. He will also keep you firm to the end, so that you will be blameless on the day of our Lord Jesus Christ. God is faithful, who has called you into *fellowship* [participation; *koinōnia*] with his Son, Jesus Christ our Lord. (emphasis mine)

In this brief passage Paul highlights the benefits the Corinthian believers share because they are "in Christ." The grace they have received (an overarching term for God's saving actions) is given "in Christ Jesus" (*en Christō Iēsou*, 1:4). Every blessing they have received—speech, knowledge, gifts—comes "in Christ" (*en autō*, 1:5). As Paul will make clear at the end of this chapter, it is not simply that believers received these benefits through Christ. Rather, it is because believers are themselves in Christ that they received all that overflows from the work of Jesus (1:30; see also Rom. 8:1; 2 Cor. 5:17). Paul uses "in Christ" here and elsewhere to signal participation.[15] Union with Christ results in an identification with his person and work in such a way that believers truly participate in, and so benefit from, Jesus's faithful life, death, and resurrection. As Anthony Thiselton frames it, they are shareholders in the life of the Messiah.[16] This is the *koinōnia*, or participation, that Paul emphasizes when he assures the Corinthians that their faithful God, who has called them into *koinōnia* with Jesus, will keep them to the end (1 Cor. 1:8–9).[17]

The picture of participation sketched so far lacks the dynamic quality that permeates Paul's vision of participation with Christ. So we need to remind ourselves that Paul's theology balances the "already" and the "not yet" of God's saving work. Quick to highlight the "already" of God's work in Christ, Paul lays emphasis on the communal participation with Jesus the Messiah that believers already share and experience in the Spirit.[18] Yet Paul speaks quite readily about sufferings that believers will experience in the time before consummation and resurrection (Rom. 8:18–25; Phil. 3:7–11). He also urges the community of believers to live into what is already theirs in the Messiah—into his life, death, and resurrection (see Phil. 3:10–11). For example, he calls the Roman believers to count themselves "dead to sin but alive to God *in Christ Jesus*" as the basis of their saying no to sin in their lives (Rom. 6:11–12). In Colossians we hear that the behavior of believers should come in line with the reality that they have "taken off [the] old self [*anthrōpon*, alluding to Adam in Gen. 1:27] with its practices and have put on the new self [referring to Christ], which is being renewed in knowledge in the image of its Creator" (Col. 3:9–10, see 5–8).[19] Identity in Christ is both a present reality and a promise to be fully actualized in the final day. Christians are to live into that final-day reality more and more fully in the present (Phil. 3:12–14).

In fact, living into the reality of being in Christ defines discipleship. Conceptually, participation is both a noun (a present reality) and a verb: believers are to live a life of daily participating in Christ, and the center of this active participation is trust and loyalty.[20] For Paul, being a believer in Jesus means trusting and committing in loyalty to him, the fully faithful one. Jesus faithfully lived out the truly human life in love on Israel's behalf and died to make this kind of life available to Jew and non-Jew alike. It is Jesus's faithfulness, even and especially in his missional death, that brings believers into right relationship with God, into life and freedom (1 Pet. 3:18). As Christians trust in Jesus's death for their forgiveness, they also trust in his faithfulness as the power and pattern of their own loyalty. They ride Christ's coattails, as it were, from his faithfulness to their own (Rom. 1:17).[21] "To live by the faithfulness of the Son of God . . . is to live in such wholehearted devotion to God that it expresses itself in sacrificial, or cruciform, love for others"—in the pattern set by Jesus and in the power provided by his Spirit.[22]

Participation in Jesus the Messiah forms the believing community into his image, fulfilling humanity's vocation to image God. In the New Testament vision Christ reveals God to be cruciform, since God's truest self is revealed at the cross (1 Cor. 1:18–25).[23] If Christ images the invisible God (Col. 1:15; see 2 Cor. 4:4; Heb. 1:3), then God's image is cross-shaped.

> When we speak of "following Christ," it is the crucified Messiah we are talking about. His death was not simply the messy bit that enables our sins to be forgiven but that can then be forgotten. The cross is the surest, truest and deepest window on the very heart and character of the living and loving God.[24]

So being conformed to the image of Jesus the Messiah is about "cruciformity"—a self-giving to others in love in the pattern and power of Jesus. According to the New Testament, being formed into the image of Christ is the end goal of Christian formation.

> For those God foreknew he also predestined to be conformed to the image of his Son, that he might be the firstborn among many brothers and sisters. (Rom. 8:29; see also Col. 3:9–10)

> For God, who said, "Let light shine out of darkness," made his light shine in our hearts to give us the light of the knowledge of God's glory displayed in the face of Christ. (2 Cor. 4:6)

Messiah Jesus imaged and images God through his perfectly faithful and loving life and death. Christians are to take the shape of this Jesus as they participate in and benefit from his faithfulness and love.

So the story of humanity's creation, fall, and redemption leads us to a vision of ongoing human formation. We have seen that, while God's purposes for creating humanity embed formation or growth into the human trajectory, human sin and idolatry have complicated this intended pathway. Instead of enjoying relationship with God and willingly participating in imaging God and serving the creation, humankind has followed the path of idolatry. Yet

God's work of re-creation, first in Israel and then concentrated in Jesus as Israel's faithful representative, invites humanity into returned relationship and restored formation and vocation focused on imaging God in Christ.

An Eschatological Vision of Becoming

The end of the biblical story also informs an understanding of human formation. While the New Testament is clear that the arrival of Jesus the Messiah has brought the end into the "now" of human history (1 Cor. 10:11), it also affirms a final renewal of all creation still to come. The biblical story concludes with this picture of ultimate restoration, of "a new heaven and a new earth" (2 Pet. 3:13; Rev. 21:1), or what Paul refers to as the liberation of creation (Rom. 8:21). The contours of this final eschatological vision are only broadly indicated in the New Testament or else expressed symbolically—not surprising, as the New Testament writers attempt to express the ineffable quality of what is still to come. Yet the following facets of this vision relevant to human formation emerge from a reading of the New Testament.

First, the formation of God's people into Jesus's likeness will no longer be deterred or marred by the presence of evil and death (1 Cor. 15:25–26, 49). Fullness of life and wholeness will mark God's people and all creation. The seer of Revelation draws on the symbols of eating from the tree of life (2:7; 22:2, 14, 19) and drinking from the water of life (21:6; 22:1, 17) to express this superabundance of life. A glimpse of communal fullness of life for God's people emerges from John's description of the church as "a great multitude that no one could count, from every nation, tribe, people and language," worshipping God in thanksgiving (Rev. 7:9–10). "The *imago dei* is . . . ultimately communal."[25] And the shape of that community is wonderfully multiethnic.

Also, wholeness and healing are evoked when the author of Revelation writes that in the final day "God will wipe away every tear from their eyes" (Rev. 7:17; also 21:4). Pain will be no more; grief and mourning will be replaced by comfort and blessedness (Matt. 5:4). New Testament authors use language of blamelessness to signal the moral wholeness that will characterize God's people at the final restoration (Eph. 5:27; Phil. 1:10; 1 Thess. 3:13; 5:23). For Fretheim, despite significant continuity between the original and the new creation, at least one difference will be that disobedience will no longer be possible (Jer. 31:31–34).[26]

Finally, full knowing of God will come to believers in that great day. As Paul expresses his longing, "For now we see only a reflection as in a mirror; then we shall see face to face. Now I know in part; then I shall know fully, even as I am fully known" (1 Cor. 13:12). Paul speaks here of relational seeing and knowing that will come to fullness in the final restoration. Being able to finally see God is likewise implied in Revelation 21:22, where the holy city has no temple "because the Lord God Almighty and the Lamb are its temple." The relational quality of this seeing and knowing does not necessarily lend itself to the notion that humans will finally achieve infinite knowledge. While Scripture doesn't speak to whether humans will continue to learn, create, and grow (in other words, continue becoming) in the renewed creation, the fact that human becoming is grounded in creation might suggest that it will continue even after fullness of life, wholeness, moral perfection, and seeing God have been granted. In fact, there might be just such a longing for becoming built into our finite creatureliness; at least I hope so.

> If heaven is perfection, I'll get my deepest questions
>   answered.
> Like a child tears into wrappings to a Christmas tune.
> But in that great hall, let there be a bright red ribbon . . .
> that stays wrapped around the mystery of "someday soon."[27]

Telling the biblical story in this way raises some central implications for human becoming. Our creaturely finitude means that we are and will be on a journey of change, growth, and becoming. The human inclination toward idolatry means that God's intervention is necessary to "re-turn" humanity. It also means that fundamental human responses to God's covenanting initiative include repentance (a corresponding returning to God) and a renewed participation in God's intentions for humankind to be image bearers. The Christian gospel is that Jesus the Messiah has taken on this human role and vocation and has become the image bearer par excellence. In essence,

God in Jesus lives the truly faithful human life so that those who trust and put their allegiance in Jesus share in his faithful cruciform life, death, and resurrection. By embracing Jesus they embrace a life committed to loving the other sacrificially. The Bible's eschatological vision of a restored and whole humanity—freed from sin and death, freed for fullness of life—means that hope is a cardinal Christian virtue. This hope is not wishful thinking. Christian hope is a robust and active stance that seeks to live in light of what is still to come (1 Pet. 1:13). And since what is still to come is guaranteed by what Jesus the Messiah has already accomplished, Christian hope arises from the deepest conviction.[28]

Cultivating Ways of Becoming Whole and Holy

A number of implications for Christian formation have emerged from this telling of the biblical story. God's initiatory and ongoing commitment to humanity invites us to a responsive kind of living that involves participating in God's creational and redemptive purposes. A remaining question is, How do we as Christians cultivate a life of this kind of responsiveness to God's ongoing, saving work? Rather than attempt a comprehensive answer to this important question, in the concluding section of this chapter I offer two broad rubrics of Christian responsiveness to God's work that have captivated me as I read the scriptural witness concerning human formation, and as I attempt to live responsively. These rubrics are *dependence* and *discernment*.[29]

Dependence arises from the human story portrayed in Scripture. It is a proper stance of finite people in relationship to an infinite, personal, and covenant-making God. Because of the fall humans chafe against dependence. Yet God has continued to call and woo people back to a relationship and condition of dependence. Psalm 131 captures this well.

> My heart is not proud, LORD,
>   my eyes are not haughty;
> I do not concern myself with great matters
>   or things too wonderful for me.
> But I have calmed myself
>   and quieted my ambitions.

> I am like a weaned child with its mother;
> > like a weaned child I am content.
> Israel, put your hope in the LORD
> > both now and forevermore.

A description of dependence as the antithesis of pride and ambition, and as the basis for contentment and hope, emerges from the psalmist's portrait of Israel, God's people, as a satisfied child in its mother's arms.[30] While grounded in the biblical story and text, my interest in attending to dependence for understanding and motivating what it means to be becoming also emerges from my own journey. I am thoroughly embedded in a cultural context that prizes individualism and autonomy. From my youth I have breathed these in and made them my own. Yet the biblical affirmation of human finitude and the story of what happens when life is lived as if the true God doesn't matter call into question my allegiance to my own independence. Scripture paints an alternate vision of human beings in a healthy dependence on God and interdependence with one another.

How does dependence contribute to spiritual formation? Being dependent elicits a different set of questions about Christian growth. Dependence assumes that God is already at work, so a centering question that emerges is Where is God in this? In whatever situations, questions, or experiences we encounter, we can ask how God is already present, involved, and directing us precisely in the middle of these life experiences. This question—a foundational one in the practice of spiritual direction—is quite different from the one I intuited in my early Christian learning: What do I need *to do* to grow in God? The latter is encapsulated in the commonplace refrain: If you're not feeling close to God, guess who moved? The onus for growth implied in this question is the Christian self, with the emphasis on autonomy rather than dependence.

Dependence also contributes to formation by inviting others into the spiritual journey. In fact, the communal contexts from which the Scriptures were written make it difficult to sustain any picture of human becoming apart from human community. Models of growth that emphasize the individual in relationship with God can lose sight of the communal nature of personal and spiritual formation. For good or ill we are formed by and in relationships with others.

The Christian community is intended to be the context of wisdom and nurture for growth into Christlikeness (Eph. 4:1–16). "From him the whole body, joined and held together by every supporting ligament, grows and builds itself up in love, as each part does its work" (4:16).

Dependence, however, is not passivity, as if I have nothing to do with my own formation. It lives closely with trust. As we have seen while exploring the biblical story of human becoming, trust placed in Jesus's faithful work is central to our participation "in Christ." His faithfulness to and trust in God provide the pattern for, and activate our own responses to, God's work in our lives. Each of the four Gospel writers makes the connection between Jesus at the cross and the portrait of the faithful yet suffering person of Psalm 22. Like that psalmist Jesus trusts God to act when it seems that God is absent (Matt. 27:39–46; Mark 15:29–34; also Luke 23:34–36; John 19:24–28). As believers seek to trust and depend on God, they can do no better than to watch and emulate Jesus's example of absolute trust in Yahweh (1 Pet. 2:21–23).

Dependence upon God is a fundamental stance that ought to characterize humans as they realize their finite, creaturely existence in relation to an infinite though personal and caring creator. Dependence is fundamentally a relational conviction, as envisioned by the psalmist's portrait of a contented child with her mother. Dependence flows from and contributes to trusting God in all things, even and especially when trust doesn't come easily. It flows from and contributes to revering God as God, with the recognition that we are not the masters of our own fate but are at every turn dependent on the mercy and covenantal love of God poured out for us in Christ.

Dependence naturally leads to the second response, discernment. We see the connection between the two in the words of Proverbs 3.

> Trust in the LORD with all your heart
> and lean not on your own understanding;
> in all your ways submit to him,
> and he will make your paths straight. (vv. 5–6)

A stance of trust and dependence upon God's ways leads to God's direction in one's life. Discernment is a lifelong pattern of listening for and living out God's direction for life. It is a posture of responsiveness and attention to God's voice and ways; it is having our antenna tuned in a God-ward direction. Building on the assumption that God is already at work in our lives, discernment is the process of watching for God's work, listening for God's voice, and following God's lead.

Because of humanity's propensity toward idolatry, following God's lead is not always our first inclination. In between the fall and final redemption God's people have always had to struggle to discern God's ways. "There is a way that appears to be right, but in the end it leads to death" (Prov. 16:25). God's way is not always, or even frequently, immediately obvious. We must *discern* the right way to go. Yet discernment is less like a GPS system and more like a compass, setting our course in a God-ward direction.

The New Testament witness affirms that, in spite of the kingdom of God's arrival in Messiah Jesus (the "already" of God's reclamation of creation), believers need to discern God's ways in this time before the final consummation (the "not yet" aspect of the kingdom). The tension between the "already" and the "not yet" provides the context for Christian living and discernment. This tension makes sense of New Testament exhortations that speak to both the reality of what believers in Christ have already experienced and the need to keep living—and thus discerning—in light of that reality. For example, Paul writes in Galatians: "Those who belong to Christ Jesus have crucified the sinful nature with its passions and desires. Since we live by the Spirit, let us keep in step with the Spirit" (Gal. 5:24–25). The call to keep in step with God's Spirit is based on the reality that believers who participate in Christ's cross now live by that Spirit, that is, live in the new time signaled by the enduring presence of God's Spirit (Joel 2:28–29). Yet the call to keep step with the Holy Spirit presumes the need for discerning where the Spirit is leading (Col. 3:1–4).

The practice of discernment arising from an acknowledgment of our dependence on God is integral to a biblical vision for humanity. As we live between the Christ event and our final renewal with the rest of God's creation, we are on a journey of becoming. This journey involves discerning what it means to return to and image the one, true God, what it means to live out participation in Christ

81

and all that he has accomplished for us, and what it means to live by the Spirit, who is the foretaste of our renewal to come.

Dependence and discernment, it must be remembered, are human responses to God's already initiated redemption in human history. Our responses to God are truly that—responses. We respond to God's prior work of covenanting by returning to that relationship. We respond to God's saving work of redemption by participating in salvation in Christ. We respond to God's daily leading with dependent discernment. And in those moments when we more fully realize all that God has worked to return us and love us, we fall on our knees in gratitude for such goodness and grace.[31]

6

WHOLENESS AND HOLINESS
Toward Communal Fullness of Life (Jeannine)

Given a biblical perspective of human becoming (chap. 5), in this chapter I will focus on holiness and wholeness as the goal of becoming. My own introduction to the concept of holiness arose within a pietistic, evangelical church context in which holiness was primarily conceived as abstinence—often focused around illicit sexual activity and "unholy" language. For me a fairly individualistic and negatively defined picture emerged, in which the believer's goal of holiness was disconnected from wholeness or any other ultimate goal.

While this picture was certainly drawn from aspects of the scriptural witness, the message about holiness I intuited was not expansive enough. The biblical testimony about holiness is rich and complex and warrants a closer look. This chapter will explore that testimony, examining positive and negative rubrics of holiness (holiness as likeness to God as well as distinctiveness of behavior); the communal nature of holiness (God's people as called to a corporate holy identity); and holiness as a penultimate goal for the Christian, resulting in authentic, holistic, and missional life. This final horizon will lead us into an exploration of wholeness in a biblical perspective as closely aligned to holiness.

Holiness in the Witness of Scripture

Holiness as a quality to describe God and mark human beings is a broad and rich biblical theme that cannot be exhausted in this chapter. For our purposes I will highlight three key ideas that are central to a biblical picture of human holiness. Holiness derives from notions of both distinctiveness and likeness; it is expressed in covenantal community; and it leads to life and mission.

Holiness: Distinctiveness and Likeness

In the previous chapter I sketched an overview of the biblical story of God's interaction with humanity in relation to human becoming. This same story informs and gives structure to the biblical concept of human holiness, especially as it relates to both distinctiveness and likeness: for Israel, distinctiveness from the nations of the ancient Near East and likeness to God. These dual aspects and bases of human holiness arise from God's holy nature. As Hannah Harrington indicates, "[T]he term, *Qadosh*, takes in both the transcendence, or separation, of God from his creatures as well as his undeniable nearness, or presence among them."[1]

There is an implicit tension involved in Israel's call to be like Yahweh (Lev. 19:2). Israel is called to image God in holiness (Gen. 1:26–27; Lev. 19:2), yet God's people are to avoid the sin of attempting to be "like God," to which humanity succumbed in the garden (Gen. 3:4–5; cf. Isa. 47:10). As we saw in the last chapter, Israel's mandate is really a return and recommitment to the *imago Dei* (the image of God). As restored humanity, Israel was to image God to neighboring peoples. Israel was to live in light of God's redemption by manifesting the original intention for all humanity: to image God and act on God's behalf within the created order (Gen. 1:26–27; Ps. 8:5–8).[2]

Yet holiness as a canonical concept is essentially about distinctiveness. A common definition of the Hebrew word *qadosh* and the Greek word *hagios* (both most often translated "holy") is to be set apart or distinct. God's expectation for Israel to be holy meant living in distinctive ways from surrounding nations and peoples. The Israelites were to be set apart to God and for God's service, which included mission to other nations. Israel was to be "a contrast-society in the world."[3]

Key to holiness as distinctiveness is Israel's mandate to avoid idolatry (Exod. 20:2–6), setting God's people apart from surrounding nations (Deut. 7:5–6; 2 Kings 17:14–15). Christopher Wright describes idolatry essentially as the human propensity to "deify our own capacities, and thereby make gods of ourselves and our choices."[4] According to rabbinic reflection, idolatry is "the quintessential enemy of holiness."[5] As Israel lived in holiness, it would truly reflect and so honor God alone. Israel was to reject the impulse to make God in its own image or in an image of any created thing (Deut. 4:15–20; Isa. 40:18–20; Hab. 2:18–20; see Rom. 1:23). Rejecting idolatry enables living into the image of God. "Since idolatry diminishes the glory of God, and since humans are made in the image of God, it follows that idolatry is . . . detrimental to the very essence of our humanity."[6]

Obedience to the Torah helped foster and remind Israel of its distinctive identity. While its covenantal stipulations range widely, a fundamental orientation to care for one's neighbor infuses the Torah. According to the biblical story the covenant arises out of Yahweh's redemption of Israel from Egypt. For this reason the Israelites were never to forget that they were once "slaves in Egypt and the LORD [their] God redeemed [them]" (Deut. 15:15). Their care for one another, especially their care for the poor and needy, was to be energized from the memory of an oppressed past (Deut. 15:1–15).

> For the LORD your God is God of gods and Lord of lords, the great God, mighty and awesome, who shows no partiality and accepts no bribes. He defends the cause of the fatherless and the widow, and loves the foreigners residing among you, giving them food and clothing. And you are to love those who are foreigners, *for you yourselves were foreigners in Egypt.* (Deut. 10:17–19; emphasis mine)

Walter Brueggemann cites this passage as a powerful expression of "[t]he link between the holiness of YHWH and the concreteness of neighborliness."[7] Orienting themselves to care for their neighbor—

the orphan, widow, and stranger—would mark the Israelites as distinct from the oppressors of the past and the dominant powers of the present. In fact, according to Deuteronomy, if the poor, needy, aliens, orphans, widows, and Levites were not provided for, Israel would have failed at being God's people.[8] Obedience to love of neighbor was a defining, holy act.

Holiness language also emerges in the Torah particularly in the stipulations that address purity. For the ancient Israelite the order of life was embedded in these commands and stipulations. What was holy (e.g., a sacrificial animal) could not come into contact with anything or anyone unclean (e.g., someone with a skin disease).[9] What was clean (the normal state of most things) could be rendered holy by certain procedures or rituals. What was clean might also become unclean through illness, contact with corpses, sin, or other "contaminants." Through their interaction with purity regulations and expectations Israelites would have been regularly reminded of their relationship to their holy God and their own call to be a distinctive people.[10]

How does the New Testament build upon this theme of Israel's call to holiness? In what ways is this theme reshaped in the context of the arrival of Messiah Jesus? First, the New Testament authors return to the language of the *imago Dei* to speak about the reality of Jesus fully imaging God (e.g., 2 Cor. 4:4; Col. 1:15; Heb. 1:3).[11] Jesus images God, and as a result of their participation with Jesus, believers are shaped into the image of Christ (Rom. 8:29). Second, holiness continues to be a hallmark of the community that trusts in the Messiah. The call to holiness from Leviticus 19:2 is cited by the author of 1 Peter (1:16; also Matt. 5:48) in his early exhortations to primarily Gentile believers living in Asia Minor. Israel's distinctive identity as a holy people now extends to all who trust in the Messiah (1 Pet. 2:9; cf. Exod. 19:6). The commonplace designation of believers as "holy ones," particularly in the Pauline letters (e.g., Rom. 1:7; 1 Cor. 1:2; 2 Cor. 1:1; Eph. 1:1; Phil. 1:1; Col. 1:2), indicates the importance of an identity of holiness for the messianic community centered around Jesus.

The parameters of the holy community are broadened by New Testament authors to include Gentiles who trust in Jesus.[12] Yet at least two features of holiness that are basic to the Old Testament picture continue to be emphasized: aversion to idolatry and avoidance of sexual immorality. Drawing on Acts 15, Robert Wall notes that the Jerusalem edict for Gentiles focuses on these two facets of Old Testament holiness: "[W]e should write to them, telling them to abstain from food polluted by idols, from sexual immorality, from the meat of strangled animals and from blood" (15:20).[13] These two facets are emphasized frequently in the New Testament epistles and are, at times, tied together (1 Thess. 1:9; 4:3–8; also 2 Cor. 6:14–7:1). Rejection of idolatry and various kinds of sexual immorality distinguished Jews from their Gentile neighbors in both the ancient Near Eastern world and the Greco-Roman world. Thus, it is not surprising to hear these Old Testament concerns echoing in the New Testament.

It may also be the case that these two areas are highlighted because of their fundamental connection to covenantal loyalty. Allegiance to God alone and marital loyalty form a pattern of faithful relationship between humans and God, and humans in relationship with one another. It is intriguing in this regard that the author of 1 Peter aligns a call to holiness with an exhortation to love those in the community of faith (1:15–16, 22), pointing to their purification as the impetus for communal love. Covenantal loyalty to God and others is characteristic of the holy people of God before and after the arrival of the Messiah.

However, the New Testament authors envision the holiness of the believing community in some ways that are distinctive from the Old Testament picture. As Stephen Barton puts it, "[H]oliness of a different kind comes to the fore."[14] First and foremost, the renewed messianic community lives in the presence and fullness of the Holy Spirit. While God's presence with Israel is a central Old Testament affirmation,[15] the Old Testament prophets anticipate a future time when the Spirit of God will be poured on God's people, signaling final restoration of creation and humanity (Isa. 44:1–5; Ezek. 36:24–28; Joel 2:28–29). According to the author of Acts, this Spirit-signaled restoration begins at Pentecost (Acts 2:14–36), so that the Holy Spirit indwells the community believing in Jesus as Messiah (Eph. 1:13–14), making that community into "a holy temple in the Lord" (Eph. 2:19–22). It is the Holy Spirit that sanctifies—makes holy—the believing community (2 Thess. 2:13; 1 Pet. 1:2).[16]

Another central difference between Israel's holiness and that expected of the New Testament church is the defining parameter of God's people. While the Torah defined Israel's identity, the New Testament church is defined by Jesus himself (as the climax and fulfillment of the Torah; Matt. 5:17–20; Rom. 10:4). Ethnic distinctions that set Israel apart from Gentiles, ones the Torah regulated (e.g., circumcision, dietary regulations, and Sabbath observance), are no longer central identity markers for the renewed people of God.[17] Instead, a "holiness of solidarity" emerges in which trust in Jesus and his faithfulness defines the New Testament church as it grows into the likeness of the Messiah.[18] It is allegiance to and participation with Jesus as Messiah that form the basis for the church's distinctiveness in the world. Holiness is "expanded to mean something like sharing in the story of Jesus the crucified. Holiness is taking on a cruciform shape."[19]

Holiness in biblical perspective is expressed as both taking on the likeness of God (and later of Christ) and being distinct from the ways of life of nonbelievers for the purpose of mission. What is particular to that distinctiveness differs from Old Testament to New because of the different contexts in which God's people find themselves and because of the new work God does in Jesus the Messiah. Jesus begins God's restoration of all creation, signaled in the outpouring upon the church of the Holy Spirit, who acts as the guarantor of final restoration to come and as the sanctifier of God's people.

Holiness: Covenantal and Communal

Holiness is utterly covenantal and communal, tied to God's covenant with Israel and Israel's responsive loyalty (Deut. 26:16–19).[20] As a people, Israel was called to be holy because of God's own holiness. It is no accident that holiness characterizes Israel's God-given identity at the inaugural moment of the covenant with Yahweh.

Then Moses went up to God, and the LORD called to him from the mountain and said, "This is what you are to say to the house of Jacob and what you are to tell the people of Israel: 'You yourselves have seen what I did to Egypt, and *how I carried you on eagles' wings and brought you to myself*. Now if you obey me fully and *keep my covenant*, then out of all nations you will be my treasured possession.

88

Although the whole earth is mine, you will be for me a kingdom of priests and *a holy nation.*' These are the words you are to speak to the Israelites." (Exod. 19:3–6; emphasis mine)

Obedience and faithfulness to the covenant charter—the Torah—will demonstrate that Israel belongs to God as a holy people—communally set apart uniquely for God. Yet this faithful obedience comes in response to God's redemptive work in bringing Israel out of Egypt. Israel's identity as a holy nation is based on God's prior redeeming and relational act. In this way the Old Testament concept of holiness is integrally connected to God's gracious redemption. The post-Reformation tendency to create a divide between obedience (law) and redemption (grace) is difficult to sustain within the Old Testament covenantal framework for Torah obedience.[21]

The New Testament picture of holiness also emerges within this covenantal framework. We see this clearly in the use of Exodus 19 language in 1 Peter 2:9–10. The author applies the description of Israel as "a holy nation" (Exod. 19:6) to his primarily Gentile hearers (1 Pet. 2:9) and goes on to speak of their identity as "the people of God" (2:10). The appropriation of Israel's distinctive identity language now applied to Gentiles as well as Jews in the messianic community is quite striking. The language is also, not surprisingly, deeply covenantal.

This New Testament passage also highlights the communal nature of holiness, which characterizes it in both testaments. These holy believers in Jesus are a holy *community*. First Peter 2:4–10 envisions God's holy presence in the midst of the messianic community by using temple imagery (2:4–5) and corporate language for believers' holy identity (2:9–10). The metaphor is of many stones being built into a single temple—"a spiritual house to be a holy priesthood, offering spiritual sacrifices acceptable to God through Jesus Christ" (2:5). Only as a corporate entity does the temple emerge and arise from individual stones (see Eph. 2:19–22 for a similar picture). While biblical authors assume that individuals within the believing community are to pursue and live into holiness, the emphasis in Scripture clearly is on holiness as corporate.

This communal vision for holiness can provide an important corrective to the individualized version of holiness that is fairly widespread in the contemporary Western church. A corporate identity of holiness counteracts an extreme individualism that might actually undermine the scriptural pattern of holiness. In his essay on a Christian "practice of a peculiar identity," Brueggemann speaks of the Western "ethic of individualism that issues in social indifference and anti-neighborliness."[22] As we will see in the next section, a notion of holiness that is cut off from its larger purposes can lead in the direction that Brueggemann fears. Such holiness is in danger of becoming an end in itself, leading to privatization of faith or even a possible means of excluding the Other.

Holiness: Leading to Life and Mission

While holiness is a central expectation of God's people in the time before and after the Messiah's arrival, it is not an end in itself. "Israel was not to pursue purity for purity's sake."[23] According to the biblical witness, God intends holiness to lead to life and mission. The purpose of holiness as invigorating or resulting in life is evident in Leviticus 18:1–5.

> The LORD said to Moses, "Speak to the Israelites and say to them: 'I am the LORD your God. You must not do as they do in Egypt, where you used to live, and you must not do as they do in the land of Canaan, where I am bringing you. Do not follow their practices. You must obey my laws and be careful to follow my decrees. I am the LORD your God. *Keep my decrees and laws, for whoever obeys them will live by them.* I am the LORD.'" (emphasis mine)

Fullness of life, or what James Bruckner calls "thriving," is a result of obedience to the Torah (Deut. 6:1–2; 28:8–16; 30:15–19).[24] The purity regulations of the Torah, in their focus on avoiding or cleansing impurity arising from contact or association with death, point to the connection between holiness and life. "In all of its forms, impurity represents death, therefore we can claim that holiness represents life. . . . [D]ivine holiness is equated with life at its finest."[25] The contours of this fullness of life involve "a sustainable community within which forgiveness and mercy can be practiced."[26]

In Matthew's Gospel, Jesus understands the commandments of God as leading to life. So he tells an inquiring rich man, "If you want to enter life, obey the commandments" (Matt. 19:17; also John 12:49–50). Yet the testimony of the New Testament authors connects Jesus himself to the gift of life. "I have come that they may have life, and have it to the full" (John 10:10). In fact, John's Gospel affirms that Jesus brings eschatological life—his death and resurrection usher in the renewal of creation.[27] For Paul, too, creation's renewal begins in Jesus (2 Cor. 5:17; Gal. 6:15).

According to the biblical story mission also provides a larger purpose for holiness. Israel's mandate emerges in the call of Abraham to be a blessing to "all peoples on earth" (Gen. 12:1–3; also 18:18; 22:18; 26:4; 28:14). According to Deuteronomy God intends Israel's covenantal loyalty to serve a missional purpose to the nations (Deut. 4:5–7; also 1 Kings 8:41–43).

> See, I have taught you decrees and laws as the LORD my God commanded me, so that you may follow them in the land you are entering to take possession of it. Observe them carefully, for this will show your wisdom and understanding to the nations, who will hear about all these decrees and say, "Surely this great nation is a wise and understanding people." What other nation is so great as to have their gods near them the way the LORD our God is near us whenever we pray to him?

The book of Isaiah emphasizes the missional purpose of Israel's call. In Isaiah 41:8–10, Israel is identified with "the servant of Yahweh." Then in Isaiah 42 we hear the words of Yahweh to Israel as servant: "I will keep you and will make you to be a covenant for the people and a light for the Gentiles" (42:6; cf. 42:1–9). Israel's role as light-bearer is emphasized in this part of Isaiah and fits well God's missional purposes for Israel in Genesis and Exodus (also Isa. 49:5–6).

New Testament writers find fertile ground for understanding Jesus's messianic mission in Isaiah's servant motif. Matthew applies the early verses of Isaiah 42 about Yahweh's servant directly to Jesus's ministry of compassionate justice (Isa. 42:1–4, in Matt. 12:18–21). This is the longest Old Testament quotation in the first Gospel, and it is surely no accident that it twice refers to the servant's mission to the Gentile nations: "[The servant] will proclaim justice to the nations. . . . In his name the nations will put their hope" (Matt.

12:18, 21).[28] Luke alludes to Isaiah 42:6 (quoted above) in Simeon's speech (Luke 2:29–32): "For my eyes have seen your salvation, which you have prepared in the sight of all nations: a light for revelation to the Gentiles, and the glory to your people Israel." For these and other New Testament writers, Jesus fulfills Israel's vocation to be a light to the nations (see also John 4:1–9; 8:12; 9:5; Gal. 3:8–29; Rev. 21:22–24).

By extension the followers of Jesus (with the spirit of Jesus in their midst) become a light to the Gentiles. According to the author of Acts, Paul and Barnabas pursue a mission to Gentiles because they (presumably along with the church more broadly) are commanded by God to fulfill the mission of Isaiah 42:6: "I have made you a light for the Gentiles, that you may bring salvation to the ends of the earth" (Acts 13:46–47; also 26:17–18, 23). We see the missional vocation of Jesus's followers as well in John 17, where holiness language (the verb "sanctify") occurs in the context of mission. Jesus's prayer in John 17 reflects a dialectic between separation from the world and mission to it. Holiness is the cohesive thread:

> My prayer is not that you take them out of the world but that you protect them from the evil one. They are not of the world, even as I am not of it. Sanctify them by the truth; your word is truth. As you sent me into the world, I have sent them into the world. For them I sanctify myself, that they too may be truly sanctified. (John 17:15–19)

Holiness in Summary

The perspective on human holiness offered in this chapter is intended to expand a view of holiness tending toward individualism that is primarily defined by behavioral abstinence. In the Old Testament holiness forms the center of Israel's vocation to image God and be distinctive in the world through exclusive loyalty to Yahweh, in committed care for neighbor, and as a light to the surrounding nations. The New Testament witness evokes Israel's call to holiness and centers its expression in Jesus, Israel's messiah who fulfills Israel's vocation to image God in a life of loyalty to Yahweh and of mercy and justice to neighbor, thus bringing God's salvation to the nations. Jesus embodies holiness perfectly and calls the community that trusts in his work to faithfully enact his pattern of holiness by the power of the Holy Spirit.

Wholeness in the Witness of Scripture

The concept of wholeness is a rather diffuse theme in Scripture and not limited to a narrow set of terms. Instead, the concept is tied to a number of other biblical concepts that overlap with one another to various degrees. In order to frame this discussion of wholeness with the earlier paradigms of holiness, I introduce this section with a brief New Testament passage that has rich associations with human wholeness. In 1 Thessalonians 5:23–24, Paul writes:

> May God himself, the God of peace, sanctify you through and through. May your whole spirit, soul and body be kept blameless at the coming of our Lord Jesus Christ. The one who calls you is faithful, and he will do it.

From this blessing we can hear the intersection of a number of biblical motifs that helpfully inform our discussion of human wholeness: peace (*shalom*), holiness (here "sanctify"), completeness ("whole spirit, soul and body"), and blamelessness. A discussion of these motifs can be ordered under two broad rubrics: wholeness in relation to holiness, and wholeness as integrity or completeness. Also, God's faithfulness in making believers holy and whole emerges as foundational.

Wholeness and Holiness

I begin with holiness, a connection to the previous discussion. Paul himself aligns holiness and wholeness in 1 Thessalonians 5:23 when he prays that God would make them "wholly holy" (my translation). The language "through and through" (TNIV) translates *holoteleis*, which denotes completeness. Paul's affirmation of a holistic response is in line with Old Testament covenantal holiness. For example, in a number of Old Testament books we hear of the exemplary model of Caleb, who "followed [the Lord] wholeheartedly" (Num. 14:24; 32:11–12; Deut. 1:36; Josh. 14:8–14).[29] The psalmist of Psalm 86 prays a compelling petition: "Unite my heart to reverence you"

(86:11, my translation).[30] It seems that the psalmist knows the heart is prone to conflicting directions. It takes a unifying act—here, on God's part—to bring the wholeness of the human heart into true worship. The same essential language is used in Ezekiel to express what God will do for Israel in the coming days: "I will give them an undivided heart" (Ezek. 11:19), which will result in covenant loyalty ("they will follow my decrees . . . they will be my people").

Holiness as a means to fullness of life can be seen in 1 Thessalonians 5:23 as it resonates in the phrase "the God of peace." This reference to peace likely evokes the Old Testament concept of *shalom*, which has rich Old Testament associations with fullness of life for the community of Israel.[31] One way we see the Old Testament concept of *shalom* intimately connected to communal wholeness is by noting the words that occur parallel to *shalom* in Hebrew poetry. *Shalom* is partially defined by *tsedaqah* ("justice" or "righteousness") in Isaiah 48:18 and 60:17.[32] Psalm 85:10 expresses beautifully the close association of these two concepts in relation to God's salvation: "[R]ighteousness and peace kiss each other." *Shalom* is also closely linked with language of covenant (*berit*) in Ezekiel 34:25 and 37:26:[33] "I will make a covenant of peace with [Israel]." The covenantal quality of *shalom* is also clear in Aaron's blessing upon Israel (Num. 6:23–26).

> The LORD bless you
> and keep you;
> the LORD make his face shine on you
> and be gracious to you;
> the LORD turn his face toward you
> and give you peace.

With these associations to justice and covenantal community, *shalom* necessitates "right harmonious relationships to other *human beings* and delight in human community."[34] It is about communal wholeness and harmony.[35] *Shalom* is another way of picturing the fullness of life that is the purpose of holiness.

Wholeness as Integrity or Completeness

Paul's prayer for the Thessalonians also illustrates the connection between wholeness and integrity or completeness. "May your whole spirit, soul, and body be kept blameless . . ." (5:23). Paul refers to the whole person or self with the language of spirit, soul, and body. Paul uses this range of terms describing the human person (along with the adjective for "whole," *holoklēron*) to emphasize that it is the entire person—the person in wholeness—who will be kept blameless by God's power. We see a similar way of expressing the whole person in the *Shema* (Deut. 6:5): "Love the Lord your God with all your heart and with all your soul and with all your strength."[36] In contrast to a divided self, Paul's eschatological prayer is for the preservation of the unified, integrated person in community (again, the plural "your" is important). Rather than dichotomizing the human body and soul in relation to wholeness or holiness, this multifold language is used to connote the unity of the whole person in eschatological perspective.

The notion of completeness as a picture of human wholeness also emerges in the use of *teleios* language in the New Testament. A compound form related to this word is used in 1 Thessalonians 5:23, where Paul prays for the Thessalonians to be completely holy (*holoteleis*). Though at times translated "perfect," the sense of *teleios* typically is maturity or completion (James 1:4).[37] The word "*teleios* conveys the sense of something reaching its end and therefore its 'completion' . . . a sense of undivided wholeness of heart before God."[38] The church as communally complete and thus mature is pictured in Ephesians 4:12–13, where leaders are given to equip the whole church for service "so that the body of Christ may be built up until we all reach unity in the faith and in the knowledge of the Son of God and become mature [*teleios*], attaining to the whole measure of the fullness of Christ." The community of believers pictured in Ephesians 4 is not divided but complete, mature, and focused together in unity—an integrated and mature community.

Wholeness as integrity also resonates in the "blameless" language of 1 Thessalonians 5:23. In the Old Testament, physical blameless-ness describes the whole and unblemished nature of whatever is devoted to God, what we could call its integrity.[39] For example, animals sacrificed at the altar must be without blemish or defect (e.g., Lev. 22:21; Num. 19:2). A New Testament reformulation of this concept focuses on Jesus as the blameless and whole sacrifice who enacts God's redemption (1 Pet. 1:19) so that believers can be morally blameless, whole, and undivided (Eph. 5:27). "Now [God] has reconciled you by Christ's physical body through death to present you holy in his sight, without blemish and free from accusation" (Col. 1:22). God's work in Christ produces human holiness and wholeness (blamelessness).

This emphasis leads to a final yet crucial observation about wholeness, beautifully captured in Paul's prayer in 1 Thessalonians 5:23–24. The answer to Paul's prayer for believers' wholeness and holiness, integrity and blamelessness, comes from God's covenantal loyalty. "The one who calls you is faithful, and he will do it" (5:24). Human wholeness and holiness do not happen apart from God's initiating and sustaining relationship with humanity. "I am the Lord who makes you holy" is a frequent refrain in Leviticus (e.g., 20:8; 21:8, 15, 23).[40] Drawing on another Old Testament picture, it is God who promises to circumcise Israel's heart, according to Deuteronomy 30:6. In a companion command the Israelites are to "circumcise [their] hearts" (Deut. 10:16). In other words, God's people are to have a responsive posture to God's initiating and ongoing work in their lives. As we saw in the previous chapter, Christians participate in what Christ has already accomplished by faithfully responding to his faithful life and sacrifice on their behalf.

Conclusion: Becoming Whole and Holy

In these two chapters we have been exploring scriptural resources for understanding what it means to become whole and holy. In conclusion I offer a composite sketch of human becoming toward the goal of Christian holiness and wholeness.

According to Scripture, the believing community is on a journey of becoming. Journeying or becoming is inherently part of the human experience because God created humanity as finite and wired for growth. Becoming is also a given because of humanity's fall and subsequent propensity toward sin and idolatry. In this light human becoming is best conceived as responsiveness to God's initiating and ongoing covenantal and redemptive work that culminates with Messiah Jesus, so that faith and faithfulness form the pattern of Christian becoming. That pattern distinguishes the Christian community from its surrounding environment and marks the community with the image of God in Messiah Jesus. This pattern of faith and faithfulness identifies the community as holy. Yet holiness in itself is not the final goal. Holiness, rightly pursued and enacted, leads to mission to the world and fullness of life or wholeness.

The New Testament witness portrays Jesus as bringing fullness of life and communal wholeness. The eschatological vision is of a *shalom* community that practices mercy and justice and is made up of restored human persons without divided loyalties or selves. This community is centered in unity around Jesus the Messiah, whose life and death on behalf of others makes possible holiness that leads to wholeness.

Yet this idealized picture of the "already" of God's final restoration is not yet fully realized. In this time of "already" and "not yet," the Christian community lives in *dependence* upon God's work and God's promises to restore all things in the final day. The church also lives a life of *discernment*, since the pattern of holiness as covenant faithfulness will need to be prayerfully discerned in relation to the ever-changing realities of culture and mission. When faithfulness to the triune God calls for resistance to cultural conformity, and when that same faithfulness calls for appropriation is, as Brueggemann puts it, "hidden from us."[41] Discernment seeks to bring God's ways and wisdom to light in the particularities of our own contexts. It seeks to hear Scripture's narrative in relation to the stories of our world, our times, and ourselves, so that we may live faithfully into and toward Scripture's alternate story of holiness and wholeness.

RECEPTION AND INTEGRATION OF OFFERINGS FROM HERMENEUTICS

A Response (Carla and Wyndy)

Our integrative method for this project includes reception of what another colleague has offered from her discipline area, in order to move toward more holistic integration. In this chapter, then, we (Carla and Wyndy) respond to Jeannine's offering from Scripture and hermeneutics, listening for areas of possible integration as well as divergence from our fields of expertise and our own understandings. As we bring these three disciplines into conversation, we trust that authentic points of integration for further discussion will emerge.

Reception and Integration from Social Science (Carla)

Jeannine,

I want to say first that I enjoy the passion so apparent in your writing. Your love for Scripture and, in this case, for what it offers us in terms of understanding becoming, wholeness, and holiness is contagious. (In fact, at some points I found myself getting excited

99

about something I'm pretty sure I didn't understand!) And yet you continually point us beyond Scripture to the God of Scripture, inviting us into worship, awe, and relationship. Thank you.

Thank you, too, for allowing me to reminisce about all the expectations for behavioral abstinence that I have encountered in my life (chap. 6). How did I know, even as I was sitting out square-dancing lessons in fourth grade, that holiness was bigger than what I didn't do? Your expansive view of holiness is a much-needed corrective to what so quickly devolves into negative, avoidance-oriented faith. The irony is that, as social science helps us understand, avoidance as a strategy for transformation is quite unsatisfactory. Discipline, of course, is essential, but discipline can support our efforts to focus on what is true, noble, right, pure, lovely, and admirable (Phil. 4:8). Holding an accurate conception of Christlikeness in our minds seems like a more powerful motivator for change than holding an image of what we should not be thinking or doing. When we deliberately place our attention somewhere, our action is more likely to follow. Change is more likely for a person who holds a clear image of what she wants to accomplish or achieve than an image of what she is trying to avoid.

On the other hand, what would this mean for the distinctiveness aspect of your definition of holiness? Perhaps one reason "behavioral abstinence" is such a tenacious worldview is that being known for what we don't do is easier in some ways than being known for our love. First of all, determining the loving thing can be a complex enterprise (more on discernment in a moment). And second, living out the loving thing may, in some situations, put us at odds with the abstainers in our lives, leaving us vulnerable to criticism or suspicion (see Rom. 14:1–15:13).

Another somewhat related point of resonance: As I read your section on idolatry, it occurred to me that there might actually be a similar dynamic within fundamentalism as relational process (chap. 2). Rules, standards, or worldview hold a place of primacy rather than God, and violation of them puts the relationship at risk. It seems that in such a case, the rule, standard, or worldview has become an idol. I will ponder this more.

When you describe wholeness as wholeheartedness (chap. 6), I wonder if you would find similarities in the idea of wholeness as *congruence*. I believe congruence—correspondence between our internal and external realities, a state of harmony rather than compartmentalization; in other words, integration—is an essential relational skill. For example, if I tell you I'm not angry with you but I really am, can we really expect authentic intimacy in our relationship? Or if I remain in a job in which I am continually being expected to violate my own moral boundaries, what kind of toll will it eventually take on my sense of integrity, and even my sense of self? Parker Palmer, in his book *Let Your Life Speak*, invites us to "live divided no more." He uses the example of Rosa Parks and her revolutionary way of challenging unjust social structures in what may have seemed like an isolated, individual act. Yet this act came out of a sense of congruence, a decision to no longer conspire in her own diminishment.[1] Perhaps growth in this kind of personal congruence, along with a sense of the unity of my embodied and transcendent selves, is also part of wholeheartedness.

I appreciate the corrective that Scripture and theology can have on a social-science understanding of hope (which you call a cardinal Christian virtue). Forty years ago Ezra Stotland defined hope as "the expectation of success in attaining goals."[2] Much research on hope since then has operationally defined it as a group of three features: goal, pathway, and agency.[3] In order to have hope I must be able to see a desirable outcome, identify a strategy to get to it, and have a sense of personal agency or efficacy. Certainly that is one kind of hope. But what of situations involving terminal illness, or oppressive governments, or genocide? In such situations part of the despair or potential hopelessness involves the very fact that we do not (and, realistically, could not) have a sense of efficacy. So, Jeannine, when you say hope is not simply wishful thinking but an active way of living "in light of what is still to come" (chap. 5), you offer an alternative that adds much to a traditional social-science perspective. We can understand hope as the process of making meaning, accepting truth, and being willing to stay in the midst of the struggle—all because our hope is located in God and God's character. Lament then becomes an act of hope and trust rather than an expression of despair.

In fact, this is one place where I might extend further your observation about dependence. You note that, as part of our dependence, we should emulate Jesus as a faithful yet suffering person with absolute trust in God's willingness and ability to act, even when it seems God is absent. In my experience this expectation is often communicated to other suffering persons as an expectation that they should suffer in silence, or at least with patient acceptance. I would suggest, again with the idea of congruence in mind, that faithful suffering might be noisy. As I look at Job's whole-self response to his calamities, I am struck with his congruence. He does not stand to sing the doxology until he has argued with God, expressed his deep despair (even what seem to be suicidal thoughts), and turned away the unhelpful help of his friends (not what I usually hear as a pattern for righteous dependence). However, at the end of Job's story God honors him for being honest with and about God and tells Job's friends to ask Job to intercede for them. Apparently, absolute trust and absolute honesty can coexist as authentic dependence.

I am intrigued by your eschatological vision for becoming (chap. 5). Two observations: as you describe the fullness of a whole and holy community, I see many points of connection between it and my emphasis on hospitality. I think this will have relevance in our conversation about immigration (chap. 11) as well. Second, I find myself hoping with you that continued becoming will be part of our experience in the renewed creation. The question that emerges for me in that regard, however, is, Becoming what? I'm curious about the nature of becoming that would be beyond "fullness of life, wholeness, moral perfection, and seeing God" (chap. 5).

I am curious, enthusiastic, and fascinated by many other dimensions of your offering, Jeannine, but will end with some thoughts about discernment as a strategy for becoming (chap. 5). It seems to me that discernment, both individual and communal, could be considered an essential and possibly inevitable part of one's experience in the crucible. Where is God in this? is a question that can be asked with a broad range of emotional tones: wonder, confusion, grief, anger, numbness, and confidence. Two cautions I want to hold clearly in mind as we think of discernment, generosity, or hospitality as pathways for becoming are (a) that we not define them solely as individual qualities or processes but that we see them as being inextricably linked with community, and (b) that we not allow them to become ends in themselves. I will offer an observation from Rose Mary Dougherty to serve as a gentle reminder to me of the end of our becoming: "Somehow . . . we have separated the will of God from God, and discernment has come to mean a search for God's will which we must find in a game of hide-and-seek. We often equate discernment with a skill which we must master rather than the gift of God's love which guides us home to Love."[4]

Thank you, Jeannine, for so much here that I haven't been able to respond to. Your caution that "any claims to absolute knowledge ironically and inevitably mirror the fall" is not often heard in the evangelical world, and I appreciate its invitation to humility. Perhaps I'm in need of more invitations in this regard, because I also heard one in your statement that "human knowledge is most possible within a set of commitments that do not place knowledge as the only or highest goal. . . . [T]rue knowing comes to those who have taken the prior ethical stance of love toward others." I will be holding these invitations in my own discernment process for some time.

Oh, and by the way: thank you for challenging the notion that if I don't feel close to God, I must have moved (chap. 5). For those who are becoming in the desert or during a dark night and are desperately seeking God, you have provided a ray of hope (as defined earlier) that has the potential to challenge false guilt, self-recrimination, and any redoubled efforts to become in our own power.

Reception and Integration from Ethics (Wyndy)

Jeannine,

Thanks for these clear and profound insights on becoming, wholeness, and holiness from the perspective of hermeneutics and Scripture. Let me respond by identifying the rich offerings I have received from you, how they are and should be integrated in Christian ethics and practices, and then ask one question.

You remind us that Scripture must be read and understood as a narrative. This is such a helpful reminder of what Scripture is. Perhaps understanding what Scripture is helps us better understand what becoming, wholeness, and holiness might be. This connection is important in our attempts to provide thicker and more integrative proposals for becoming, wholeness, and holiness.[5] We started our project because the three of us have heard assumptions about becoming, wholeness, and holiness that were often just that—assumptions. In spite of the enormous and important place Scripture has in our theological traditions, it does strike me as odd how little we talk about what Scripture actually *is*, its relationship to God, and the many reasons why it comes to us as God's gift. Just as we need thicker definitions of morality and formation, we need thicker definitions and ways of reading Scripture. You have offered this to us in your valuable reminders of what Scripture is as a story, and how it invites us into "the greatest story ever told."

Your articulation of the story of Scripture offers us a counter-narrative to the American narratives of individualism and freedom. I find this helpful for rearticulating the very social dimensions of formation that extend beyond "just personal piety" and "just personal transformation." I think this is an important contribution to counteract some narrow ideas and trends in how we understand becoming and formation. I find myself having to press students on their rather thin notions of the relationships between Scripture and formation, which show up in phrases such as, "The Bible is about transformation, not information." On one level I understand this. But when working toward thicker ideas of what this statement means, I often receive blank stares when I press on: What is transformation? Why is transformation a goal? For what purpose? Into what are we to be transformed? Does information not matter? Is there no content—dare I say information—which Scripture offers that may actually be crucial for whole and holy formation?

This thin description of the Bible's purpose seems to reflect the highly individualized ways of reading and using Scripture that assume God is concerned with (only) *my* transformation. I take from your chapters that Scripture continually forms us if we actually pay attention in our reading and take it seriously. Reading Scripture, therefore, becomes a moral practice.[6] Your insights help me find a way through this simple and somewhat dangerous dichotomy separating process from end, and formation from a particular shape, content, and direction. They also contribute to reexamining the overused and assumption-loaded lingo of "transformation" that is so common in Christian rhetoric. And they remind me of the corporate dimensions of formation that are deeply relational and social, starting with our willingness to place ourselves in a relationship with Scripture that is ongoing, deliberate, and open to this Other, as you so eloquently state both here and in your previous book, *Scripture as Communi-*

cation. You offer language, content, and a framework that grounds our becoming, wholeness, and holiness in a larger context of the purposes of God as narrated in all the rich and complex dimensions of Scripture. I so appreciate your telling the story of humanity's sin (another area needing some thick redemption), along with the hopeful story of our re-creation in Christ, and our becoming more like Christ, as the goal of wholeness and holiness. I can now respond to some of these thin assumptions of the Bible's relationship to formation by saying, "Here, read this!"

I too gravitate to this concept of story. Your offerings, however, push me to be clear about which story we believe and tell in our actions and practices. This seems important in our postmodern context, enamored as it is with *my* story as the primary one worth telling and the only one that matters, with very few indications of how my story may be interrupted, changed (dare I say converted!), and continually made new by the story of God. It's also important to consider how Scripture's formative power might shape our identity, direct our calling, and form our character. Scripture and Christian moral formation through the lens of story remind me that formation is ongoing, and that our being and becoming do not involve isolated attitudes and acts that kick in at moments of crises and conundrums. We are always being formed, whether we realize it or not. This is the contribution virtue ethics has made: attending to "who we are" and "what we should do" requires vigilance and intentionality. It seems important as you remind us that we are invited to read Scripture with vigilance, intentionality, *and* wonder. Scripture invites us to wonder who we are and who we can become, and how we should be in relationships with God and others.

Your contributions to our common work on becoming, wholeness, and holiness have important intersections with theology, Christian moral formation, and ethics. Narrative ethics is an important method that is gaining greater attention due to the renewed interest in virtue ethics (which requires narratives) and Scripture's role in moral formation beyond a rulebook mentality.[7] It also reaffirms for me that theology is essentially telling the "good story" as we work toward coherence between what we believe and how we live. To speak about God is to understand the purpose and authority of Scripture; to engage with the Scriptures is to learn the story of

Jesus; and learning and living the story of Jesus shapes our humanity and directs it to its ultimate *telos*. We are invited by God in Christ into a particular kind of life, a life marked by righteousness and justice, one made possible by the Holy Spirit, who is continually forming us into the divine image. These have been helpful moves in theology, ethics, and hermeneutics, providing a way for ethicists, theologians, and biblical scholars to forge ahead on common work that enriches and holds our disciplines accountable to fundamental and pressing questions about God, our humanity, and what it means to be and become more human. It has been great to be in this conversation with you and Carla not only as an academically trained New Testament scholar and social scientist, but also with friends who I know practice their art with skill and integrity, for the sake of others and in light of their own practiced commitments to wholeness and holiness. They help this academically trained ethicist and friend desire to do the same.

I was (happily) surprised at your discussion on dependence and discernment (chap. 5), since discernment has such a crucial role in ethics. The connections you make between human independence and idolatry helped me give a presentation on artificial reproductive technologies to the bioethics committee (of which I am a member) at our local hospital. How uncomfortable we are with our own finitude and limitations, and to what extremes we go to counteract our bodies, which are mortal and will disappoint us. I was immediately drawn to integrate your offerings in my reflections on forms of technology as idolatries that we use to counteract our finitude, dependence, and disappointments, and why discernment is needed to assess these attempts to ameliorate our limitations and dependence.[8] I am not arguing against technology per se. But I am concerned about the assumption that just because we can do something means we should do it.

Therefore, I think the connections you make between dependence and discernment are interesting. Discernment helps us find our way through the moral mazes of technologies that often become forms of idolatry and redefine what it means to be and become human, or to cease being such. In Christian moral thought discernment is often seen as practical wisdom. It helps us navigate life's complexities when what we should do is not always clear. In ethics doing what we know is right takes moral courage; failing to do what we know is right and just is moral failure, and I would even say constitutes our contribution to evil. However, not knowing what to do requires us to admit our limitations and finitude, and to depend on God, others, and Scripture for the moral wisdom and discernment to find our way.

I greatly resonated (as you might expect from an ethicist) with your insights on the missional, moral, and corporate purposes of wholeness and holiness (chap. 6). Again I was reminded that what we think about these ideas will inform how we put them into practice (or not). In returning to the scriptural story and the dialogical relationships between wholeness and holiness, spirituality and morality, faith and ethics, you offer an important perspective and a corrective for the ways we have appropriated the modernist narratives of fragmentation, bureaucratization, specialization, and the over-privatization and over-personalization of Christian faith. I was drawn to your descriptions of holiness as a form of witness to the world that is tangible and visible. They also help me explore the reverse: what wholeness and holiness are not, which I find a helpful starting point to reframe conversations.

I am left with a question related to formation, one you broach early in chapter 5. We have attempted in our work together to identify our own perceptions, locations, and limitations to our knowledge. I think we all know at some level, at least cognitively, that God's perspective and ways of knowing are different than ours, because we are largely bound by our own locations and the limits they place on our epistemologies. These are uncomfortable acknowledgments to make, especially in our theological circles. Yet it seems important to acknowledge our own finitude and limitations, our own creaturely dependencies. Doesn't this confession say something about our own formational commitments as Christians and as scholars? So perhaps what I'm asking is this: Why are we uncomfortable about our own limited perspectives, especially when it comes to interacting with and appropriating Scripture? Why do we crave certitude and absolute know-ability when a core virtue for Christians is the practice of faith?[9] What does the demand for certainty say about our willingness to trust God and others? Does this demand truncate formation and say something about our actual commitments to the process of formation and its envisioned end? I raise these questions for further dialogue and look forward to thinking about them with you and Carla, because they are central to how we read Scripture and conceive of the moral life in the context of formation, wholeness, and holiness.

BEING AND BECOMING
The Trinity and Our Formation (Wyndy)

We are making deliberate attempts in our work to be explicit about what our respective disciplines contribute to a thicker[1] understanding of wholeness, holiness, and how we become. We are also committed to leaving room for one another to speak into, speak about, and reflect upon our offerings for their implications on our own formation and that of others. My contributions to our project are informed by my commitments as a Christian social ethicist and by central affirmations of Christian faith that have enormous moral implications for how we understand God, ourselves, and other selves; how we become; and our conceptions of wholeness and holiness.

I see an integral link between ethics and our theological understandings about God and humanity. If one is asserting a claim about God, such as "God is Creator," then intentionally or by default one is building on the implications of this belief for how he or she actually lives. However, there are important differences between theology and ethics, even as there are significant and important intersections. Theology, or "words about God," is our attempt to articulate what we understand about God through various sources—a primary source being Scripture—in conversation with tradition, reason, and experience. It is the attempt to systematize and create an interlocking and "intricate web" of belief that "shapes our lives,"[2] a web that is coherent, faithful, defensible, and practical in that it provides guidance not just for what we believe but, equally important, for how we should live. Theology therefore has a greater purpose than "just getting it right" in the crossing and dotting of theological t's and i's. Its purpose is to guide us in the ways of wise, faithful, and righteous living, and to produce faithful Christian communities where we can become and live more whole and holy lives, reflective of the story of the Christian faith.

Christian ethics, while relying on theology for fundamental points of orientation and guidance, is a separate discipline with its own sets of questions, concerns, and language. Ethics provides us with the questions and tools to make our fundamental moral claims concrete in actual practices and strategies that move toward what ought to be. Ethics extends and operationalizes our moral frameworks, helping us work toward a greater consonance between what we profess to believe about what is good and how we actually live. Christian ethics is not the final chapter in a series of systematic theology classes, in an arrangement that assumes that right thinking will lead to right action or that defending right beliefs is our ethical task. Christian ethics is a necessary and integral part of theological reflection as we pose real-life questions to our theology and wonder about the implications for how to live. Ethics also relies on the insights of the social sciences for sources of understanding and analysis of issues confronting us. Ethical issues are far more complex than problems with one cause and a single solution. Ethics is multifaceted, begging the need for expanded avenues of understanding human nature; the dynamics of social systems and structures; economics; analyses around race, gender, and class; and cultural anthropology. Carla's contributions as a social scientist and Jeannine's as a biblical interpreter are apt and fitting for my contributions as a Christian social ethicist, helping me see issues from fresh vantage points. Their contributions are critical for helping me understand becoming, wholeness, and holiness from an interdisciplinary perspective.

In this chapter and the next, I will offer ideas on how we become, on ethical formation, and wholeness and holiness from a theological and moral perspective. I will start by probing the fundamental assertions Christians make about God as Trinity, moving beyond the usual debates and yet interacting with and revisiting them as needed. I am concerned with how this primary picture of God provides the model for becoming whole and holy Christian persons and communities. What does our belief in the trinitarian God mean for understanding our own humanity, how we become more human, how we become in fundamental relationships, and how we become more whole and holy persons?

The Trinity and Theological Anthropology

I think back to my systematic theology courses in seminary and remember our student eagerness to "take every thought captive to Christ" in order to demonstrate our theological prowess. This prowess was particularly challenged when it came to understanding the mystery we call the Trinity. One of my church history professors, Dr. Timothy Weber, would remind us that those who could fully explain this grand and central mystery of the Christian faith would be assigning themselves a place as the fourth member of the Godhead. Yet acknowledging something as mystery does not relieve us from the responsibility of careful exploration and thoughtful reflection upon its practical implications. Historical Christian thinking has provided our creedal affirmations of the Trinity—particularly in the Apostles', Nicene, and Chalcedon creeds—that have for centuries guided the church's thinking about God and life with God.[3] We are indebted to our church parents, who worked hard on our behalf to articulate as best they could what we today affirm about God the Father, God the Son, and God the Holy Spirit. We continue this work by reflecting on the implications of trinitarian thought in our context, especially since the "philosophical turn to relationality."[4]

My seminary education helped me understand the historical development of the doctrine of the Trinity. I learned about its roots in scriptural descriptions and texts, the various ways of articulating the oneness of God, and the distinctions and relationships between the three persons of the Godhead in the economy of salvation. It is likely that the intended end of this study was to affirm orthodox Christian thinking on the matter. Little if anything was made of how the Trinity shapes our understanding of our humanity, who we are and who we are to become, how we are to live, and the nature of our relationships within the Christian community and in society. There were very few contemporary and contextual connections made between the doctrines of the Trinity, humanity, and the church, even though these connections have been central in the church's movement toward a coherent theology. The "philosophical turn toward relationality" has offered us important ways to construe the Trinity and investigate more deeply the relationships between this model of God and our own humanity.[5] It is this connection that I will explore, examining some of our trinitarian beliefs for their implications for how and what we become and how we start to retrieve more robust understandings of wholeness and holiness.

Being Human Beings

A central affirmation of Christian faith is that God is the Creator of all. This Creator is not an amorphous and ethereal cosmic force or a civil deity hidden behind the world, but a particular God who spoke creation into being and continually sustains it in love, with gracious and merciful power, and for a divine purpose. Most Christians agree that the apex of God's creative activity was humanity, recorded in the first chapters of Genesis.

> Then God said, "Let us make human beings in our image, in our likeness, so that they may rule over the fish in the sea and the birds in the sky, over the livestock and all the wild animals, and over all the creatures that move along the ground." So God created human beings in his own image, in the image of God he created them; male and female he created them. (Gen. 1:26–27)

This original depiction of the source and purpose of our humanity offers us important insights into what it means to be human and made in the image of God. The first is that our creaturely, embodied existence as male and female is the creation and gift of God. Contrary to many Western philosophical narratives, passed along from Plato and Aristotle (and unfortunately appropriated by some Western theological traditions), our entire existence—male and female, with flesh and bone, minds, spirits, and creative capacities, all that makes us who we are—is central to our humanity. God created us and it is God who declared this creation to be "very good" (Gen. 1:31). There is no sense in the creation narratives that there is a more important part of our humanity called "spiritual," a more privileged person called male, a subordinated position occupied by woman, or that we are just confined to the drudgery of an earthly existence with no connection to transcendence, divine calling, and purpose. It is the complexity, difference, and wonder of human beings that make us truly human. The gift of our humanity is not something to be overcome or denied. It is something we accept as creatures, in an appropriate response to the God who calls us into being. This is at the center of what it means to be a human being, "to stand in relation to God as one's maker and to the rest of the created order as a fellow-creature."[6]

Being a finite human being, therefore, is an intentional gift of God, not a problem to overcome. I believe that denying this created limitation and the finitude of our humanity is sin, a refusal to acknowledge and accept the importance of ourselves and other selves as created by God, beloved yet dependent creatures. We deny who we are as human beings when we usurp the rightful place of God in our lives and the lives of others by denying our creatureliness and acting as gods over others.

One of the primary boundaries established in the creation narratives is the boundary between the Creator and what is created, a boundary that must remain intact if we are to truly live as human beings before God. The Scriptures recount through historical narratives, Wisdom literature, and the prophetic materials the chaos and turmoil that ensued after Genesis 3, when that which was created "exchanged the truth of God for a lie, and worshiped and served created things rather than the Creator" (Rom. 1:25). Our existence as creatures ought to be a source of delight and joyful dependence on God, as it releases us from the anxieties and desires to be more than we are or to assume prerogatives that do not belong to us as creatures.[7] In other words, we need not apologize for being "only human."[8] Instead, as Paul Wadell reminds us,

[I]t is actually the case that our freedom begins the moment we acknowledge and embrace our dependence. Accepting my life as a gift

113

frees me from the burden of having to establish myself or from having to give my life meaning and legitimacy. I do not have to make myself count, I do not have to make myself matter. I matter because I am loved, and I live on account of that love.[9]

For a Christian ethicist, any conversation about becoming, wholeness, and holiness must start with the recognition that all persons are created in the image of God and therefore have worth and dignity *because* they are human beings. In a globalized economy that values and treats humanity as no more than consumers, producers, and means to others' ends, a renewed commitment to the inherent dignity and worth of human beings is badly needed. In a technological society that interprets and mediates when life begins, when it ends or should end—in a society that can engineer and modify creation, procreation, babies, and genetic makeup—we need to be told again that life is not a market commodity or something that mirrors our wishes and ideals of perfection.[10] In a world of stringent racial, ethnic, and national divisions into "us" and "them," Christians—whose primary scriptural identity-metaphors are sojourners, pilgrims, and aliens in this world—have something transformative to offer that breaks the power of personal and national self-interests that systematically exclude the Other. When we overextend ourselves and assume prerogatives that do not belong to us, we need to be reminded that just *being* human is a gift common to all human beings and the source of dignity, worth, and freedom to be and become the persons God intended.

Being and Becoming More Human

In order to become, we first need to "be." The creation accounts affirm the goodness and giftedness of our creaturely existence that God called into being. These accounts also ground our creaturely existence in a source beyond the self. The one who creates us is also the one in whose image we are created: "in the image of God he created them; male and female he created them" (Gen. 1:27). There are intricate connections between our understanding of God and how we understand our own selves and other selves as human beings. This God in whose image we are created is the trinitarian God of Christian faith. This is the picture, the icon for how we better understand and live out our humanity, becoming more human and more whole and holy persons.[11]

A detailed exploration of the fourth- and fifth-century creedal debates about the Trinity is too lengthy for the immediate concerns of this chapter. Instead, I offer a brief summary in order to contextualize my argument and to make the connections between the Trinity as the model of God and what it means to become more whole and holy persons.[12]

As the early church moved out of the periods of persecution and into the Constantinian[13] era in 313, church leaders increasingly had the luxury of time and the support of Constantine to articulate more specifically the doctrinal claims of Christian faith. The need for more precision about what Christians believed was pressed by a number of challenges. First, Christianity had emerged out of Judaism and was now an official religion of the empire and no longer regarded as a sect of the Jewish faith. Second, the Roman Empire was radically pluralistic and polytheistic, with a pantheon of gods readily available, believable, and acceptable. Christianity found itself in this space, adhering to the radical monotheism of its Jewish roots but needing to affirm the divinity of Christ and the Holy Spirit without becoming polytheistic in belief and practice. In this context Christians needed to respond and provide an answer to what made Christian faith "Christian," different from Judaism and polytheism, particularly when it came to the relationships between Father, Son, and Spirit and the divinity and humanity of Jesus Christ. Third, there was already a diversity of belief in the church, some of which caused confusion and schisms in the church and the empire. Theological controversies mirrored geopolitical divisions and power struggles. A united empire needed a united church, and a church with emerging power needed the resources and legitimacy of a powerful state.

In response to these challenges, various proposals were presented to resolve and articulate in creedal form what Christians officially believed about the Father, the Son, and the Spirit, particularly an affirmation of the full divinity and humanity of Christ.[14] In short, the points of reconciliation were centered on these related questions and issues: How do we affirm the divine essence of the three persons of the Trinity as God? How do we affirm that God is one and yet acknowledge the divinities and distinctions of the Son and

115

the Holy Spirit? How are the members of the Trinity related to one another? How can Jesus be fully divine and fully human? What does his divinity say about what it means to be fully human, and what does his humanity reveal about the divine? What was offered us by the pastor-theologians of the church regarding these questions became known as the Nicene Creed, made official in 325. The Nicene Creed affirmed the full deity of the members of the Godhead and their relatedness in the work of salvation. Later the more expanded Chalcedon Creed in 451 reaffirmed the Council of Nicaea.

This historical and theological legacy has left us with a way of understanding the Trinity as both the way in which God exists as a community of three in one and how God is revealed and works as three persons constituted both by their relatedness to and distinction from one another. The Trinity reveals the fullness and cooperative relationships between the members of the Godhead. It is the Trinity that makes God known and does the work of God in the world. It is the Holy Spirit who reveals Jesus to humanity (Matt. 3:16–17; John 14:15–21, 25–27); Jesus is the "visible expression of the invisible God" pointing us to the Father (John 14:6–14; Col. 1:15–19); and it is the Father who created us in this trinitarian image for both divine and human community, making whole and holy participation in both possible. As Kathryn Tanner eloquently states, "From the Father, through the Son, in the Spirit, is the world created, saved, and brought to its end or consummation. By the breath of his mouth and in the image of his Word, the Father creates, preserves and saves the world; the Father brings into being, orders, and redeems, using, as Irenaeus would say, his two hands, Son and Spirit."[15]

The technical word used to describe this relationship of communion and relationality within the Trinity is *perichoresis*. Deriving from the Greek *peri*, which means "around," and *choreiō*, or "dance,"[16] it expresses "the idea that the three divine persons mutually inhere in one another, draw life from one another, 'are' what they are by relation to one another. *Perichoresis* means being-in-one-another, permeation without confusion."[17] The three members of the Trinity are inseparable yet distinct, unified in purpose in mutual giving relationships with one another, opening themselves to the world without losing anything. They exist as a "community of being"; we know them as a community of being in and through their relationships, and they are known to us because of their relationships.[18] It is the Spirit who reveals Jesus to us, Jesus who points us to the Father, and the Father who embraces us in divine love and acceptance. Catherine LaCugna explores the language of *perichoresis* with an eye to its implications for humanity. She writes, "*Perichoresis*, embodied in inclusiveness, community and freedom, is thus the 'form of life' for God and the idea of human beings whose communion with each other reflects the life of the Trinity."[19] Miroslav Volf also notes the implications of *perichoresis*, seeing in it the means by which God and humans maintain separation from each other in a way that retains for us a life-giving interdependence. He writes,

> At the ecclesial level (and at the creaturely level in the broader sense), only the *interiority of personal characteristics* can correspond to the interiority of the divine persons. In personal encounters, that which the other person is flows consciously or unconsciously into that which I am. The reverse is also true. In this mutual giving and receiving, we give to others not only something, but also a piece of ourselves, something of that which we have made of ourselves in communion with others; and from others we take not only something, but also a piece of them. Each person gives of himself or herself to others, and each person in a unique way takes up others into himself or herself.[20]

What are the implications of this theological foundation for conceiving of our humanity as created, finite, relational, and interdependent as good gifts of God? How can we be and become informed by Christian faith rather than conceptions of autonomy and individualism that characterize so much Western thought regarding personhood? I see two interrelated components for understanding our being and becoming more human in this trinitarian image, and its implications for our wholeness and holiness as we "participate in the divine nature" (2 Pet. 1:4).[21] The two ideas are relationality in general and righteous relationality in particular.

God's Relationality and Ours

Central to our claims about God and humanity is the concept of relationality, the notion that human beings only come into existence as a result of relationships and can only survive and thrive in these relationships. Relationality connotes an awareness of our existence as both dependent and interdependent creatures. When these relations are ignored or broken, social pathologies arise that plague our environment and our commitments to others. Affirmation of our relationality implies that our destiny is bound up with the relational God and with others. It has deep roots in our Christian narrative, which must be recovered in order to understand how we become and how we should live. The trinitarian God creates us in the *perichoretic* image, calls us into existence, and gives us the gift of being. Affirming that we are created in God's image is not an abstract theological claim but a fundamental assertion of our humanity as relational and social. Tom Smail writes, "Genesis is not about origins, but about our relationships to the God who made us, to the other people around us; and its revelational and anthropological authority lies in its exposition of God's purposes for these relationships."[22] If we take God seriously in our attempts to understand our identity and becoming, then this trinitarian image is central for grasping the shape, purpose, and moral dimensions of our humanity. How might this be important and applicable?

We come into existence in relationships—with God, parents, and nurturing communities. Also, it is only by relational connections that we can become as well as be. This is a central thesis of Arthur Dyck's "moral bonds of community."[23] Rights are not abstract political concepts that are realized without sustained practices of love and justice. Commitments to other human beings are embodied in actual communities that recognize rights as forms of responsibilities to others. Existence in and protection by communities are critical for our being and becoming at their most basic levels. Dyck writes,

Human agents only exist because other human agents cooperated to conceive, nurture, love, and instruct them; and because they cooperated to prevent and rectify potential and actual harm to those former agents. The lives of all individual human beings are gifts bestowed and sustained by others. The gift of life is daily reaffirmed and rendered possible by the responsible behavior of all those who refrain from killing us, who protect us from those who would harm us, and who stand ready to save our lives whenever it is necessary and possible. Even the remotest hermit is not without a history of parental love, for without love in the form of some attention and fondling no human will live and grow in infancy. . . . Hermits, like all other individuals, are here at everyone's mercy and, like all others, share the responsibility to ask themselves how to use the gift of life in ways that honor and express gratitude to those who nurtured them, both family members and that larger protective and sustaining community and communities.[24]

Like the trinitarian God who gives us life and sustains it, our various communities offer us gifts that protect, sustain, and enable us to flourish. Just as the members of the Trinity work together for the good of the world that they love, so we, who live in this trinitarian image, work to structure our communities around concrete practices that recognize our comprehensive connectedness and responsibility to others in ways that enable them to be and become all God means them to be and become. This is why the moral quality of our relationships and communities is so central to our ideas of becoming, wholeness, and holiness—a claim I will explore more fully below and in the next chapter.[25]

It is in relationships that we understand not just our dependence and interdependence but also our difference from others. Interdependence and difference must be affirmed and protected in whole and holy communities. As noted previously the early christological debates concerned how to maintain consonance with our heritage in Jewish faith and practice around the oneness of God, alongside the distinctions between the members of the Trinity revealed in light of Jesus the Messiah and the gift of the Holy Spirit. The proposals that were condemned as heresies either collapsed the members of the Trinity into one mode of being, thereby erasing the distinctions between the three members, or they privileged the distinctions between them, severing their equal sharing of the divine essence as God. This tension in maintaining wholesome and holy connectedness and differentiation strikes me as an important implication of trinitarian thought for how we become, how we view ourselves in relationships, and how we view and treat others.[26]

In reflecting on 1 Corinthians 4:7, Linda Woodhead reminds us that "for Paul, as for much Jewish thought, human identity is not the creation of each individual, but is bestowed by God and by fellow-humans. It is the gift of God and it is the gift of those who have shaped and formed us, both directly and through the texts and institutions they put in place."[27] To locate these ideas in a reflection on my life, I come to realize that there is so little about me that has anything to do with me apart from others. For example, I did not choose my parents, though I'm glad they chose to conceive and give birth to my siblings and me. Being birthed into a particular family at a particular historical moment, at the tail end of the baby-boom generation, socialized me into particular ways of seeing the world. Being born an American citizen offered me a worldview informed by American history and various interpretations of what that history means. My father's employment and my mother's carpooling skills made possible myriad opportunities for extracurricular activities. Involvement in the arts, educational programs, and eventual employment advantages were a result of growing up in a white middle-class family. Being raised in the church meant I was likely to accept the Christian faith as my own, which I eventually did. By staying rooted in the church I continually learn (I hope!) how to be and become more fully human by accepting and living into the counter-narratives of the Scriptures embodied in Christian community. I made choices along the way about what was offered me in these relationships with God, family, spouse, and friendships, choices that may not have been possible without these relationships. I continue to become a person intimately connected with these life-giving relationships but also differentiated from them. I am not my siblings, though we share traits that reflect the essence of our biological family. I am not my husband, though I understand how to be a better partner and life companion because I live with him and because our lives are interdependent. I am not identical to my colleagues, but I hope my unique perspective contributes well to our common vocation in theological education.

Even though there is correspondence between our understandings of the Trinity and how we exist in our own relationships, Kathryn Tanner reminds us of the limitations of perfect correspondence between God's relations and ours. Because of human finitude and our creatureliness, she writes, "[O]ne should avoid modeling human relations directly on Trinitarian ones, because Trinitarian relations, say, the co-inherence of trinitarian Persons, simply are not appropriate as they stand for human relations."[28] While the Trinity is the normative theological and moral model for human relationships, it is important to remember that we cannot perfectly model trinitarian relationships as does the perfect divine community. For instance, the Trinity is not becoming and so offers a stable referent for human becoming. We are and will always be becoming in relationships, understanding our true selves as we understand all that God is in trinitarian relations. The wholeness and completeness of these divine relationships are settled yet open to the world without losing anything; and because they are, they provide the stability and *telos* for what we are to become. We too can be open to the Other without losing anything in ways that reflect the relationships of the Trinity. In fact, it is only by openness to the Other that we can gain understanding necessary for being and becoming. As Smail notes,

> We become human in the way that we do through our receiving from others. It is in our relationships with them that we become aware of ourselves as persons capable of and obligated to committed responses to other people and to God, who is the ultimate source of the giving and receiving that structures our life—all that is the reality and the sign that we are created in the image of God.[29]

Affirming human creation in the trinitarian God and understanding our being and becoming in this light help us confront two aspects—threats or impasses, if you will—to becoming more whole and holy persons. First, divine and human relationality provides a way through the polarities of seeing humans, on the one hand, as autonomous, rugged individuals, a primarily Western narrative of what it means to be human; and the ideologies, on the other, that deem us little more than social constructs and products of our environment. The first pole (humans as autonomous) robs us of our connections and responsibilities to others. The second pole (humans as social constructs) relieves us from our own sense of moral agency and ways of responding to our "subjection to the accidents of history."[30] The creation and formation of our selves is social—a dialectic between our uniqueness, difference, and individuality as it is shaped and brought forth by our various relationships and contexts.[31] We are both social and individual; we are both connected and different; and we are shaped by—and we shape—the contexts in which we live. Similar to a dynamic tension in the trinitarian debates about oneness and distinction, we rest in the middle tensions that must affirm both aspects of what it means to be a person created in the image of God. We must recognize this in order to become and also to allow others to become as we provide relational connections for them.

A second issue that we confront in our being and becoming in this trinitarian image is the one-sided circumscription of relationality to women. This is reflected in assumptions that women are more relational, more nurturing, more connected to others than are men. This supposition has the perhaps unintended consequence of reducing women to the sum of their relationships in ways that men are not and assigning a meaning and purpose to women's existence that is wholly referential to male figures.[32] These ideas about the unique relationality of women may be derived from contexts that socialize women into roles as caretakers and nurturers, whose primary purpose for existence is to allow others to become who God intended them to be.[33] Given that our understandings of ourselves are shaped by the contexts we inhabit, it is important to question the sources of these assumptions. The Scriptures affirm both men and women as created in the image of God. There is little if any indication in Scripture of specific traits that are male or female, except for physical ones. The Scriptures do not, in my view, provide a blueprint or pathway for being and becoming more feminine or masculine. Rather, they draw us to images of being and becoming that are more like God and less like our various cultural construals and expectations of being female and male. Miroslav Volf suggests that "instead of setting up ideals of femininity and masculinity, we should root each in the sexed body and let the social construction of gender play itself out guided by the vision of the identity and relations between divine persons," the norm for all human relations.[34]

I raise this issue because of the grip these polarizing gender ideologies—portrayed in popular expressions like "men are from Mars and women are from Venus"—have on our ideas of being and becoming the persons God creates us to be. These poles are not helpful for either men or women. They disregard the myriad ways in which humans are different from and similar to one another. These ideologies also betray a gender-biased special pleading, because they reduce women to the substance of their relationships, while ignoring the ways in which maleness is informed by equally rigid and idealized social constructs of masculinity. These notions also damage the being and becoming of men who do not fit such molds. The Scriptures do not idealize a certain type of maleness or femaleness as transcultural, ahistorical, or universal.[35] Rather, they urge us to understand ourselves and root our theological anthropology in our relatedness to God and to others, and to recognize the fundamental relationality of both sexes worked out in our Christian communities, where we all can become and grow into the wholeness and holiness of the divine image.

The Trinity's Right Relationships and Ours

The Trinity does not just provide us a model for human relationality. It also gives us a way to make moral assessments about the quality of these relationships by contributing to our understanding of justice, righteousness, protection of being and fostering of becoming, and the renewal and re-creation of God's intended purposes. The work of the Trinity makes reconciliation with God and righteousness possible, and it does the same for human relationships. Part of imaging the Trinity, according to Mary Catherine Hilkert, is working for a "new future" for our "interpersonal relations and social and political structures."[36] Such a future would be characterized by equal concern for all "according to Trinitarian paradigms of radical equality and mutuality."[37] For Hilkert human communities image God by living in "right relationships" characterized by mutual love, respect, equal regard and concern, justice, and solidarity with others in the work of God in the world.[38] This is what the Trinity does in maintaining unity and distinction; perhaps these right relations are also ways in which we as God's creatures can better live with our differences and common commitments.

We model trinitarian commitments in the ways we relate to other persons, since their destiny is bound up with ours. For Nicholas Wolterstorff the attachment of love found in trinitarian relationships must translate into commitments and practices that attend to the well-being of others. The primary way in which we attend to this is through a justice that acknowledges the worth of others, not in intangible affirmations but in concrete practices that take seriously what others need to exist and become. Does the Trinity have anything to say about justice? According to Wolterstorff, the answer is a resounding yes, since

> God's doing of justice in human affairs reflects the justice internal to God's own life; God's love of justice in human affairs reflects the justice that incorporates love that is internal to the Trinity. Accordingly, when we treat each other justly, we neither merely obey God's injunction to act justly nor merely imitate God's doing of justice within creation. We mirror the inner life of the Trinity.[39]

Conclusion

Tom Smail writes that "to image the life of God is to mirror in our humanity the initiation of the Father, the obedience of the Son, and the creativity of the Spirit as the harmonious but distinct expressions of the free love of God within a human life and a human community."[40] God initiates loving relationships and redeems the world through gracious acts of creation and merciful compassion that sustain human life. Jesus provides the ultimate embodiment of God's triune life in his humanity, the means by which we know what God is like. His life of obedience is "mirrored in our relations with others as we live a life of service to God's ends."[41] It is the Holy Spirit who offers the good gifts that we, in turn, offer to the world. It is the Trinity that gives us life and enables us to be. And it is in relationship with the Trinity and trinitarian communities that we become, so that "out of the fullness of the Father by way of Christ and in virtue of his Spirit in us, we are to provide others with all good things for their good."[42] How we become more whole and holy persons by actively participating in this divine life is the subject of the next chapter.

9

WHOLENESS AND HOLINESS

Christian Moral Formation (Wyndy)

In the last chapter I proposed that the Trinity is the model for human relationships. As such it contains rich sources for understanding what it means to honor human beings and for becoming more human. The Trinity invites us to participate in the divine life of Father, Son, and Holy Spirit. The Trinity is not just a central theological affirmation of Christian faith describing what God is like. The triune God also provides normative moral criteria for how we should pattern our lives, for how our desires and communities should be ordered, and for how we should be and what we should become. In this chapter I want to explore the implications of this claim for the concerns and aims of Christian ethics. How might we establish normative moral criteria for human wholeness and holiness? I will start by exploring ideas of the Good and goodness in moral theology. I will then make more-explicit connections with our participation in the divine life of the Trinity, God's own moral goodness, and the formation of whole and holy virtues.

Conceptions of the Wholly Good in Christian Ethics

In ethics, the life well lived is often referred to as the good life. Paul Wadell poses the question, "How can we plan our lives so they can be lived as well as possible?"[1] This question contains important assumptions for ascertaining the purposes of human life and for clarifying our ideas of goodness. One assumption concerns the degrees of intentionality by which we plan how to live as well as possible. Living well-lived lives must be an aim, something we aspire to, attend to, and even plan for. In other words, Christian morality, goodness, wholeness, and holiness do not just happen. They require attention, deliberation, discernment, self-examination, and practices that enable us to live out what we believe in order to make a difference in the lives of others and in our own.[2] A second assumption is that living well-lived lives is a good thing, worthy of pursuit itself, not just for its results, but for the qualitative difference that well-lived lives mean for others and for us.[3] Becoming good by becoming more whole and holy requires due diligence in Christian faith and practice, not out of a begrudging sense of obligation, but flowing from a deep desire to be and become the kinds of people who wholly participate in the holy divine life of the Trinity, for the sake of the *shalom* of the world. This is a good thing to do.[4] What is the Good and what is the content and purpose of goodness? Three interlocking ideas of the Good and goodness are important in Christian moral thought for expanding our ideas of wholeness and holiness. They are (1) our ideas of happiness and wholeness; (2) the ultimate Good as God; and (3) practiced consonance between means and ends while participating in the divine life of the Trinity.

Our Ideas of Happiness and Wholeness

The good or well-lived life is one of happiness, satisfaction, harmony, and wholeness—terms I take to be related and will use synonymously in this discussion as descriptions of processes toward, and ends of, completeness. In philosophical discourse *eudaimonia* (often translated "happiness") is a Greek concept that encompasses ideas of moral excellence and goodness by bringing together all aspects of a person's life into a whole, and harmonizing them as they direct us to ultimate aims and purposes. As Alasdair MacIntyre notes, *eudaimonia* "is the state of being well and doing well in being well, of a man's [*sic*] being well-favored himself and in relation to the divine."[5] In philosophical ethics happiness is not a fleeting feeling based on moods or life's circumstances. It is instead a reasoned, deliberate approach to life based on ultimate desires that bring true, long-lasting happiness and satisfaction about who we are and the kinds of lives we choose to live long term. True happiness requires an "examined life" that functions at the attitudinal and interpretive levels. John Kekes notes the dynamics of these two functions:

> The attitudinal aspect of happiness is more than a succession of satisfying episodes. For the attitude requires that the significance of the episodes be appraised in terms of our whole lives. This appraisal need not involve conscious reflection, although it frequently does. It may simply be an unspoken feeling of approval of our lives and a sense that particular episodes fit well into it. The episodes may be goals achieved, obstacles overcome, experiences enjoyed, or just the seamless continuation of the approved pattern of our lives.[6]

Happiness in moral thought is related to an integrative wholeness, this "seamless continuation of the approved patterns of our lives," this "state of being well and doing well." This conception of happiness from a moral perspective provides greater and more stable connections between who we are, how we want to live, and how we should live.

Christian ethics provides us the resources to reflect on and practice becoming whole and holy based on the grand scriptural vision of *shalom*. *Shalom* is both a moral vision and a practiced way of life that embodies God's intentions for what is good for all that God created. *Shalom* guides us to seek to restore and reconcile what has been lost through acts of justice, mercy, and compassion. Thus, Christian ethics is about what is good, about being good, and about doing well in our pursuit of *shalom*—the wholeness that God intends for all that is created in the good image of the trinitarian God. This wholeness in ourselves reflects a consonance between who we are, what we are becoming, what we love, and how we live. *Shalom* enables us to interpret and reflect on the episodes of our lives, and it informs and directs our actions to establish "an approved pattern of our lives." What we care about, how we view life, what narrative we choose to live by (or which narrative chooses us), and how we perceive God's ultimate purposes are moral matters and crucial for our conceptions of wholeness.[7] Our lives will be oriented around what we love and what we view as good. We need to think about our moral lives and reflect on why and what we desire in order for there to be a "seamless continuation," a wholeness between who we are and how we live. This is why it is so important to be clear in our understanding of the Good and deliberate in its pursuit.

The pursuit of wholeness is a good journey in and of itself, even as it remains incomplete in its pursuit of the Good. That it is incomplete is not a moral problem; only the refusal to desire or pursue the journey is. The misguided assumption that we have arrived at our final destination of wholeness and holiness is also a moral problem because it leads to a cessation of pursuing the Good. It is the epitome of human hubris to conflate our smug definitions of what is good with God's ultimate goods, as if these were totally attainable by humans. Wadell writes:

> As human beings we are never anything other than pilgrims because we never fully possess what we desire. We move toward wholeness, but we never know it completely. We strive for happiness and satisfaction but are never so content that we don't reach out for more. . . . This is especially true when what we are reaching for is the love and goodness of God. The Christian life is a pilgrimage, an always unfolding quest whose destination is lasting communion with God. But it is a happiness which must also be pursued, but never fully possessed, because it requires the ongoing transformation of ourselves in the goodness of God, and at no point is that conversion complete. We strive for this goodness, we grow more deeply into it, but we are never perfectly conformed to it. The "not yet" character of life abounds in the Christian life because the remaking of ourselves in holiness will always be unfinished.[8]

Becoming whole—becoming good—is both an active pursuit and a reflection of our deepest desires. It is both externally and internally driven. In moral language the extrinsic Good orders our intrinsic desires, our deepest affections. Perhaps one of our deepest desires is to be whole in the midst of fragmentation. The quest for wholeness and *shalom*, and all the various forms that quest takes—even unhealthy ones—defines being human. Is desiring to be whole and holy part of what it means to be human? In moral theology the answer is yes. We are what we desire; and we order our lives, intentionally or not, around what we see as ultimate goods. It matters, therefore, what we desire and how we see ultimate purposes in our vision of wholeness.

God as the Ultimate Good

For Christians the ultimate extrinsic Good is God, the one who orders all other goods, and gives shape, purpose, and meaning to our lives. Unlike Greek philosophical thought, in Christian thought the Good is not a transcendental idea—the Form that remains abstract, aloof, and ethereal. The Good in Christian ethics is not a set of ideas about what is good or a series of moral platitudes about goodness. The Good in Christian moral thought is about a way of life in friendship with God, the source of all that is good. God "calls us to a distinctive way of life," and it is radically different from visions of the good offered to us by our contemporary culture, and even in many of our churches.[9] The Good is embodied, concrete, visible, and offered to us most completely in Jesus Christ. As Stephen Long notes,

> [T]he specificity of the form through which this goodness is revealed to us is indispensable. That form is Jesus of Nazareth. He is our way to the goodness that is God. Only in him do we have the infinite in the finite in such a way that the latter is not destroyed by the former but restored, preserved, and maintained. . . . [I]n the Christian incarnation, our finite participation in the infinite makes possible participation in a goodness beyond us, a goodness that is transcendent, an infinite goodness. For Christian theology, to desire Jesus is to desire the good.[10]

In Christian ethics and theology it is the Holy Spirit who makes the pursuit of God and the desire for Jesus possible, through divine power and the continual shaping of our affections.[11] This brings us back to the Trinity as more than just the description of what God is like. It is the Trinity that reshapes our notions of goodness, our understandings of wholeness and holiness, and the purpose of our existence. The Trinity—Father, Son, and Holy Spirit—now becomes the means by which we pursue and participate in the Good by participating in the very life of God. This happens through the process of *sanctification*, or becoming holy, and *theōsis*, or participating in God's own nature, two theological ideas with rich moral import for becoming more whole and holy.

If there is one predominant metaphor in Christian thought, it is that God is holy and wholly Other. The Scriptures are replete with this self-reference of God by God and the acknowledgment of God's holiness by others (Lev. 11:44; 20:26; Ps. 99; Isa. 6:1–3; Rev. 4:8–11). Holiness broadly conceived describes God's nature, God's very being and difference from all that is created. God is majestic and awesome, set apart from all other gods and from creation. God is morally perfect, complete, just, and righteous in acts of compassion and mercy. God's holy being is known by what God does, or how God acts, because God is whole and complete. There is perfect consonance between who God is and what God does. In other words, God is not just holy; God acts in holy ways. God's holiness is perceptible in what God does and how God responds to persons with justice, right dealings, compassion, mercy, and grace. God's ways, God's own manner of conduct, have a particular form and purpose intricately related to God's own moral character (Exod. 33:12–13; Ps. 25:4–11) that is visible and tangible, eliciting reverential awe when seen by others (Gen. 32:22–30; Exod. 19; Isa. 6:1–5). God shows God's self holy by acts of righteousness and justice (Isa. 5:16). Isaiah "saw" God's holiness and responded appropriately in light of what he saw by crying out both "woe to me" *and* "send me" as a witness to others (Isa. 6:1–8). Central to Christian faith is the belief in Jesus as the "visible image of the invisible God" (Col. 1:15). Those who have seen Jesus have seen the Father (John 14:9–14). Jesus is the tangible, visible expression of what God is like and how God acts. It is in the Incarnation, in Jesus's own humanity, in what Jesus does and how he acts, that we see the nature, character, and actions of the one holy God made manifest and concrete.

Holiness is not only a description of God but also a prescription for human behavior for those who see God's holiness in action. Holiness becomes a moral criterion for how the people of God should be and act because we are in relationship to this holy God through Jesus. "Be holy for I am holy" (Lev. 11:44 NRSV; 1 Pet. 1:15–16). This is a holiness informed by God's own conduct of holiness, care and concern, and commitment to *shalom*, as opposed to some kind of super-spiritual, other-worldly gnostic holiness reserved for the elite few and hidden from public view. Christian holiness is an incarnated, lived holiness. It has a shape, a content, and a purpose. It is a visible holiness that embodies—albeit imperfectly and incompletely—the concerns and character of God, both practicing and pointing the way to God's intended *shalom*. The importance of this kind of embodied holiness, patterned after Jesus, is a result of our "being clothed with Christ" (Rom. 13:14), what Kathryn Tanner calls our "assumption by Christ." She writes:

> Our assumption by Christ has as its whole point such a correspondence in action between Christ's life and ours: we are to live our lives in community with Christ's life as that is demonstrated in all that we think, feel, and do. Our lives are to be the reflection in action of our assumption into Christ, in virtue of their taking on the mode of Sonship. Our assumption in Christ is to become visible as our lives show forth, in action and in deeds, the form of Christ's own life, the mode of Sonship. Thereby, the glory of God's own triune superabundance shines forth, not in a static epiphany, but from all that it is that we do for the good, from our efforts to instantiate and further the good of others.[12]

The Christian moral life has its source in the goodness of God, the normativity of Jesus, and the working of the Holy Spirit, giving it a concrete triune shape and purpose. The Christian life is about becoming more whole and holy in the image of the trinitarian God. As Mark O'Keefe notes, "[T]he task of the Christian life . . . is to orient one's life toward God, and over a lifetime, to dispose oneself more fully toward God so that one may come to love God with one's *whole* heart, soul, mind, and strength."[13] This theological idea called sanctification is understood as the process of growing into Christ-likeness and becoming more holy. This process has important moral dimensions, in that growth in holiness is manifested in particular behaviors and attitudes that are visible and practiced in the context of communities. When Jesus prays for the Christian community's sanctification (John 17:17–19), his desire is that we may be unified and that the love of God supremely expressed in Jesus will be in us and visible to the world. They will know us by our love (John 13:34–35). We are to try to be holy, to live lives that reflect the goodness and concerns of God (Heb. 12:14–17). We are to present our bodies as "living sacrifices, holy and pleasing to God" (Rom. 12:1–2). It is this sense of embodiment that elevates the moral dimensions of becoming holy, because it is in and through our bodies that we interact with God and other persons.

The point I want to stress is this: becoming more holy has an important visible, bodily dimension, just as God's holiness does in the incarnation. From the perspective of Christian ethics, becoming holy involves patterned ways of seeing and living with God and others. Holiness is not a description of an unattainable attribute of human existence. Perfect holiness is reserved for God. But like God our becoming holy is manifested in what we practice doing over a lifetime in our embodied existences. Becoming holy is a work of the Spirit, "the agent of sanctification applying the benefits of Christ's sacrifice to the believers *in their common life*. The Spirit produces those gifts, fruits, and infused virtues without which the Christian moral life cannot make sense."[14]

The fruit of the Spirit inculcates and cultivates the virtues that shape our lives and enable us to become more whole and holy. Virtues in Christian ethics are moral qualities, characteristics, and dispositions that are infused, learned, and practiced.[15] They are often associated with character ethics that give attention to the kinds of persons we desire to be, who we are becoming, and the means by which we become more virtuous persons. I've already mentioned that the pursuit of the Good involves both extrinsic and intrinsic desires. Our ultimate extrinsic Good is God, who offers us the orienting vision of *shalom* as a gift of grace, out of God's own desire for justice and right relations between everything God created. The necessary intrinsic component is the Holy Spirit, cultivating in us the intrinsic goods of the virtues that are part of God's own moral character. It is important, however, not to relegate these intrinsic goods or virtues to a private, interior space of our lives, lest they be solely understood as some kind of inward journey. The cultivation and practice of the virtues are deeply social and always embodied. They are learned, practiced, and developed. They involve habits that work on both our attitudes and behaviors. They carry with them the visions of *shalom* to which they point. They are visible, and they contrast with what the apostle Paul calls the acts of our sinful nature (Gal. 5:13–26). We are to walk, conducting ourselves by following in the ways of Jesus and giving attention to the kind of lives we are called to live. In this walking the Christian life has a distinct and visible pattern characterized by love, joy, peace, patience, kindness, goodness, faithfulness, gentleness, and self-control (Gal. 5:22–23). These virtues are whole because they contribute to *shalom*. They are holy because they reflect the life of God. We are not just called to be these things; we are called to learn, practice and do them.

Virtues are intrinsic goods that enable us to participate in the good that is God's own moral excellence. They are important for becoming whole and holy because they are the bridge that helps us put into practice what we believe about God, fostering a more "seamless continuation of the approved pattern of our lives."[16] Virtues are the means by which we participate in God's own moral goodness, in God's very nature (2 Pet. 1:3–11). This idea of *theōsis*, sharers of the divine nature, reminds us that the purpose of the Christian life is not just about "getting saved."[17] *Theōsis* provides a much clearer connection between morality and our salvation, a connection that tends to be unintentionally bifurcated in Protestant articulations of the *ordo salutis* of regeneration, conversion, justification, adoption, sanctification, and glorification.[18] This order offers an overly neat, almost linear description of the process of salvation that puts sanctification too far along in the process. The end of our lives is communion with God, whereby we will be made completely whole and holy. Yet because of the Trinity, we even now are

> given . . . everything we need for a godly life through our knowledge of him who called us by his own glory and *goodness* [can also be translated as "virtue"]. Through these he has given us his very great and precious promises, so that through them you may participate in the divine nature [have communion in the divine nature], having escaped the corruption in the world caused by evil desires. (2 Pet. 1:3–4)

We are called out to participate in God's divine nature, reminiscent of the call to be holy because God is holy. Peter goes on to elucidate the means by which we participate in God's own moral excellence. It is by making every effort (2 Pet. 1:5) to add to our faith these moral qualities or practiced virtues: goodness, knowledge, self-control, perseverance, godliness, mutual affection, and love.

According to O'Keefe, "participation in the divine life—both as the ultimate goal and as proleptically present—impacts the moral life of the Christian in a number of ways."[19] It does so by bringing together the ultimate Good with the ways in which we live, "at both the level of decisions and the level of character—what contemporary Christian ethics refers to as the 'ethics of doing' and the 'ethic of being.' "[20] Participation in the divine life of the Trinity does not privilege being over doing. Instead, it more tightly connects who we are and what we do as a response to the grace of the God who calls us in love and pleasure. Participation in God's divine life encompasses both, recognizing that we are human beings and doers. Becoming whole and holy requires attention to both who we are and what we do. This participation in the divine nature of the Trinity is also social since, as O'Keefe notes, "the human person is inherently relational—in relationship with other persons. This reality flows from the creation of humanity in the image of the triune God," who is also social and who acts for the redemption of the world in morally excellent ways.[21]

Practiced Consistency between Means and Ends

The Good in Christian moral thought is God, and the means for becoming whole and holy—like God—is the ongoing formation of our lives into the image of the Trinity through the Spirit-inspired and grace-given virtues, and through participation in the divine nature. Virtues provide the bridge between who we are and the more whole and holy persons we can become. Virtues foster a deliberative and necessary consistency important for formation and for living more whole and holy lives. In this section I will explore two virtues, learned through our participation in the divine life of the Trinity, which I see as crucial for practicing an embodied holiness and for concretizing the vision of *shalom*. They are the virtues of generosity and justice, which "arise naturally out of an understanding of the embodied, communal, and trinitarian dimensions of Christian faith."[22] They are depicted in the rich iconic portrait of the holy Trinity, prompting Catherine LaCugna to make these observations about its generosity and justice:

> The most famous artistic portrayal of the Trinity is the icon painted by Andrei Rublev early in the fifteenth century in Russia. It depicts three angels seated around a table on which there is a eucharistic cup. . . . The icon was inspired, as the greatest works of Trinitarian art have been, by the story of Genesis 18 of the visit of the three men to the home of Abraham and Sarah. Abraham met the strangers outside, and despite not knowing their identity he called upon Sarah, and together they showed the visitors extraordinary hospitality. . . . In the process of sharing the resources of their household, the identity of the visitors was revealed to be Yahweh and two angels.[23]

LaCugna elevates the importance of this iconic image of the Trinity for our own lives and ways of being in relationships, describing it as "God's economy" of mutuality, justice, respect, and generosity. Michael Gorman also explores the particular shape of trinitarian holiness.[24] There is not just an inner quality to holiness, such as sexual purity and distinctive ways of life, familiar to many of us in certain streams of American Christianity. The Trinity also calls us to public holiness, which is *"counter-intuitive, counter-cultural, and counter-imperial"* based on Christ's *kenotic* life on behalf of the world and the inherent mutuality and right relations between the members of the Trinity.[25] One of the results, according to Gorman, should be a "holy politics," which also "requires a corollary vision of life in the world that rejects domination in personal, public, or political life—a mode of being that is often considered realistic or 'normal.'"[26] Again, the Trinity is not just descriptive of God but also provides the normative model for how we should be and act in the world. This public face and expression of trinitarian holiness is the paradigm of hospitable generosity—an openness that invites others in and grounds our relationships in the mutuality, respect, cooperation, and justice needed for *shalom.*

Generosity is the willingness and capacity to give of one's self and what one has without coercion or strings attached. It is a response of gratitude to the generosity of God who "gives freely."[27] Volf notes the important contrast between the "gift-giving God" and a "Santa Claus God." He observes, "A Santa Claus God gives simply so we can have and enjoy things; the true God gives so we can become joyful givers and not just self-absorbed receivers. God the giver has made us to be givers and obliges us therefore to give."[28] The Trinity has given humanity and the whole of creation all that is needed to survive (be) and thrive (become), and now calls upon those in this divine relationship to be generous just as God is, in order for others to survive and thrive. Others are dependent on our generosity as we are on theirs, as well as all are on God's. We can be and should be generous because God is generous. As recipients of God's generosity, we now become the conduit through which God's generosity flows to the world. The practiced virtue of generosity is rooted in God's own generosity to all God has created. God gives out of abundance for the good of humanity, losing nothing by giving. Generosity is a necessary virtue for creating and maintaining the conditions of *shalom* for a harmonious sharing of the goods that God offers us for our well-being, for justice, and for peace. God's generosity is manifest in and flows through the generosity of God's people to others. Generosity is an embodied response signaling our willingness to practice the virtues necessary to realize *shalom* in our relationships and in our communities.

> Generosity necessarily involves the physical act of giving in some minimal form. There is no such thing as a purely inward and spiritual act of generosity. Generosity inevitably involves our participation in the creaturely realm of physical acts. Generosity is also a mode of participating in the world because it is a means of building human community. . . . By acting generously we proclaim we are members of the human community and not beings that are exempt from its needs and constraints.[29]

As Dave Toycen notes, generosity is "the lubricant that smoothes our daily living in a way that affects other moral virtues. . . . [G]enerosity is the first car in a train of virtues. Without it, the other virtues are unlikely to ever get started or be fully expressed."[30] Generosity is a social virtue necessary for the maintenance of whole and holy communities, in places of shared spaces, where our lives are wrapped up in a "tissue of mutual dependencies" and where our "gratitude expresses our dignity as creatures of God whom he made to depend on one another."[31]

What are the forms of God's generosity, and therefore what forms can our generosity take? For Volf, our capacities to be generous start with faith in the God who is generous and who provides. We are recipients of God's generosity in a relationship with God the giver and so must "ascribe(s) to God what is due."[32] God's generosity to us is out of the abundance, mutuality, and completeness of God's own trinitarian life. Our generosity starts with this sense of an abundant life appropriated by faith, which is also a practiced virtue crucial to generosity. We can be generous because God is faithful; therefore, practicing generosity as a virtue is also practicing our faith. While generous people may experience satisfaction and joy in giving, generosity is an important way of addressing "fundamental human needs in response to and in light of God's active presence for the life of the world" and based on God's *shalom*.[33] Meeting fundamental human needs has a variety of forms—there are very tangible needs of resources, finances, and material possessions. There is the generous sharing of time and space to the lonely and dispossessed. There is generosity to meet immediate as well as long-term needs. There is the sharing of ourselves, allowing other persons to enter our communities, just as the Trinity has invited us into the divine society of Father, Son, and Holy Spirit. This form of generosity, patterned on the generosity of God, is a means of becoming whole and holy through the participation in God's own divine life, all the while contributing to conditions that are more "whole and holy," reflective of *shalom*. Volf refers to this as "right giving."

> We give when we *delight* in someone. . . . We also give when others are in *need*. A stranded stranger receives a helping hand; we aid the sick or those recently laid off from work get what they need. Finally, we give to *help others give*. We give to people who work for good causes in which we believe—we give to educational institutions (maybe to build and maintain a good library) and churches (perhaps to pay their ministers), to relief organizations (say, to help alleviate the global HIV/AIDS crisis). . . . In all three types of situations, we give because we seek the good of another. In all three we imitate God.[34]

137

What keeps us from being and becoming more generous and from practicing this right kind of giving described by Volf? Practicing generosity as a social virtue is difficult, which is all the more reason for us to be attentive and diligent in the ongoing process of forming virtues.[35] Virtues are not meant to be easy when understood in light of God's goodness and the practices for creating and maintaining *shalom*. They force us to practice what we might not naturally be inclined to do. I think, however, that there is a more pernicious aspect to our failure to practice generosity, one that involves the lack of a desire to be generous. In moments of brutal honesty we probably feel that certain persons are not worthy of generosity, while others are (including ourselves). Certain accounts of justice focus on retaining what we feel is rightly ours out of fear of what we might lose if we were generous and just. Justice becomes what we seek for our own well-being, as opposed to a practiced virtue on behalf of others, and in response to the generosity and justice of God. For many of us, our ideas of justice are inexorably linked to ideological assumptions inherent in our legal and political systems. In this economy, justice is about rewarding good and punishing wrongdoing. Concepts such as freedom, rights, fairness, and equal opportunity are also bundled into conversations about justice, as if these terms were synonymous.[36] While these are important aspects of justice, to collapse it into these concepts is to miss the important relationships between the purpose and shape of God's justice and our works of justice as we participate in God's divine life. God's justice is about restoring the wholeness of *shalom*, in right relationships between God and humans, between fellow human beings, and between humans and other parts of the created order. Justice is something we *do* in relationship to others.

The virtue of justice is about commitment and sustained practices to make things whole; it is a mark of our becoming more holy persons. "To be holy is to be just. For if all human living is a matter of relationships—to God, to people, to earth [some would add, to one's self]—then, good, loving, intimate relationships mirror in a finite way trinitarian life and love."[37] Justice conceived in this way is the active participation in the goodness of God based on the grand vision of *shalom*. Acts of justice contribute to the re-creation of the conditions of *shalom* that the trinitarian God intended for creation in the first place. Justice involves working toward establishing and maintaining harmony, wholeness, and righteousness within the entirety of the created order. It is our work, in cooperation with God, to help our communities become more whole by becoming more just. Jim Wallis writes:

> In the Hebrew Scriptures, one finds the more holistic concept of *shalom* as the best definition of justice. It is a deeper and wider notion than the security of individual human rights. The vision of shalom requires us to establish "right relationships." It is a call to justice in the whole community and for the entire habitat. Shalom is an inclusive notion of justice extending even to the rest of God's creatures and the whole of the creation. Restoring right relationships takes us further than respecting individual rights. It pushes us to see ourselves as part of a community, even as members of an extended but deeply interconnected global family, and ultimately as strands in the web of life that we all share and depend upon. The biblical vision of shalom could be a basis for a new politics of community and the social healing we need so much.[38]

Practices of justice are about becoming more whole and contributing to the wholeness of all creation. Becoming more holy and embodying the holiness of the triune God are intricately linked with our commitments to the shape and concerns of God's justice, which involve reconciliation and restoration. There is a formative dimension to justice that must not be overlooked. Our unwillingness to see our complicities in and contributions to injustice and our reluctance to be formed into more just and holy persons are both morally and spiritually problematic, since "genuine spirituality involves an external expression of the internal experience. So too for the holiness that is justice. It demands involvement not only with God but with God's people and God's material creation."[39] Both generosity and justice are whole and holy virtues because of the ends to which they point, and for the good that they carry in their formation and their practices. They carry the good intentions of the whole and holy trinitarian God even as they help to form persons and communities that are more whole and holy.

Conclusion

The collaborative work of this book is to offer an integrative approach to becoming, wholeness, and holiness, and to speak out of ourselves and disciplines by offering new perspectives and language about these areas. Part of the task of Christian ethics is to offer a framework and a language to talk about becoming, wholeness, and holiness from a moral perspective. I have attempted to do this by exploring the descriptions of God's trinitarian life and the inherent quality of the relationships between Father, Son, and Holy Spirit as the model for being and becoming more human. The other side of the task probed how this model of the Trinity provides the normative criteria for who we are and how we should act. Being and becoming more human, and being and becoming more whole and holy, are formative processes that extend beyond ourselves because they are not just about ourselves. They are the means by which God's good purposes are realized in the entire creation as it is being made whole by the holy acts of God and by those who wholly participate in the divine life of the Trinity.

From the perspective of Christian ethics we must make commitments to human *beings* a starting point for allowing all persons to *become*. Becoming happens in a web of relationships—with the trinitarian God and with others. The quality of these relationships has a huge impact on who we become. What the Trinity offers us is a whole and holy model that informs and guides our commitments to just, caring, mutual relationships with others, as well as our commitment to their becoming. Becoming whole and holy occurs in our ongoing participation in the divine life of the Trinity, and through our attention to and practices of virtues, those habits that form us and help us to integrate what we believe with how we live. Desiring consonance between who we are becoming and how we live is the expression of lives moving toward an embodied wholeness and holiness, that which enables us to attend to the needs of others based on God's vision of *shalom*.

RECEPTION AND INTEGRATION
OF OFFERINGS FROM ETHICS
A Response (Carla and Jeannine)

I n this chapter we (Carla and Jeannine) reflect on Wyndy's offering from the discipline of Christian ethics. Again, in our methodology for this book one colleague's offering leads to reception by the others, attending to points of potential integration as well as possible divergence between vantage points based in our distinct disciplines. While bringing the fields of social science and biblical hermeneutics into conversation with Wyndy's insights from theology and ethics, we continue to center our conversations around the topics of becoming (human formation), wholeness, and holiness.

Reception and Integration from Social Science (Carla)

Wyndy,

I find myself so energized as I read your offering—partly because I see several places for constructive engagement between our disciplines and partly because I feel called to mercy, justice, and humility in ways that seem more possible and hopeful because of the way you articulate the invitation to the good life. Thank you!

Something in your reminder that the Trinity does not "become" sparked an awareness in me that you, Jeannine, and I have perhaps been talking about becoming these past many months with what may be an unarticulated assumption that the best or right kind of human becoming is intentional. We have been discussing less a deterministic, inevitable kind of development that happens because of chronology than we have a becoming that you and Jeannine highlight, one that incorporates the concepts of relationality, dependence, finitude, and so on. Your offering reminds me that I also want to be careful to leave room for formation that takes us by surprise.

A couple of questions that emerged made me wish I was reading in your presence so I could ask, "So what about . . . ?" One concerns how non-Western ethicists and theologians understand the Trinity as a model for human becoming differently than do Western ethicists and theologians. What might this additional perspective highlight that we miss, being located in our Western narrative? You've inspired me to add to my "to-read" list! Any suggestions?

I would add that rugged individualism has not held up well in social-scientific explorations of healthy relationships. Differentiation of self is often misunderstood to mean becoming a more effective lone ranger, when in reality it incorporates the capacity for both authentic connection and appropriate self-regulation. The importance in human development of attachment and attunement—both inherently relational concepts—has been well documented. You seem to affirm this relationally oriented corrective from the perspective of your field as well, citing Volf, for example, as one who emphasizes the idea that we become ourselves in communion with others.

I completely agree with your critique of the simplistic, stereotypical gender categories (chap. 8) that have been received with what I find to be a troubling lack of critical thinking on either scriptural or empirical grounds. Whether framed as "planetary problems" (the Mars/Venus dichotomy) or as reified culturally bound lists of what men and women "need," these restrictive, one-dimensional categories contribute to confusion, resentment, disappointment, and power struggles for couples who regularly show up in the offices of marriage and family therapists. In fact, I concur about the adverse effects on men who don't fit the mold of culturally defined masculinity, and would add that men who *do* fit the mold are also negatively impacted by the explicit and implicit messages in our culture that women know how to relate and men do not. Part of my work with couples often involves challenging the notion both parties have been handed that it is the woman who is "doing the relationship right." This example you raise is an important one that needs the corrective both of particularity and relatedness.

I'm struck with how resonant your descriptions of generosity are with mine of hospitality. For example, you name generosity "a social virtue necessary for the maintenance of whole and holy communities, in places of shared spaces, where our lives are wrapped up in a 'tissue of mutual dependencies'" (chap. 9). You note that our generosity is inspired and sustained by God's prior generosity to us; I believe the same is true of hospitality. I see the distinctives of both concepts but find myself wondering if the shared core represents an even deeper virtue or theme. With apologies to George and Ira Gershwin: "You say 'generosity,' I say 'hospitality'; let's call the whole thing 'love.'"

Two sociological theories consistently emerged as places of potential engagement with your ethical perspectives: conflict theories and symbolic interactionism. With regard to the first set of perspectives, your sobering assessment of our lack of desire to be generous might be seen as competition for scarce resources, combined with the application of a "justice rule" that specifies that those who contribute more should receive more (as opposed to one that says those who need more should receive more). This theoretical perspective may help us describe what conflict theorists see as an inevitable (and, in itself, neutral) reality of human relationships.

I would suggest that there is also an element of "just-world" thinking in our stinginess: that people basically get what they deserve. If I have enough, I must deserve it. If you don't, you must not deserve it. This is not a new phenomenon, of course—witness Job's friends and their unhelpful willingness to determine what he had done that had brought unbelievable calamity to his life.[1] God—the Good, Creator God—challenged their assumption (one we may share) that there is a one-to-one correlation between what I have and what I deserve (Job 42:7–9). .

The second theoretical framework, symbolic interactionism, came to mind at several points in my reading of your chapters. One such moment was your emphasis on being shaped by community. You cite Volf's description of "something we have made of ourselves in communion with others. . . . Each person gives of himself or herself to others, and each person in a unique way takes up others into himself or herself."[2] You confirm his insight by saying, "The creation and formation of our selves is social. . . . We are both social and individual" (chap. 8). Along with the echo of differentiation, some basic elements of symbolic interaction help describe this process. Symbolic interactionism posits that we become human through interaction with other humans. This takes place partly through a process known as the looking-glass self, in which our sense of ourselves is formed by feedback from others.[3]

Another place for mutual engagement between ethics and social sciences might be expressed in the symbolic interactionist axiom that "if a thing is perceived as real, it is real in its consequences." Your emphasis on the importance of being clear in our understanding of the Good and of God's ultimate purposes is consistent with the quality of authentic piety I described in chapter 3, which requires us to hold our representations of God up for illumination by the Holy Spirit. As I noted there, we serve and introduce others to the God we imagine. Your definition of our perceptions of life, of God's purposes, and of our heart's desires as moral matters is underscored by this symbolic interactionist principle.

I would hypothesize that a point of concern might also arise between you and a symbolic interaction theorist. You describe a danger of "ideologies . . . that deem us little more than social constructs and products of our environment" (chap. 8). This would be applicable to a purist, constructivist, symbolic interaction perspective. However, I would suggest that a Christian working within a symbolic interaction framework might posit that there is indeed absolute truth, but that what we know and believe about it is socially constructed. A Christian sociologist may commit to metaphysical absolutism and epistemological relativism, the inverse of what a typical sociological perspective might suggest.[4]

Reception and Integration from Hermeneutics (Jeannine)

Wyndy,

It is so clear to me as I read your chapters that you are gifted as an ethicist. Clearly this is no surprise to anyone who knows you well,

144

including me, but I was impressed by the strength of your contributions consistently arising from the moral framework and foundation that you have developed through much intentional reflection and action—from understandings of theology as "ways of wise, faithful, and righteous living" (chap. 8). I want to begin my responses by indicating what resonated between our respective chapters, so that we will not miss the common ground between our disciplines, and between you as a particular ethicist and me as a particular biblical scholar. After exploring these resonances, I will reflect on certain ideas you develop that seem to be fertile ground for further conversation, and some which provide a balance and counterpoint to my own work.

Your grounding of holiness in God's own holiness enfleshed in the life of Jesus accords with themes from my chapters. I am impressed that we both so strongly stress the crucial notion of human finitude for understanding human being and becoming. Your affirmation that human being is a gift rather than a problem fits well with my sketch of the biblical story, which locates finitude within creation rather than the fall (chap. 5). I also hear our similar emphases on *shalom* as being communal, entailing both righteous relationships and justice. This gives both of us one way to speak of and sum up wholeness. Yet you helpfully lay emphasis on *shalom* as "both a moral vision and a practiced way of life" (chap. 9). At every turn you remind me that the *shalom* vision of Scripture is meant to enliven our current practices. It is to be incarnated in our world.

All three of us also draw upon the *imago Dei* as a key resource for understanding human being and becoming, which you especially connect to human relationality. I appreciate your significant contribution on the implications of humanity created in God's image for the way we treat fellow humans. Rather than capitulating to cultural patterns that encourage us to treat other human beings as commodities or enemies, you call us to affirm the worth and dignity of all because we all bear the divine image. In light of the creation of all people in the image of God, we must recognize our human, moral obligation to the Other (chap. 8).

A contribution that you share with Carla is offering a relational dialectic in defining human wholeness and holiness (Carla's terms: *particularity* and *relatedness*). As I noted in my response to Carla (chap. 4), I am intrigued by the fruitfulness of that dialectic for hermeneutics as well as for human becoming. Your framing of the dialectic arises from historical trinitarian deliberation, which sought to do justice to the polarities of *relatedness* and *distinction* between the persons of the Trinity. You offer this dialectic as a way of understanding what it means for humanity to image our triune God. And, not surprisingly, you draw upon this dialectic to ground ethics—to navigate between the extremes of living the narrative of "humans as autonomous, rugged individuals" and humans as "little more than social constructs" (chap. 8). I am wondering if this dialectic might also offer some insight into our deliberations on immigration in chapter 11, particularly in relation to how we choose to engage the Other as both related to and distinct from ourselves. Might this dialectic inform our tendencies to either assimilate or reject those who are different from us?

I also appreciate your emphasis on the embodied nature of wholeness and holiness, something Carla has referred to as "vertical integration"—our integration within our embodied self (chap. 3). This is an area I explored less than I would have liked in my chapters, so I'm thankful that it recapitulates through your work (and through Carla's chapters). You assert that holiness "has an important visible, bodily dimension" based in the incarnation and on the bodily nature of our interactions with God and others (Rom. 12:1–2; chap. 8). Your reflections are particularly important given the level of ambivalence toward embodiment in historical theological deliberation as well as in contemporary culture (with two teenage daughters keeping me aware of this ambivalence on a daily basis). I think of Michael Horton's words: "[B]oth body and soul are included in [the] image-bearing task."[5] I am convinced that an evangelical theology able to take seriously the embodied nature of human being and becoming, wholeness, and holiness would have a winsome message in a cultural context that alternately idolizes and then demonizes the human body. I would love to explore this aspect of holiness and imaging God with you more fully, especially in your significant interaction with contributions from feminist theology.

I was intrigued by the fact that we both introduce *participation* as an important biblical-theological category, yet with different emphases. I have drawn upon the Pauline concept of believers' participation "in Christ" as the means of their receiving all the benefits that come from Jesus's own faithfulness in life and death (chap. 5). You draw upon the Orthodox concept of participation as *theōsis*—a participation in the divine nature through the practice of virtues (chap. 9, with 2 Pet. 1:3–11). Participation in these two configurations is wonderfully complementary.[6] While the notion of participation in Christ focuses on what believers become and receive through the work of Jesus, participation as *theōsis* emphasizes human action for participation. While I have noted Paul's parallel call to live into what is already theirs in Christ, Paul's participationist language emphasizes what Christ has accomplished for believers. As you demonstrate, *theōsis* emphasizes the moral action of believers (though I'd love to hear from you how this concept engages God's actions toward Christians). In your words, "virtues are the means by which we participate in God's own moral goodness, in God's very nature" (chap. 9).

I appreciate your expansive discussion of Christian virtues (not a favorite Protestant term, as you note) that includes a whole range of moral imperatives. Virtue has, at times, been limited to a description of sexual purity, an association that was brought home to me a few days ago when watching the movie *Doubt*. A priest who is accused of sexual impropriety refers to mean-spirited people who "kill kindness in the name of virtue." You wonderfully demonstrate that virtue includes kindness, generosity, and justice, as well as what has traditionally been associated with the term. Your robust vision of Christian virtues includes the affirmation that they are "deeply social and always embodied," as well as the means of sharing the divine life of the triune God (chap. 9).

Some of the most intriguing offerings from your work are in the same general areas where I found Carla's offerings particularly fruitful for further conversation: your contributions to my ongoing interests and questions in hermeneutics and human identity.

You suggest an interesting connection when you indicate that, for philosophical ethics, true happiness requires reflection and integration. "True happiness requires an 'examined life' . . . and is related to an integrative wholeness" (chap. 9). You note that a sense of coherence between one's experience, actions, and goals is at the heart of this wholeness or integration and that some attention to this coherence (or its lack) is important, whether that attention occurs at a cognitive or an emotive level or both (chap. 9). I am intrigued by the idea that to move toward wholeness one needs to engage in some level of second-order reflection. I need to consider myself in my world as an object of reflection, specifically in relation to my construal of lived coherence. A hermeneutics of self—the awareness of myself as acting, thinking, feeling, and being as a (coherent) self within my contexts—is necessary to my quest for wholeness and well-being. Yet even as I write these sentences many questions flood my mind. How do our communal and individual stories construct coherence as well as reflect experiences of coherence? What if I am unable to tell a coherent story of my life experience due to trauma or significant relational disintegration? Does this keep me from achieving a sense of well-being? And, as Carla has indicated, does well-being necessarily signal integration and formation? Your introduction of these connections affirms the importance of hermeneutics, and not just focused on biblical texts, for making sense of life, all the while raising some questions that will require further conversation with you and Carla.

Another hermeneutical question came to mind as I read your helpful description of the contextual influences surrounding the church's trinitarian debates of the fourth and fifth centuries. You note the early church's need to locate its theology in relation to Jewish monotheism and in distinction from Roman polytheism. You also observe that the church's "theological controversies mirrored geopolitical divisions and power struggles" within the empire (chap. 8). By highlighting the setting of these debates and councils, you raised for me the question of how or whether the church's formulations are fully adequate for our contemporary understandings. What might their context have hidden from them as well as illuminated for them?

As one whose primary lens for exploring trinitarian theology is New Testament studies, I find myself reframing the questions of the church councils in comparison to the questions that New Testament writers seem to be asking. You note that trinitarian discussion of Jesus's identity focused on such questions as, "What does [Jesus's] divinity say about what it means to be fully human, and what does his humanity reveal about the divine?" (chap. 8). It seems to me that New Testament writers, while certainly providing initial (and more often than not implicit) answers to these questions (e.g., Phil.

2:5–11; John 1:1–18), are to a greater degree (or at least just as) interested in the question, What does Jesus's humanity say about what it means to be *fully human?* For them Jesus represents Israel by faithfully living in covenant with Israel's God (chap. 5). By doing so Jesus demonstrates and fulfills God's intention for humanity. This New Testament picture provides a direct link to Christian wholeness and holiness. Jesus is model humanity; he embodies what holy and whole humans are to look like. Yet my own church tradition has so emphasized Jesus as divine that Jesus as the representative human being often gets lost. I wonder if there might be a point of historical discontinuity between our two disciplines' perspectives on the theological significance of Jesus's humanity. So a few of my questions for exploring this discontinuity are How did the early councils frame this contribution of Jesus's humanity to our humanity? In your estimation, did the church in its two-natures discussion do justice to the New Testament vision of Jesus as the representative human? What historical resources might help the contemporary church in reengaging the humanity of Jesus for our own moral reflection?

Finally, as I shared in response to Carla's work, I continue to explore the question of an anchor for human identity, from the assumption that humans as finite beings are always changing and becoming. Carla's contribution to my ongoing wondering was the truth that being beloved by God might provide such an anchor. You have offered another wonderful resource. You speak of the Trinity in perfection —the one who does not change—as offering "a stable referent for human becoming" (chap. 8). Your offering drew me immediately to Paul's language in 1 Corinthians 8:5–6, where Paul sets his shared confession with Corinthian believers (evoking the *Shema*, Deut. 6:4) within their polytheistic world.

> For even if there are so-called gods . . . yet for us there is but one God, the Father, from whom all things came and for whom we live; and there is but one Lord, Jesus Christ, through whom all things came and through whom we live.

For Paul, God is the source and purpose of human existence; all things are from God and for God. And Christ is the means: humanity came into existence and continues to exist through Christ. This picture seems to resonate well with your affirmation of the Trinity as the anchor for human becoming.[7]

Perhaps God's trinitarian self as supremely stable, and God's love for humanity as utterly constant, together provide the anchor for human being and becoming. As I continue to reflect if there is anything that might anchor becoming from within humanity, I am also drawn to Dan Stiver's way of expressing a contribution from Ricoeur: "The self's *commitment to something* [i.e., the promising self] provides a kind of self-constancy that also provides an answer to the question of identity."[8] Human loyalty in dependence upon God's triune self and God's own covenantal love and loyalty might provide a more-than-adequate mooring for human identity.

INTERFACE

An Integrative Conversation around Immigration

We have framed our final chapter as a conversation, a fitting conclusion for the work we have been doing in this book. In this chapter we interact with one another and with our respective disciplines around a moral issue (immigration), a biblical text (Acts 10:1–11:18), and a formational practice (prayerful listening). As we have discovered and emphasized throughout the book, there is no single, proper place to begin this conversation.[1] In this final conversation it made sense to us to begin with the topic of immigration, since ethical conundrums often draw Christians into engaged (and sometimes heated!) conversations. Also, given the complexity of this ethical dilemma, it provides a web of issues (economic, legal, racial) that highlight possibilities and tensions for human being and becoming.

Wyndy begins our conversation by offering an account of a recent experience teaching about immigration in a local church setting. The case she presents gives the three of us opportunity to engage immigration issues with the resources of Scripture, spiritual practices, and various disciplinary insights already emerging from our conversations in our earlier chapters. This is not a final word that attempts to tie up all loose ends, but a more or less open-ended conversation that models the dialogical method we have introduced in this book: *offering, reception,* and *integration.*[2]

As a reminder, we are working with descriptions of wholeness, holiness, and becoming that have emerged over the course of our work together. We would summarize these integrative descriptions in the following ways.

Descriptions of Key Concepts

Becoming

God has created humanity as finite and thus on a journey of becoming or change. The nature of change may be incremental or transformational (or both), forward or backward (or both), and is potentially evidenced in every domain of life. The context of human becoming is relational; it emerges from commitments to and in relationship with God, others, and self. The quality and trustworthiness of these relationships significantly impacts what and how we become.

In light of human sin—the propensity toward idolatry—a Christian vision of formation involves returning to God in loyalty based on God's covenanting initiative and love. Thus, becoming is an invitational and responsive process. Formation involves knowing God's love for us deeply, responding to God's covenantal invitation to us, and participating in imaging God in Christ—following the pattern of Jesus the Messiah through the Holy Spirit.

The Trinity in relationship provides the analogy for human relationality and leads toward just, loving, and mutual relationships. There are constraints to human becoming, given both our finite nature and personal and relational limitations. Yet Christian hope is forward looking, a longing for the fullness of restoration in Christ that will lead to life and to knowing God fully in relationship.

Holiness

Holiness involves being like our holy God, while also recognizing God as qualitatively distinct from us. It also entails living in ways that are sometimes distinct from cultural norms, while still participating in and contributing missionally to society. As such, holiness is about living rightly in relation to God and in our contextual and relational networks, ever aware of the dialectic between distinctness and connection. Holiness means embodying and practicing virtues, those moral habits that form and integrate us. Holiness is a means toward the goals of Christian becoming: intimacy with the triune God, mission to the world, and communal, personal, and eschatological fullness of life (or wholeness).

Wholeness

Christian wholeness occurs in ongoing participation in trinitarian life and in responsiveness to the initiating work of God. Wholeness as a vision for human becoming involves communal well-being and equity (*shalom*) as well as personal completeness and integration—an undivided self that exhibits full consonance between who one is and what one does. Wholeness is marked by maturity, though this does not imply the absence of pain, suffering, or experiences of disorientation. Wholeness (and holiness) relates to all dimensions of a person's life—physical, emotional, spiritual, relational, intellectual, sexual, financial, and so on—and is oriented toward healthy relationship with God and others. Key markers of both holiness and wholeness are just and right relationships, as well as hospitality, generosity, and love as intersecting Christian virtues.

A Case Study: Immigration

Wyndy: The ideas we have presented are not merely academic for us. We regularly find ourselves confronted with issues and in contexts that present challenges to the integration of Christian faith and practice. I had such an encounter in the past year, when I was asked to speak on the topic of immigration. Immigration seemed a fruitful topic for our integrative dialogue, since it encompasses the multifaceted themes of our work related to formation, being, and becoming—with responses ranging from an engagement with the Other, to a rejection of the Other, to a desire to protect one's own sense of ethnic, national, and personal identity by excluding the Other. It is also an issue that pushes against the boundaries we erect between the personal and the political, and the spiritual and the embodied, with their limiting effects on a more integrative approach to wholeness and holiness.

As I started thinking and preparing for this presentation, two things occurred to me. One is that there is no one Christian response to immigration. Two, there have been some Christian responses to immigration that have been less than Christlike, with this particular issue causing sometimes volatile reactions. My preparation and presentation took a fairly modest tack by wondering how Scripture might inform how we think and talk about immigration and guide us as Christians in our moral deliberations and responses.[3]

The group gathered for this presentation was from a church that had a strong interest in exploring current issues in light of Christian faith. It was a mixed group of men and women from white middle-class backgrounds with an estimated average age of fifty-five or so. I started by telling a story about a group of people with no homes and no land of their own who began a lengthy migration across seas, foreign countries, and deserts because of their hope—hope for community, hope for security, hope for a place to call home, hope for their families and children, hope for a future that was yet unknown. During this migration they were met with hostility, danger, a shortage of food, deaths among family members, and the hard work of just staying alive in the face of such difficulties. Some gave up. Some yearned to go back to where they came from, not because it was ideal but because at least it was familiar. But many pressed on toward new possibilities and the fulfillment of dreams, not just for themselves but for future generations. Finally they arrived. Yet their struggles for belonging, identity, and community continued, and their efforts met with both great success and abysmal failure. They continued to live as strangers in strange lands. Even as they looked ahead to a future, the experience of migration and immigration stayed with them and defined who they understood themselves to be well into the future.

A question I posed in light of this narrative was, Whose story does this tell and represent? Many responded that it paralleled their own families' stories of leaving parts of Europe and making the exodus to the United States in hopes of freedom and better futures. I was surprised that no one identified this as the exodus narrative of the Old Testament or indicated that the images of sojourners, aliens, and citizens of God's kingdom reminded them of biblical metaphors for the Christian life. In fact, they were quite surprised when I made this connection.

I went on to explore other stories of migration and immigration in Scripture, like the story of Abraham, who was called by God to leave his own country and his own people for a new land (Gen. 12:1–9). A famine forced Abraham's descendants to migrate again, this time to Egypt, where there was food (42:1–43:34). Israel was enslaved in Egypt, ushering in the story of Moses (Exod. 1–2). Moses witnessed firsthand the injustice and violence of slavery against his own people and the exploitation of their labor by those in power. The exodus is the story of the people whom Moses, Aaron, and Miriam led on a mass migration to a promised land. Another biblical story about immigrants is the story of Ruth, a hated Moabite and the consummate foreigner, who married into the family of Elimelech and Naomi when famine drove them to Moab. The men of the family died, leaving the women vulnerable and making Naomi a foreigner in a strange land. When the famine lifted, Naomi and Ruth migrated back to Judah, where Ruth became a stranger in a strange land. Another biblical story of immigration is the story of Jesus, who left his Father's throne, took on human flesh, had no place to lay his head, and who was consistently treated with hostility and fear, even as he welcomed cultural outsiders such as Samaritans, prostitutes, the disabled, and lepers.

Even though I was clear in acknowledging the complexities around public and social policies about immigration, areas in which I am by no means an expert, our discussion quickly moved to rather simplistic affirmations about these issues with no point of connection to any of the scriptural narratives I had just presented. For most in the audience, these stories seemed to have little or nothing to do with how we might think about the topic or how Scripture might actually guide our attitudes and responses to other people, in spite of our disagreements on larger social policy issues.

Sadly, the responses were somewhat predictable and also quite telling. One individual suggested that we could solve the current U.S. immigration problem by ceding Texas and New Mexico back to Mexico. I raised the problematic nature of how these territories were acquired by the United States in the first place, though my words didn't have quite the moral resonance I had hoped they would. Another person assured me that she knew firsthand that "these" people were sitting in "our" emergency rooms and classrooms using "our" tax dollars. I asked for clarification on the identity of the "we" in a country founded by immigrants, none of whom were native to this country.[4] Given that many of the participants had made connections between the scriptural injunctions to take care of widows, orphans, and aliens and their own families' histories, I was surprised at the lack of empathy surrounding today's immigrants, especially given the multiplicity of reasons why persons emigrate and seek asylum and employment outside their countries of origin.[5] Many in the audience made their own families' experience of immigration normative. They came from Europe, committed themselves to learning English, worked hard, and became legal citizens. "Why can't 'they' do the same?"

This was an interesting experience for me, but it still leaves me rattled and puzzled. I left with more questions than answers, particularly about what the experience says about our capabilities for and interests in being guided by Scripture (remember, this was a church group), our identification of moral dimensions in various issues, and our quite vehement defense of "us" (this was an all-white, middle-class audience) against a "them" perceived as threatening and harmful to our well-being. I was curious about a sense of threat imposed by the Other and wondered exactly what was being threatened: Economic well-being? Safety? National identity? Social resources? Our borders? I couldn't ignore the racial overtones of the conversation when many references to "them" were immigrants from Mexico and Latin America.

I turn to you, Jeannine and Carla, for help in elucidating the dynamics I observed and wondering about better ways of integrating our reading of Scripture, understanding ourselves, and responding to others. I begin with these questions:

- Why was Scripture seen as largely irrelevant to this conversation about immigration? What keeps us from connecting with Scripture in our deliberations on social ethical issues such as immigration?

- What is the source of threat? Why is there a need to keep boundaries between us and the Other? What parts of ourselves are we afraid of losing?
- What does this response say about our humanity, our sense of being and becoming? Are there more "whole and holy" ways of responding to the issue of immigration, as well as other issues, that are more integrative in our approach to Scripture, formation, and our moral capacities?

Jeannine: Wyndy, I am captivated by the case that you raise for our reflection and have been pondering your question of why Scripture and its story of God's people as sojourners and aliens (much of the Old Testament; see 1 Pet. 2:11) was fairly irrelevant to the committed Christians who were part of this conversation on immigration. Two reasons come to mind. First, the church in some circles has held the Old Testament at arm's length. My Old Testament colleagues at Bethel Seminary often say they need to work with our students to show them the relevance of the Old Testament for their lives and ministries. Israel's story can be viewed as quite separate from the story of the church. This is understandable to some extent, but also quite ironic. The New Testament writers regularly appropriate Israel's story as the story of their Jewish *and* Gentile audiences. In 1 Corinthians 10:1–14, Paul draws on Israel's story in the wilderness to warn his primarily Gentile hearers. Then Paul writes an amazing thing: "These things happened to them as examples and were written down as warnings *for us*, on whom the culmination of the ages has come" (1 Cor. 10:11; emphasis mine). Israel's story *is* the church's story.

A second possible reason for the inability to identify with Israel's story as a wandering, exilic people is our tendency in Western readings of the Bible to individualize and over-spiritualize (or even allegorize) biblical narratives. Regardless of one's view of the historical nature of Old Testament narrative, when it comes to application our tendency is to draw analogies between individuals within biblical stories and our own lives. We are less likely to apply these stories on a corporate level, where Israel's group story might inform ours. In the contextualizing impulse we also tend to over-spiritualize Old Testament stories. Rather than seeing Ruth as a displaced person in poverty and reflecting on that social category in our own world, we tend to move to only "spiritual" categories to understand her and to bring her story into interaction with our own lives. Ruth is a Moabite, so she's not a Jew, not a part of Israel at the beginning of the story. The story of Ruth is about her inclusion among God's people. And it is about her covenant loyalty to Israel's God and to Naomi. While this rendering of the story is certainly true to the narrative, it misses the socioeconomic issues of the story that might inform our own understandings of the Other in our worlds. When evangelicals move to social issues, it is more likely that we will use the story of Ruth to affirm values related to family (e.g., Ruth as good daughter-in-law), rather than turning toward other social realities of her story that confront contemporary disparities of privilege and wealth.

Wyndy: Jeannine, this is a helpful contextual reminder for how the Scriptures are both perceived and used in our context. I team teach a class at Ashland with one of my Old Testament colleagues titled "Theology of Scripture in Ministry." We spend quite a bit of time talking about what Scripture is, as well as various approaches to its interpretation and use. This class, plus the experience I had in the presentation on immigration, remind me that what we understand Scripture *to be* will influence how we read it and use it. If the Bible is perceived as a personal devotional book, then it will be read as such. If it is understood to be a book of rules, then it will be used as such. If Scripture is understood as a tool in evangelism, then we will use it to communicate information people need to "be saved." If we think it is about spiritual issues only, then, as you note, we will miss its hugely important social dimensions. Perhaps we can acknowledge that Scripture speaks to both spiritual and social dimensions of human existence.

Using Scripture in ethics and for moral deliberation can be tricky. In Christian ethics the dispute is not about Scripture's authority but about method—exactly how the Bible is authoritative for moral deliberation, ethical choices, and positions, given the huge gap between the worlds of the Bible and our contemporary one. Because of various ways of perceiving and using Scripture (some noted above), social ethical issues tend to get "bracketed." The result seems to be twofold. First, we draw on other sources for moral deliberation. So in the case of making moral assessments about immigration we default to the primary narrative of national security: "our" borders and "our" resources. It becomes more about "us" than about entering into the narratives of Scripture and allowing them to take us where they lead us. Your response highlights the second result, which is a very individualized and privatized way of reading Scripture that reduces morality to just the personal, disabling us from seeing social contexts as moral spaces.

Jeannine: Wyndy, I just need to say at least once in this book that I love the way you can turn a phrase: "seeing social contexts as moral spaces" gets my moral imagination moving.

Carla: Wyndy, I have been reflecting particularly on your third question about the case.[6] I'm thinking about the kinds of prayerful listening that would be helpful and relevant for our conversation about immigration (as if there were a kind of prayerful listening that *wouldn't* be helpful or relevant?). "Prayerful listening" is the phrase I prefer for the kind of being with God, others, and self that is sometimes also described as "group spiritual direction" or "theological reflection."[7] Rose Mary Dougherty describes prayerful listening as "'wasting time with God together'—being with God without [a] specific agenda."[8] It is a "deliberate slowing down of our habitual processes of interpreting life in order to take a closer look at [our] experience and at our frameworks for interpretation."[9]

I believe God uses the practice of prayerful listening to speak both to us and through us in the formation process. I set aside my desire to correct or to be "helpful" or profound in order to "hear the other into speech."[10] Together we listen for God; together we listen to our hearts. Psychoanalyst Ana-Maria Rizzuto says, "Listening is the core action for any transformative process."[11] This listening stance seems to me foundational for formation. After all, if formation is invitational, responding to the invitation requires first hearing it.

For our conversation around this important issue of immigration—which has so much to do with justice, hospitality, and generosity—prayerful listening holds a way for me to allow God to bring to my awareness my stinginess, my fear, and my ignorance. It also holds a way—particularly if I am intentional about incorporating the Other into my community and therefore into the prayerful listening process—for God to teach me about the lived experience of the Other, about the effects of oppression, exclusion, and silencing on his or her formation and spirit. And if I am given the grace and find the courage to stay in this listening stance past the point of my discomfort, perhaps those two ways meet, making a place where the invitation of God and the reality of the Other join to form me and my communities.

Jeannine: Carla, as I read your description of prayerful listening my imagination went immediately to the story of Peter and Cornelius (Acts 10:1–11:18), which has some important points of resonance with the immigration issues we are discussing. (It doesn't hurt that I am correcting about fifty papers on this passage at the time of writing.) Both Peter and Cornelius experience visions from God during their times of prayer (cf. Acts 10:3 with 3:1; 10:9). Whether or not Peter or Cornelius had an agenda in prayer at those moments, God used their availability and faithfulness to initiate something new with them, though something that was not fully clear by the end of their visions. While we don't have explicit indication in the story that prayerful listening happened in community, we certainly hear a fascinating conversation about and experience of the work of God there (Acts 10:25–48). Cornelius reports his experience in prayer (10:30–33), and Peter responds by affirming a new understanding of who God is (one who "does not show favoritism," 10:34). Even as Peter is still speaking the good news of Jesus to Cornelius and his household, the Holy Spirit falls upon them (10:44). The interplay of Cornelius, Peter, and the Holy Spirit sounds something like your description of prayerful listening: God speaking both to and through Cornelius, to Peter and through him. The significance of Peter's reassessment of Cornelius and his household from Other to equals in this text heightens the importance of prayer as discernment, it seems to me.

Carla: I think it does, Jeannine, particularly when we hold the communal dimensions of discernment in mind as well. It is the "to/through" you identify that reminds us that individual, internal discernment must always be held up for correction, expansion, and refinement by others who are also listening carefully to God and to one another. Prayerful listening, it seems to me, almost by definition requires a community.

Wyndy: Carla, I'd like to weigh in on your contribution on prayerful listening as well, particularly how prayerful listening may be a practice in which our participation might move us in particular directions. I wonder, therefore, about the possibility that what we pray for may form us in important ways. So, might praying for immigrants change our attitudes, heighten our moral sensitivities, and enlarge our capacities to care about others? Perhaps the adage, "We are what we love," can be applied to prayer: "We are what we pray."

I raise this question for two reasons. One, based on your insights from neurobiology, Carla, I have been increasingly interested in prayer as a moral practice. So, might what we pray for somehow change us? I also raise it because of a recent transition in churches. My husband and I have gravitated back to a more liturgical church for a variety of reasons. One of the reasons that I am finding a revitalization in my own life is because this church context "forces" me to hear Scripture actually read in worship services in a systematic and thoughtful way. Following a lectionary means I do not get to pick and choose which parts of Scripture I want to hear and read. It has also provided a structure for corporate prayer that I have missed. Our corporate prayer starts with the world. Current events are named in prayer. The needs of the world are presented before us as calls to participate in God's redemptive work. Requests for God's mercy, justice, and wisdom are made as an acknowledgment of our own frailties and limitations in understanding issues. And consistently, in the Wesleyan spirit, we are reminded that we demonstrate God's love in very tangible ways: "There is no holiness but social holiness."

Carla: Related to your question about what we pray for, prayerful listening is different from intercessory prayer in the way that I learned the latter and experience it in most contexts. In intercessory prayer we typically decide what would be helpful or desirable for a person or situation and ask God to do it. I think this is a very valid kind of praying in Scripture (the woman badgering the judge comes to mind). The kind of prayerful listening I refer to here, however, is more about listening for what God's prayer is for a person or situation, and asking how I might join God's prayer. To do so, is there something I would need to give up: a belief, a preference, some convenience? Is there something God would like me to do or say on God's behalf?[12] It strikes me, in line with your last paragraph, that this moves us more toward a "Thy kingdom come, Thy will be done" stance than does simply bringing my laundry list of expectations (though I don't mean to be making a straw person out of that approach to prayer).

Jeannine: Carla, it seems to me that Peter, in the Cornelius story (Acts 10:1–11:18), gives up a significant belief in order to participate in what God is doing with Cornelius's household, namely, the belief that those who eat unclean foods become unclean (10:28). Instead, he is persuaded that he is not to declare anyone unclean. This reorientation provides an interesting textual moment for deliberation on immigration. At the center of the story is a new word to Peter that Gentiles (specifically Cornelius and his household) are to be fully included in the people of the Messiah, without prior conversion to Judaism (no required adherence to circumcision or food laws). The rationale? Peter's words narrated in 10:34–36 provide it: "I now realize how true it is that God does not show favoritism but accepts those from every nation who fear him and do what is right. You know the message God sent to the people of Israel, announcing the good news of peace through Jesus Christ, who is Lord of all." God is not a god of favoritism in spite of his choice of Israel to bring blessings to all nations (Gen. 12:3). Now, in the time of the Messiah, Jew and Gentile come on equal terms and are equally included in the community of faith.

This story provides two foundations for this equality: Peter's affirmation of Jesus's universal lordship (Acts 10:36), and God's inclusive affirmation in the outpouring of the Holy Spirit upon Cornelius and the other Gentiles listening to Peter (10:44). As I've been thinking about these two bases for inclusion across the historic ethnic/religious divide between Jew and non-Jew, I am struck by the issues of power and access raised that might speak to immigration issues.

The need within current debates on immigration to wield power over undocumented workers, effectively determining their fate, might find an answer in this Acts passage, in the truth that Jesus is Lord of *all* (10:36). In this text inclusion trumps exclusion because of the universal lordship of Jesus. If Jesus is truly Lord of all (Jews and Gentiles, believers and unbelievers, citizens of a nation, noncitizens, and immigrants), then we might need to let go of our power over the Other in deference to Jesus's authority over them. We don't have to be in control; in fact, it would seem quite clear that we are not. And control of the Other appears to me to be part of what swirls around issues of immigration, whether explicitly or implicitly. I would add that Jesus's authority, according to Peter's words, is intimately connected to his offer of peace (10:36), which might be another helpful theme to reflect upon in relation to immigration.

God's initiation and affirmation of inclusion is made clear when the Holy Spirit falls upon the Gentiles before Peter finishes his sermon (10:44). Access to the very presence of the power of God through God's Spirit is no longer reserved for Jewish believers in Jesus (cf. Pentecost in Acts 2), but is freely given to non-Jews (making this the "Gentile Pentecost" of Acts, as some have called it). Again, immigration debates have much to do with access (as well as power). In Acts, full access to the Spirit of God is not limited to one group favored over another. And with access come blessing and benefit, another set of themes that might be good for us to reflect upon as we think about what it means to welcome the foreigner and alien into our midst. Benny Tat Siong-Liew frames the coming of God's Spirit (in Acts 10:44) in a way that reminds us of how it might impact our thinking and actions related to immigration and welcome: "If faith in Christ is like obtaining a 'green card' that grants entry and residency, the coming of the Spirit is comparable to the 'naturalization process' that (theoretically) turns a 'green card' holder into a citizen eligible for rights and benefits."[13]

Carla: I'm not sure whether we can even do the kind of welcome you're describing, Jeannine, if we have not yet moved from a worldview in which our own culture is experienced as central (monocultural) to a worldview in which we experience our culture in the context of other cultures (intercultural). This is what Milton Bennett's Developmental Model of Intercultural Sensitivity (DMIS) suggests is necessary to achieve authentic relating across cultural boundaries.[14]

I'm realizing that, in the Peter/Cornelius story, I tend to focus on Peter and the epiphany (the mystical type of quantum change) God offered him. I ask students in an introductory formation course to wonder in their small groups about what would be "on the sheet" for them in a similar experience. That's a pretty challenging question, because as I wrestle with it myself I tend to either (a) identify one of my primary commitments and pretend I could assume it to be wrong, all the while "knowing" it isn't, or (b) choose something that I'm ambivalent about because I've already wrestled with the possibility.

I find myself now wondering about two follow-up thoughts: First, are both the more "accumulative" kind of insightful quantum change and the abrupt mystical quantum change (chap. 2) equally likely and valid pathways for moving from an ethnocultural to an ethno-relative position? The DMIS certainly doesn't discount the possibility of change through more "Aha!" moments, of course, but I believe it would suggest that insightful quantum change—and maybe just good old incremental change—is the pathway for most people. That path involves acquiring new learning, being exposed to differentness, and receiving feedback about one's behavior and attitudes. Robert Kegan, in his discussion of dealing with difference, also suggests that "the goal of supporting gradual development, the evolution of consciousness, is obviously a slower and more ambitious undertaking than skills training."[15] I guess part of my wondering in this regard is that many of my clients and students hope for "Aha!" moments of change because they seem like less work. God does something amazing and—presto—we're different. I don't believe that's what happens, of course—even if we are able to sustain the change, there's the work of living differently in our communities. Even Peter found that returning to his home context required differentiation and commitment.[16]

Second, I realize that I've been more concerned with understanding, experiencing, and nurturing the kind of formation Peter demonstrates in the story than I have been with the impact of exclusion and injustice on the formation of those persons and communities who are excluded and oppressed. I seem to have put that in a different category of justice (and I'm not even sure there can truly be different categories of justice). My concern for justice in this area of immigration, I'm afraid, has been more systemic, structural, and political than personal. A sobering awareness.

Wyndy: Which relates somewhat to the question I raised earlier about the source of threat.

Carla: I believe social science helps us understand that there are multiple sources of threat when we encounter differentness. For example, "stranger anxiety" is a developmentally normal response of young children to unfamiliar people and could be a protective response in some contexts. However, I believe there is a more sinister source of threat that should not be considered developmentally appropriate, and that is the response of "superordinates" (those in a subgroup that hold a majority of resources and power) when "subordinates" (those in a less dominant group) seem to acquire power—even when it does not impact the power of the superordinate.[17]

Wyndy: These are thoughtful reflections on how the stories of Peter and Cornelius connect with our stories, and vice versa, in ways that push us beyond a one-dimensional reading. I wonder if one of the reasons why our reading of this story tends to be so flat is because our notions of conversion and salvation are so flat. So we read this story as Cornelius's conversion and miss the ways in which Peter, in the earlier part of the story, failed to embody the vision of Jesus. And yet Peter demonstrated some form of repentance after he acted (in spite of his ambivalence about actually going to Cornelius's house) and when he met Cornelius (Acts 10:34–38).

From an ethical perspective this story holds some interesting possibilities about the relationships between being and doing. Peter acted, perhaps against his own inclinations and fundamentalist process (chap. 2), and then he was changed, and I would say converted again (and again, and again). One could only speculate what would have happened if Peter had not gone to Cornelius's home. Some grand theory of God's sovereignty would say that God would still work to make sure Cornelius heard the specifics of the gospel. I can agree with that. But this may have left Peter in an unconverted state, as far as his attitude toward the Gentiles, that ultimately left him off the hook.

In my response to your chapters, Carla, I found your insights helpful for expanding our notions of conversion. I think our American religious context has sensationalized conversion experiences due to our revivalistic and entrepreneurial proclivities.[18] Conversion is not only sensationalized (just think of the people who feel the need to apologize when they tell their faith stories because of how boring they seem), but it is often seen as a one-time event. In practice I often wonder if conversion, in this one-time sense, changes anything about the way we live and how we think about issues from the perspective of Christian faith. I think this relates to your observations of our desire for the "aha" and "presto" moments. These are easy; attending to formation over the long haul is hard work. I also wonder if our Protestant heritage makes this more difficult because we are so fearful of anything that might suggest or smell of works and good deeds as part of Christian belief and practice.

Carla: Yes, yes, yes! It's very helpful to think about the resistance to slower change as being tied to some fear about works—which I believe, Jeannine, you talked about in chapter 6 with regard to a false post-Reformation dichotomy between law and grace.

Jeannine: Yes, if we can embrace and live into a more covenantal understanding of our relationship with God we will be less likely to dichotomize obligation and grace. Covenantal loyalty to God and others already presumes God's initiating and ongoing covenant action.

Wyndy: We could also look at this dichotomizing from the vantage point of the tendency in Protestant ethics to be very "law driven." What I mean is that there is an assumption that because something is legal it must be moral, and the flip side is that whatever is illegal is immoral. This explains the amount of attention given by certain subgroups of Christians to legislative changes. Now I do think laws are good and necessary: I'm glad people stop at stop signs! Yet it is rather simplistic, and even dangerous, to equate morality with legality, because laws can be immoral and morality can never be fully legislated. I can obey laws and still be immoral; I can obey all the right rules and do incredible harm; and I can disobey laws because it might be a moral thing to do (the foundation of civil disobedience). So, in the case we are exploring together this is the line of thinking: undocumented workers[19] have broken the law (hence they have done something immoral) and need to be held accountable (punished and deported). This dynamic is also informed by ideologies of justice as retribution for wrongdoing and reward for doing right. In Scripture justice is more concrete: it is something we do, informing how we relate to others in acts of mercy, compassion, and restoration. So how does our becoming more whole and holy enable us to morally discern at "higher" levels beyond the categories of legal versus illegal and punishment or retribution?

Jeannine: I am intrigued by your distinction, Wyndy, between morality and legality, and my mind (again!) went to Acts 10:28. Peter has arrived at Cornelius's household in Caesarea after seeing a divine vision where unclean and clean foods are combined in one large sheet. Peter then says to Cornelius and his relatives and friends:

"You are well aware that it is against our law for a Jew to associate with Gentiles or visit them. But God has shown me that I should not call anyone impure or unclean" (10:28). Peter distinguishes between what is lawful and what is right (what God has revealed to Peter just prior to his arrival), or, we might say, what is moral. Now the language used here ("against our law") is not referring to the Mosaic Torah (which did not forbid association with non-Jews). The term *athemitos* indicates something that violates tradition. Peter seems to be saying that what has been commonly (and rightly) avoided based on Old Testament purity ideals and regulations—namely, close association of Jew with Gentile—now has to be rethought in light of God's revelation to Peter in the new time of the Messiah (10:36). The Holy Spirit falling upon the Gentiles listening to Peter (even before he finishes his sermon!) clinches the deal (10:44). Truly, "God shows no partiality" (10:34 NRSV).

It strikes me that this passage offers a rather complex set of connections between what is legally forbidden to Jews (Torah prohibitions against eating unclean food), what is forbidden socially and culturally (Jews closely associating with Gentiles by eating with them or entering their homes), and what is right (Peter associating with the Gentile Cornelius by eating with him and entering his home). Two issues that impact what is moral or right in this passage involve (1) the difference that the arrival of Jesus the Messiah, along with the outpouring of the Holy Spirit, make in answering "what is right" (10:34–44); and (2) the nature of God as one who "shows no partiality" (10:34 NRSV). For the author of Acts, eschatology and theology shape ethics.

Wyndy: Jeannine, this is a powerful way to redirect much of our contemporary rhetoric surrounding immigration based on Scripture as a story. Both you and Carla mentioned earlier the fear of giving up unexamined beliefs (which Peter eventually did). When Peter opened himself to the Other (both the Spirit and Cornelius), he had to give up his modicum of control over the message and the meting out of the good gifts of God meant for all persons.

This offers a point of connection to your earlier comment on the power issues raised by this story. I agree that what is at stake—though what often goes unnamed—are issues of power, control, and access, especially our control and power over the Other, and our right to determine who deserves access to "our" resources. This idea of Christ's lordship is an interesting one for me. We often construct immigrant identity as Other along the same lines that we construct our own identity: based on race, ethnicity, nationality, language, and cultural location. Why don't we assume that perhaps what binds us to immigrants is Christ's lordship in our lives and in their own confessions of Christ as Lord? How might this change the conversation? I rarely, if ever, hear raised in our church discourse the possibility that immigrants are Christians, our brothers and sisters in Christ. If "Christ is Lord" is a political statement about our own ultimate loyalties and belonging, then we share it with others making the same claim, fostering this new community that crosses the natural boundaries that we construct between "us" and "them," in turn shifting (one hopes) our primary obligations. Perhaps, in reality and in practice, the formation and construction of our identity has very little to do with a desire to be formed as more whole and holy Christians, since this would change many of our fundamental understandings about our own humanity, our sense of importance and difference from the Other, and our sense of place in the world, especially those of us from more privileged locations.

Jeannine: You raise again the "us/them" dichotomizing that goes on in immigration deliberation, reminding me of the important relational dialectic that both you and Carla raise in your chapters. How does the dialectic between *alterity* and *intimacy* (Carla) or *relatedness* and *difference* (Wyndy) inform our deliberations on immigration? Might this dialectic inform our tendency either to assimilate the Other or to reject or even demonize those who are different from us in an effort to "fix" their Other-ness?

Wyndy: In response to these questions, I am reminded of Carla's insights about the insistence on a single story (in a community or family) and how this might take the shape of demanding assimilation (chap. 2). I am drawn to Miroslav Volf's insights on assimilation as a form of oppression that insists the Other give up identity while asking nothing of us.[20] So I suppose I wonder if the shrillest protests against immigration (and hence, against immigrants) come from those who have not met persons struggling with hard choices about leaving their own countries, denying parts of their stories in order to fit in somewhere or hide from someone, putting their lives at risk, and being left more vulnerable by exploitation and demonization. Like Peter, would our responses be different if we actually went and met immigrants and heard their stories? Perhaps "doing" in this regard may change us and be a form of repentance leading to conversation (again and again and again!).

Carla: I agree. Actual engagement with the real stories of real people has the potential to change us. Unfortunately, it's only the potential. Without at least some intentional receptivity, encounters with difference can be so anxiety provoking that we believe our initial fears and negative evaluations are justified. But at some point actual experience of the Other without demanding that the Other change is essential for true hospitality. Parker Palmer, in *The Company of Strangers*, summarizes this powerfully:

> Hospitality means letting the stranger remain a stranger while offering acceptance nonetheless. It means honoring the fact that strangers already have a relationship—rooted in our common humanity—without having to build one on intimate interpersonal knowledge, without having to become friends. It means valuing the strangeness of the stranger—even letting the stranger speak a language you cannot speak or sing a song you cannot join with—resisting the temptation to reduce the relation to some lowest common denominator, since all language and all music is already human. It means meeting the stranger's needs while allowing him or her simply to be, without attempting to make the stranger over into a modified version of ourselves.[21]

Jeannine: This provides a powerful expression of living with the Other in the dialectic of difference and relatedness, a theme we've raised throughout our book.

Carla: Palmer also offers a suggestion for what we can do while we are becoming ready to reach out to strangers:

> If we are not ready . . . to reach out . . . we can practice hospitality by using care when we speak of the stranger in private, a hospitality of the heart. So often we use the cover of privacy to speak words of condemnation which we would not speak in public places. . . . A private language of understanding and compassion can be a great contribution to the public life; it breeds hospitable attitudes towards the stranger even if the stranger is never invited into one's home.[22]

169

Wyndy: I am also thinking of our ongoing conversation on story from our respective disciplines and our desire for thicker ways of understanding formation, reading Scripture, and engaging in moral reflection. I was taught that this story in Acts 10:1–11:18 was really about Cornelius's conversion and the missionary nature of the church, as if there is just one story line to this narrative. Yet if I read this as a story in light of our conversation in this chapter, I am compelled to look at all elements of this story and ask whether I take Scripture seriously as a source for formation, holiness, and wholeness. So am I really Peter in this story? Am I the one who needs to be converted to new ways of seeing what God is doing and what God cares about? Is this story just as much about Peter's need for conversion and formation as it is about the gracious gifts of God offered to this Other, this Cornelius?

Carla: I think it must be. Christian formation happens in the crucible of relational challenge (chap. 2). The challenge of engaging and embracing the Other might just be our opportunity for deepest formation. Again, I find both invitation and challenge in a thought from Parker Palmer's book on Christians and the public life.

> [T]he stranger of public life becomes the spiritual guide of our private life. Through the stranger our view of self, of world, of God is deepened and expanded. Through the stranger we are given a chance to find ourselves. And through the stranger, God finds us and offers us the gift of wholeness in the midst of our estranged lives, a gift of God and of the public life.[23]

Conclusion

In a way, perhaps welcome of the Other represents what we have been trying to do in this conversation: As we truly welcome the Other—even the Other in a different discipline—we discover that there is something of the familiar in her and that there is something of the unknown in ourselves. And beyond all of that comes an energizing and reassuring sense of being found again by God, being offered an invitation to come more deeply and more authentically into relationship with God, others, and oneself.

EPILOGUE

Our Experiences of Integration

B ecause integration is something we do in community, it results not only from conversation but also from the process of that conversation. In this book we have tried to capture this process-oriented aspect of integration in our response chapters (4, 7, 10) and in our dialogue around immigration (11). In this epilogue we offer readers a glimpse of our common and individual processes during the integration and writing of the book in hopes of promoting authentic dialogue and integration.

We have attempted in writing this book to follow the integrative rubric we elaborate in chapter 1 of offering, receiving, and integrating. After working together to sketch out an introduction to the book (chap. 1), we each developed contributions to the concepts of formation (becoming), wholeness, and holiness in our individually written chapters (2 and 3, 5 and 6, 8 and 9). We then shared these contributions with one another as offerings for integration. In the response chapters to each contribution, we received, listened, tested connections, and explored areas of integration. We also acknowledged and wrestled with points of non-integration. The final chapter captured our conversation around a case study on immigration as a window into a more informal integrative dialogue among the three of us.

I (Jeannine) was surprised and formed by many moments in the process of collaborating and writing this book. One delightful observation occurred when I first read the offerings from Carla and Wyndy and realized that together we centered our reflections on some of the same theological concepts and biblical passages. It might not be surprising to note that we were drawn to some of the same biblical passages about human being (e.g., Gen. 1:26–27) and holiness (e.g., 1 Pet. 1:15–16). Yet the echoing of these passages and others (e.g., Deut. 10; Matt. 22; John 17; Eph. 4) across our work fueled my own integrative reflections. Common themes emerged as well: *shalom*, integrity, the image of God, participation, and the dialectic between our role and God's work in formation, as well as the dialectic between particularity (distinction) and relatedness. The latter became a particularly fruitful area for my own reflection.

What surprised me most, however, was the integrative potential that arose from areas of initial or seeming disintegration. To be honest, I experienced some anxiety around areas of dissonance—or at least non-integration—as I read the contributions of Carla and Wyndy. My cultural moorings (Scandinavian), gender socialization, and birth order (middle child) all conspire toward avoidance of conflict and discord. So I found myself nervous at those points where I didn't hear the possibility of integration between my discipline and those of Wyndy and Carla. Yet some of these areas of divergence proved to be fertile points for integration because they pushed me to listen more closely, draw from my discipline more carefully, and look for connections more deeply. These points of initial dissonance, once I decided to stay with them in spite of the anxiety, piqued my curiosity and pushed me to further reflection and conversation (including a few phone calls to Carla and Wyndy to ask more questions).

This leads me to my final comment about collaborating with Carla and Wyndy. I've had a few people ask if it was difficult writing on a three-person project. My answer was that is was surprisingly easy, because I wasn't simply collaborating and writing with two other people. I was writing with two colleagues and friends, individuals whom I trust deeply. That made the difference. Integration is an adventure, but it is not for the faint of heart. It involves self-disclosure, trial and error, and the risk of feeling incompetent as you venture outside your area of expertise. So it is an adventure best experienced with friends who are both honest and trustworthy. Wyndy and Carla are just such friends.

I (Wyndy) will pick up where Jeannine left off in her observations. One of the claims that we made and rediscovered throughout our writing was the inherent relationality of being, becoming, wholeness, and holiness. Our relationships as friends and colleagues provided a wonderful laboratory to test this fundamental claim. As scholars we can easily fall into the trap of believing that our questions and contributions are the only ones that really matter. We took on this project with a set of common questions posed for the three of us. In some ways this was the hardest part. I had to think about my own discipline in light of a set of questions and in an actual conversation with two people, Carla and Jeannine, as opposed to a set of abstract ideas. This is a relinquishing of control that requires honesty and openness to others, similar to when we allow students' questions to drive the conversations in classrooms instead of clinging to our own prepackaged material or ideas. But by giving up control, something not easy for me to do, I found a freedom to engage, hear, and learn from others' contributions because I knew I did not have a complete set of answers to these questions. I had perspectives and contributions to offer that were graciously received and prodded in important ways, causing me to want to think more. I was deeply moved by something I was aware of already: the professional and personal investments Jeannine and Carla have in their vocations. But to be invited to follow their progression of thought, to be a recipient of their expertise and listen to them think out loud in their writing and in our conversations reminded me of how important it is to keep on thinking, wondering, and exploring with colleagues in whatever context we find ourselves. Formation truly is relational.

Aside from the discipline and stick-to-itive-ness of completing a writing project, writing with others required and fostered new sets of disciplines and practices, reaffirming again for me how necessarily social and communal formation really is. This collaborative writing project reminded me that faith is both a virtue and a practice. We needed one another to complete our work, something that writing solo does not require. And in needing one another in such basic things as passing along chapters when we said we would and trusting that our ideas would receive a fair hearing, I learned again that needing other persons and practicing faithful interdependence is a good thing—or a "God thing," as many of my students would say; and it truly was.

I (Carla) agree with Jeannine and Wyndy that "faithful interdependence" has been an essential aspect of this project, as it has been in any integrative task in which I have participated. Such faithful (or faith-full) relationality seems to be one of the few things that enables me to take the risks that may be inherent in such a process: the risk of disagreement, of misunderstanding, of confusion; the risk that any of us might give in to temptations to abuse or abdicate our personal and/or professional authority; the risk that the carefully constructed crucible for this formative, integrative work might unexpectedly crack or "spring a leak."

In addition to this aspect of faithful interdependence, two other elements have emerged again and again for me throughout this collaboration, both of which God regularly highlights as important in my own journey toward wholeness and holiness. One is the importance of making space for the unpredictability of life. Several years ago the convergence of a number of faculty, student, and institutional crises at the beginning of the academic year made it abundantly clear that the informal curriculum will trump the formal curriculum every time. Nothing new, of course: Proverbs 16:9 declares that "in their hearts human beings plan their course, but the Lord establishes their steps." But I needed to hold this inevitable truth with humility and acceptance. Each of us was in some form of transition during this time of thinking and writing, and transition always holds a bit of unpredictability and ambiguity. Creativity and energy ebb and flow in disconcerting ways. I found that I needed to welcome life in the same way that we three authors needed to welcome one another, to receive one another's offerings, in order to live out the process we had proposed.

And that's the final element that has been significant for me. I frequently hear myself tell students and clients to "trust the process." In this project I have been encouraged again and again by peace that comes from doing just that. We spent a lot of time in the first months of this endeavor discussing, describing, and defining just what we would be doing. In long conversations full of hilarity, tears, enthusiasm, blank looks, and varying levels of energy, we came to a process that we believed could hold the content about which we were passionate. Because we had taken care in doing this "work before the work," it served as a trustworthy guide and anchor when I was stuck, unfocused, or frustrated. It provided both rest and motivation, and it held invitations for my own next invitations toward becoming whole and holy—invitations to use my voice, to speak truth, to ask for what I need, and to expect others will do the same. Trusting the process is, paradoxically, both safe and risky. Which of course comes as no surprise to me when I realize that the deepest dimension of trusting the process is actually that of trusting God in the process. And as with all our becoming, God is able to do more than we could have asked or imagined.

NOTES

Chapter 1 Location: Our Selves, Our Disciplines, Our Process

1. See Clifford Geertz, *The Interpretation of Cultures* (New York: Basic Books, 1973), 14. Geertz's concept of "thickness" is helpful for our integrative work, reminding us of the complexity of what it means to be human and the multiple sources and dynamics of human formation. See also Walter Brueggemann, "Dialogic Thickness in a Monologic Culture," *Theology Today* 64 (2007): 322–39. For Brueggemann, "thickness" is, in day-to-day terms, "*a practice of dialogue*" of many, diverse voices (323; emphasis original).

2. Dennis Hiebert, "Can We Talk? Achieving Dialogue between Sociology and Theology," *Christian Scholars Review* 37 (2008): 198–214, 202.

3. James W. Fowler, *Stages of Faith: The Psychology of Human Development* (San Francisco: HarperCollins, 1981), 5; also Fowler's *Becoming Adult, Becoming Christian: Adult Development and Christian Faith* (San Francisco: Harper & Row, 1984), 50. Fowler describes faith as one's orientation to Ultimate Realities (such as the existence and nature of a transcendent being, the reality of death, and the responsibilities humans have toward one another) and notes that all humans, in all cultures, hold such orientations. Therefore, even if my orientation is that there is nothing beyond me, nothing after death, and no moral obligations from me to others, I have faith.

4. See, for example, James E. Loder, *The Logic of the Spirit: Human Development in Theological Perspective* (San Francisco: Jossey-Bass, 1998); Jack O. Balswick, Pamela Ebstyne King, and Kevin S. Reimer, *The Reciprocating Self: Human Development in Theological Perspective* (Downers Grove, IL: InterVarsity, 2005); Robert Kegan, *The Evolving Self: Problem and Process in Human Development* (Cambridge, MA: Harvard University Press, 1982), and *In Over Our Heads: The Mental Demands of Modern Life* (Cambridge, MA: Harvard University Press, 1994); Daniel Siegel, *The Developing Mind: How Relationships and the Brain Interact to Shape Who We Are* (New York: Guilford Press, 1999), and *The Mindful Brain: Reflection and Attunement in the Cultivation of Well-Being* (New York: W. W. Norton, 2007); Louis J. Cozolino, *The Neuroscience of Human Relationships: Attachment and the Developing Social Brain* (New York: W. W. Norton, 2006), and *The Healthy Aging Brain: Sustaining Attachment, Attaining Wisdom* (New York: W. W. Norton, 2008).

5. For a discussion and definition of hermeneutics, cf. Jeannine K. Brown, *Scripture as Communication: Introducing Biblical Hermeneutics* (Grand Rapids: Baker Academic, 2007), 20–56.

6. Ibid., 135–36.

7. Paul Ricoeur, *The Conflict of Interpretations* (London: Continuum, 2004), 294.

8. Brown, *Scripture as Communication*, 232–43.

9. Joel B. Green, *Seized by Truth: Reading the Bible as Scripture* (Nashville: Abingdon Press, 2007), 173.

10. Cf. Ibid., 24; Gordon D. Fee, "To What End Exegesis? Reflections on Exegesis and Spirituality in Philippians 4:10–20," in *To What End Exegesis? Essays Textual, Exegetical, and Theological* (Grand Rapids: Eerdmans, 2001), 276–89.

11. My specific field is New Testament studies. Yet because in this book I address questions of wholeness, holiness, and becoming from a canonical perspective, I at times refer to the broader field of biblical studies. I also interact with the field of biblical hermeneutics with great interest and passion, given my conviction that we are all situated interpreters of the Bible.

12. Stanley Hauerwas, *The Peaceable Kingdom: A Primer for Christian Ethics* (Notre Dame, IN: University of Notre Dame Press, 1983), 17.

13. Allen Verhey, *Remembering Jesus: Christian Community, Scripture and the Moral Life* (Grand Rapids: Eerdmans, 2002), 20. Italics in original.

14. See Richard Hays, *The Moral Vision of the New Testament: Community, Cross and New Creation* (San Francisco: Harper, 1996), chap. 11.

15. Robert C. Roberts, *Spiritual Emotions: A Psychology of Christian Virtues* (Grand Rapids: Eerdmans, 2007), 139.

16. Bouma-Prediger delineates four types of integration: interdisciplinary, *intra*disciplinary, faith-praxis, and experiential. Our relational approach is intended to demonstrate all four of these. Steve Bouma-Prediger, "The Task of Integration: A Modest Proposal," *Journal of Psychology and Theology* 18 (1990): 21–31.

17. F. LeRon Shults, " 'Holding On' to the Theology-Psychology Relationship: The Underlying Fiduciary Structures of Interdisciplinary Method," *Journal of Psychology and Theology* 25 (1997): 338.

18. 1 Cor. 8:3 TNIV (footnoted rendering).

19. Shults, "Holding On," 329.

20. Al Wolters, "No Longer Queen: The Theological Disciplines and Their Sisters," in *The Bible and the University*, ed. David Lyle Jeffrey and C. Stephen Evans, Scripture and Hermeneutics Series 8 (Grand Rapids: Zondervan, 2007), 79.

21. Steven J. Sandage and F. LeRon Shults, "Christian Spirituality and Transformation: A Relational Integration Model," *Journal of Psychology and Christianity* 26 (2007): 262.

22. Cf. Vanhoozer's discussion on the value of judgments for assessing theological continuity: "Theology . . . is ultimately a matter of right *judgments*, not concepts." Kevin J. Vanhoozer, *The Drama of Doctrine: A Canonical Linguistic Approach to Christian Theology* (Louisville: Westminster John Knox, 2005), 344.

23. Vanhoozer, *Drama of Doctrine*, 343, citing Yeago: "[T]he same judgement can be rendered in a variety of conceptual terms." Cf. David S. Yeago, "The New Testament and the Nicene Dogma," in *The Theological Interpretation of Scripture: Classic and Contemporary Readings*, ed. Stephen E. Fowl (Oxford: Blackwell, 1997), 91.

24. Sandage and Shults, "Relational Integration Model," 262.

25. Steven J. Sandage and Jeannine K. Brown, "Monarchy or Democracy in Relation Integration? A Reply to Porter," *Journal of Psychology and Christianity* 29 (2010): 20–26.

26. This language comes from Ivan Boszormenyi-Nagy and Barbara R. Krasner, *Between Give and Take: A Clinical Guide to Contextual Therapy* (New York: Brunner/Mazel, 1986), 281–312.

27. Wolters, "No Longer Queen," 59–60.

28. Brown, *Scripture as Communication*, 90.

29. Sandage and Shults ("Relational Integration Model," 262) speak of avoiding "hegemonic power relations (i.e., one up/one down forms of relating) between our equally hermeneutical disciplines."

30. We use the capitalized version of the word Other here and throughout to denote the personhood and value of one who is different from us, whose difference might be a source of anxiety yet also a source for our own formation (cf. esp. chap. 11).

Chapter 2 Being and Becoming: A Journey toward Love (*Carla*)

1. In this chapter and the next I use "becoming" and "formation" as synonyms that both refer to the work of God in human lives that leads humans from one way of being to another. I am not referring to formation in a programmatic way.

2. William R. Miller and Janet C'de Baca, *Quantum Change: When Epiphanies and Sudden Insights Transform Ordinary Lives* (New York: Guilford, 2001), 6.

3. Hiebert, "Can We Talk?," 202.

4. William James, *The Varieties of Religious Experience: A Study in Human Nature* (Cambridge, MA: Harvard University Press, 1902).

5. Miller and C'de Baca, *Quantum Change*, 4.

6. Ibid., 35 and 71, respectively.

7. Ibid., 91.

8. For earlier approaches, cf. Erik Erikson, *Identity and the Life Cycle* (New York: W. W. Norton, 1994); Jean Piaget and Barbel Inhelder, *The Psychology of the Child*, 2nd ed. (New York: Basic Books, 2000); Brenda Munsey, *Moral Development, Moral Education, and Kohlberg* (Birmingham, AL: Religious Education Press, 1980); Fowler, *Stages of Faith* and *Becoming Adult, Becoming Christian*.

9. Kegan, *Evolving Self*; Loder, *Logic of the Spirit*; Siegel, *Developing Mind*; Cozolino, *Neuroscience of Human Relationship*.

10. David M. Schnarch, *Resurrecting Sex* (New York: Harper Collins, 2002), 274.

11. David Schnarch, *Passionate Marriage: Keeping Love and Intimacy Alive in Committed Relationship* (New York: Henry Holt, 1997), and F. LeRon Shults and Steven J. Sandage, *Transforming Spirituality: Integrating Psychology and Theology* (Grand Rapids: Baker Academic, 2006).

12. Parker J. Palmer, *The Courage to Teach: Exploring the Inner Landscape of a Teacher's Life* (San Fransisco: Jossey-Bass, 1998).

13. Martin Linsky and Ronald A. Heifetz, *Leadership on the Line: Staying Alive through the Dangers of Leading* (Boston: Harvard Business School Press, 2002).

14. Jay Haley, *Uncommon Therapy: The Psychiatric Techniques of Milton H. Erickson, M.D.* (New York: W. W. Norton, 1993).

15. Parker J. Palmer, *To Know as We Are Known: Education as a Spiritual Journey* (San Francisco: HarperCollins, 1993).

16. Diana Chapman Walsh, *Trustworthy Leadership* (Kalamazoo, MI: Fetzer Institute, 2006), 11.

17. I resonate with the caution against "evangelical behaviorism" raised by Steven Sandage, Mary Jensen, and Daniel Jass in their article "Relational Spirituality and Transformation: Risking Intimacy and Alterity," *Journal of Spiritual Formation & Soul Care* 1:2 (2008): 187, 199. They helpfully remind us that spiritual practices can be motivated by anxiety, fear, or desire for approval rather than by an integrative desire for intimacy with God or connection to one's community. For concise historical and contemporary overviews of spiritual practices, see, for example, Richard J. Foster, *Celebration of Discipline: The Path to Spiritual Growth*, 3rd ed. (San Francisco: HarperSanFrancisco, 1988); *Streams of Living Water:*

Celebrating the Great Traditions of Christian Faith (San Francisco: HarperOne, 2001); *Life with God: Reading the Bible for Spiritual Transformation* (San Francisco: HarperOne, 2008); and Foster's newer work with Gayle D. Beebe, *Longing for God: Seven Paths of Christian Devotion* (Downers Grove, IL: IVP, 2009).

18. Patricia O'Connell Killen and John de Beer, *The Art of Theological Reflection* (New York: Crossroad, 1994).

19. Siegel, *Developing Mind*, 31; *Mindful Brain*, xiv, 129.

20. For the concept of "good enough" caregiving, see D. W. Winnicott, *The Maturational Processes and the Facilitating Environment* (New York: International University Press, 1965). See Siegel, *Mindful Brain*, 204, for the concepts of repair work and earned security.

21. Siegel, *Developing Mind*, 100.

22. Ana-Maria Rizzuto, *The Birth of the Living God* (Chicago: University of Chicago Press, 1980).

23. Siegel, *Developing Mind*, 206.

24. Andrew Sung Park and Susan L. Nelson, *The Other Side of Sin: Woundedness from the Perspective of the Sinned-Against* (Albany: State University of New York Press, 2001); Cynthia S. W. Crysdale, *Embracing Travail: Retrieving the Cross Today* (New York: Continuum, 1999).

25. "Oppression leads to silence, which leads to shame, which leads to rage, which leads to outrage." Kenneth V. Hardy, "Managing Hot Moments: Strategies for Crossing Cultural Boundaries" (presentation, Psychotherapy Networker Symposium, Washington, DC, March 28, 2009), www.iPlaybackNetworker.com.

26. For a more thorough discussion of fundamentalism as a systemic, relational process, see my PhD dissertation: Carla Dahl, "A Phenomenological Exploration of the Definition and Expression of Spirituality within Families" (University of Minnesota, 1994).

27. Judy J. Johnson, *What's So Wrong with Being Absolutely Right: The Dangerous Nature of Dogmatic Belief* (Amherst, NY: Prometheus Books, 2009), 121.

28. Thomas Moore, *Care of the Soul* (New York: HarperCollins, 1992), 236.

29. Identifying characteristics have been changed to protect this family's identity.

30. Martin E. Marty and R. Scott Appleby, eds., *The Fundamentalism Project* (Chicago: University of Chicago Press, 1991–95). Particularly vol. 1, *Fundamentalisms Observed* (1991), and vol. 5, *Fundamentalisms Comprehended* (1995).

31. Miroslav Volf, *Exclusion and Embrace: A Theological Exploration of Identity, Otherness, and Reconciliation* (Nashville: Abingdon Press, 1996), 162–63.

32. Walter Brueggemann, *Interpretation and Obedience* (Minneapolis: Fortress, 1991), 300.

33. Volf, *Exclusion and Embrace*, 159.

34. Ibid., 160.

35. Ibid., 164 (emphasis in the original).

36. Ibid., 164–65.

37. Fyodor Dostoevsky, *The Brothers Karamazov*, trans. Richard Pevear and Larissa Volokhonsky, Everyman's Library (1881; New York: Alfred A. Knopf, 1990), 57.

38. Siegel, *Mindful Brain*, 130.

39. C. S. Lewis, *The Lion, The Witch, and the Wardrobe* (New York: Collier, 1973), 75–76.

Chapter 3 Wholeness and Holiness: Selves in Community with God and Others (*Carla*)

1. Two of the most accessible and innovative interpersonal neurobiologists are Daniel Siegel (*The Developing Mind; The Mindful Brain; Parenting from the Inside Out*) and

Louis Cozolino (*The Healthy Aging Brain: Sustaining Attachment, Attaining Wisdom*; *The Neuroscience of Human Relationships: Attachment and the Developing Social Brain*; *The Neuroscience of Psychotherapy: Building and Rebuilding the Human Brain*).

2. Jack O. Balswick, Pamela Ebstyne King, and Kevin S. Reimer, *The Reciprocating Self: Human Development in Theological Perspective* (Downers Grove, IL: InterVarsity, 2005), 31.

3. Kegan, *Evolving Self*, 108.

4. Siegel, *Mindful Brain*, xiv: "Attunement may lead the brain to grow in ways that promote balanced self-regulation via the process of *neural integration*, which enables flexibility and self-understanding." Siegel describes attunement as a "way of feeling felt, of feeling connected in the world."

5. Desmond Tutu, *The Rainbow People of God: The Making of a Peaceful Revolution* (New York: Doubleday, 1994), 125 (emphasis mine).

6. James Fowler, in *Faithful Change: The Personal and Public Challenges of Postmodern Life* (Nashville: Abingdon, 1996), summarizes in another way a set of "both/ands" that also highlight the relational significance of differentiation and integration as indicators of wholeness and holiness: "Individuated Identity combined with Intimate Connectedness; High Cognitive Operations combined with Emotional Integration; Grounding in a Tradition combined with Preparation for Continuing Change," 234. Balswick, Ebstyne, and Reimer nuance Fowler's understanding vis-à-vis that of Loder:

> For Fowler spiritual transformation is embedded in human development, but for Loder human development is shaped by spiritual transformation. Fowler argues that faith development is dependent on an individual's level of cognitive, moral and psychosocial growth. Loder believes that these aspects of psychological development can be determined by the spiritual transformation brought about through the divine intervention of the Holy Spirit, which brings about radical change in a person's life. In this way the spiritual growth axis acts independently from the rest of human development. (*Reciprocating Self*, 274)

7. Siegel, *Mindful Brain*, 78.

8. Ibid., 199. One of the many joys of reading Siegel is that he is a master of acronyms. COHERENCE, here, thereby becomes its own definition (164–65): connected, open, harmonious, engaged, receptive, emergent, noetic, compassionate, and empathic. Two of my other favorites are COAL (curiosity, openness, acceptance, and love, 15), and NOTO (narrative of the other, 290). I'll leave you to your own adventure of discovering what YODA's SOCK stands for.

9. Ibid., 292.

10. Ibid., 298 (emphasis mine).

11. See, for example, Killen and de Beer, *Art of Theological Reflection*.

12. Siegel, *Mindful Brain*, 301.

13. Family therapist Janine Roberts suggests that the most spacious style of storytelling, what she refers to as an "evolving" style, recognizes that our stories are different at different times in our lives, with changes in emphasis and meaning. Janine Roberts, *Tales and Transformations: Stories in Families and Family Therapy* (New York: Norton, 1994), 13.

14. Siegel, *Mindful Brain*, 309. Additionally, Siegel notes that "attachment studies reveal that one of the best predictors of a child's attachment to a parent [important for our attachment to God, as we saw in chap. 2] is that parent's life story having what is called 'narrative coherence.'"

15. Cozolino, *Healthy Aging Brain*, 266–75.

16. Siegel, *Mindful Brain*, 316.

17. Ibid., 320.

18. Eugene H. Peterson, *Christ Plays in Ten Thousand Places: A Conversation in Spiritual Theology* (Grand Rapids: Eerdmans, 2005), 219.

19. Rizzuto, *Birth of the Living God*.

20. C. S. Lewis, *A Grief Observed* (New York: HarperCollins, 1989), 78.

21. Brueggemann, *Interpretation and Obedience*, 304.

Chapter 4 Reception and Integration of Offerings from Social Science

1. The NT concept of the already *and* not yet of God's restoration also helps in this regard (cf. chap. 5).

2. As we noted in chap. 1, listening for similar judgments between disciplines rather than linguistic duplication can lead to clearer coherence in integration.

3. Walter Brueggemann, *Theology of the Old Testament: Testimony, Dispute, Advocacy* (Minneapolis: Fortress, 1997), 385–99.

4. Sandage, Jensen, and Jass, "Relational Spirituality and Transformation," 182–206. Steve, Mary, and Dan are colleagues of ours (Carla and Jeannine) at Bethel Seminary. It is a pleasure to learn formation from such an able and insightful team of scholars and therapists.

5. Cf. Brown, *Scripture as Communication*, 127, 239–40.

6. It is also the case that some students arrive at Bethel with a significant sense of distance between themselves and Scripture. They need to hear the relational pole of the dialectic. Cf. Brown, *Scripture as Communication*, 241–43.

7. "[A] 'naked' reading of Scripture" is Hart's phraseology. Trevor Hart, "Tradition, Authority, and a Christian Approach to the Bible as Scripture," in *Between Two Horizons: Spanning New Testament Studies and Systematic Theology*, ed. Joel B. Green and Max Turner (Grand Rapids: Eerdmans, 2000), 191.

8. My wonderful colleague and friend Luke Keefer has mentioned in conversation with me on a number of occasions that "there are areas in his/our lives which remain unconverted." We are always being converted. Or at least should be. I address the dangers of seeing "just getting saved" as the end of our formation in "We've a Story to Tell: Which One and Why?" chap. 4 in *Reviving Evangelical Ethics: The Promises and Pitfalls for Classic Models of Morality* (Grand Rapids: Brazos, 2008).

9. www.pbs.org/wgbh/amex/weshallremain.

10. I realize this is a large topic that I cannot fully explore, given the limitations of our project and the purposes of our responses. I do hear this phrase quite a bit, and at a very basic level I wonder *which* Christian values and biblical roots these persons have in mind: humility? charity? nonviolence? nonretaliation? mercy? communal sharing? This phrase more than likely functions as a "sacred canopy" and a means of interpreting and organizing one's desired reality. See Peter Berger's important work in *The Sacred Canopy: Elements of a Sociological Theory of Religion* (Garden City, NY: Doubleday, 1967).

11. I am also reading Miroslav Volf's book *The End of Memory: Remembering Rightly in a Violent World* (Grand Rapids: Eerdmans, 2006). For Volf it is important not just *that* we remember but that we remember *rightly* (both oppressors and oppressed) as part of the struggle for justice.

12. See William Spohn's insights on the "analogical imagination" and Christian ethics in *Go and Do Likewise: Jesus and Ethics* (New York: Continuum, 2006), chap. 3.

13. See Robert Bellah, Richard Madsen, William Sullivan, Ann Swidler, and Steven Tipton, *The Good Society* (New York: Random House, 1991), for an interesting sociological

analysis of how important institutions are in our social lives but how inadequate we are in addressing their moral dimensions because of our commitments to individualism.

14. L. Gregory Jones, "A Thirst for God or Consumer Spirituality? Cultivating Disciplined Practices of Being Engaged by God," *Modern Theology* 13 (January 1997): 3–28.

15. See also Spohn's distinction between authentic and inauthentic spiritualities in *Go and Do Likewise*, 33–42.

16. Sociologists of religion notice the prevalence of this trend in certain segments of American Protestantism. See Robert Bellah, Richard Madsen, William Sullivan, Ann Swidler, and Steven Tipton, *Habits of the Heart: Individualism and Commitment in American Life* (Berkeley: University of California Press, 1985); Wade Clark Roof, *The Spiritual Marketplace: Baby Boomers and the Remaking of American Religion* (Princeton: Princeton University Press, 1999); and Robert Wuthnow, *After Heaven: Spirituality in America since the 1950s* (Princeton: Princeton University Press, 1998), and *The Restructuring of American Religion: Society and Faith after World War II* (Princeton: Princeton University Press, 1988).

17. This question comes from a recent reading of Robert C. Roberts, *Taking the Word to Heart: Self and Others in an Age of Therapies* (Grand Rapids: Eerdmans, 1993).

18. See Mike W. Martin, *From Morality to Mental Health: Virtue and Vice in a Therapeutic Culture* (New York: Oxford University Press, 2006). This is an interesting attempt to bring together criteria for mental health and notions of the good life necessary for human flourishing. Martin attempts to draw closer connections between morality and mental health by appealing to ethicists to take more seriously mental health, and for mental health practitioners to take more seriously morality as a pathway to mental health.

19. See the following works for rich explorations of the relationships between hospitality and generosity: Christine Pohl, *Making Room: Recovering Hospitality as Christian Tradition* (Grand Rapids: Eerdmans, 1999); Elizabeth Newman, *Untamed Hospitality: Welcoming God and Other Strangers* (Grand Rapids: Brazos, 2007); and Amy Oden, ed., *You Welcomed Me: A Sourcebook on Hospitality in Early Christianity* (Nashville: Abingdon, 2001).

Chapter 5 Being and Becoming: The Scriptural Story of Formation (*Jeannine*)

1. For the assumption of a storied coherence, cf. Richard Bauckham, "Reading Scripture as a Coherent Story," in *The Art of Reading Scripture*, ed. Ellen F. Davis and Richard B. Hays (Grand Rapids: Eerdmans, 2003), 39.

2. Michael S. Horton, "Image and Office: Human Person and the Covenant," in *Personal Identity in Theological Perspective*, ed. Richard Lints, Michael S. Horton, and Mark R. Talbot (Grand Rapids: Eerdmans, 2006), 181.

3. Terence E. Fretheim, *God and World in the Old Testament: A Relational Theology of Creation* (Nashville: Abingdon, 2005), 276, cf. 41. Grenz contextualizes the *imago Dei* by noting its subversion of a royal ideology that would claim that the king is the only image bearer of the gods. The writer of Genesis universalizes the *imago Dei* so that it is the human community rather than a chosen individual that reflects the divine image. Stanley Grenz, "The Social God and the Relational Self: Toward a Theology of the *Imago Dei* in the Postmodern Context," in Lints, Horton, and Talbot, *Personal Identity*, 79–80.

4. Horton, "Image and Office," 184.

5. Richard Bauckham, *God and the Crisis of Freedom: Biblical and Contemporary Perspectives* (Louisville: Westminster John Knox, 2002), 174.

6. Fretheim, *God and World*, 9.

7. For the tension inherent in the call to image God without inappropriately desiring godlikeness, see my subsequent chapter.

8. Martin Buber, *I and Thou*, trans. Walter Kaufmann (New York: Charles Scribner's Sons, 1970), 155.

9. John Goldingay, *Old Testament Theology 2: Israel's Faith* (Downers Grove, IL: Inter-Varsity, 2006), 593, citing Prov. 16:20; 29:25 in support.

10. Different readings of 8:2–3 are found in the Greek manuscripts. The one represented here (from TNIV footnote) has very early support and appears to make the most sense of both scribal tendencies in the transmission of the Greek NT and Paul's flow of argument in 1 Cor. 8:1–6, which addresses the issue of eating meat sacrificed to idols in pagan temples.

11. Shults, "Holding On," 338.

12. Joel Marcus, "Idolatry in the New Testament," *Interpretation* 60 (2006): 152–64.

13. Fretheim, *God and World*, 146.

14. Richard Bauckham, *God Crucified: Monotheism and Christology in the New Testament* (Grand Rapids: Eerdmans, 1998), viii.

15. The phrase *en Christō* occurs over eighty times in the Pauline epistles.

16. Anthony C. Thiselton, *The First Epistle to the Corinthians* (Grand Rapids: Eerdmans, 2000), 104.

17. In Paul this participation is not only with Jesus but with all others believers; it is a communal participation (Thiselton, *Corinthians*, 104). For example, the churches Paul ministers among are "in Christ" (e.g., Gal. 1:22; 1 Thess. 2:14). It is, in fact, participation in Christ that enacts Christian unity (Rom. 12:5; Gal. 3:28).

18. I shift in this paragraph and following to using the Hebrew word that is translated as "Christ" as a reminder that the participation Paul speaks of is "in the Messiah," with the focus not on an additional name for Jesus (as if "Christ" were his surname) but on the title that defines, in part, his person and work.

19. This is Marianne Meye Thompson's translation (74); see her discussion of the corporate connection between believers and Adam and Christ in these verses (77–78) in *Colossians and Philemon* (Grand Rapids: Eerdmans, 2005).

20. "Trust" and "loyalty" are two ways of rendering *pistis*, also rendered "faith" in English. I use the former two words here to emphasize the active nature of *pistis*.

21. N. T. Wright, "Romans," in *New Interpreter's Bible* (Nashville: Abingdon, 2002), 10:425.

22. Michael J. Gorman, *Apostle of the Crucified Lord: A Theological Introduction to Paul and His Letters* (Grand Rapids: Eerdmans, 2004), 204.

23. Ibid., 118.

24. N. T. Wright, *The Challenge of Jesus* (Downers Grove, IL: InterVarsity, 1999), 94–95.

25. Grenz, "Social God," 89.

26. Fretheim, *God and World*, 9.

27. David Wilcox, "Someday Soon," *Big Horizon* (New York: A & M Records, 1994).

28. For the believer and the believing community, bodily resurrection (1 Cor. 15:20–22) and final vindication and honor (Matt. 13:43) are still to come.

29. These themes arise more implicitly from the biblical story just traced. They also are prominent in OT wisdom literature as a corpus, which focuses on the practice of living with God in godly ways.

30. Earlier in the chapter, I sketched a picture of Jesus's faithfulness and trust in his God as the power and pattern for believers' own trust (dependence) and covenant loyalty.

31. "The rhythm of grace and thanksgiving—God's rich goodness, people's glad response—goes on and on, to the glory of God." N. T. Wright, *Reflecting the Glory: Meditations for Living Christ's Life in the World* (Minneapolis: Augsburg, 1998), 36.

Chapter 6 Wholeness and Holiness: Toward Communal Fullness of Life (*Jeannine*)

1. Hannah K. Harrington, *Holiness: Rabbinic Judaism and the Graeco-Roman World* (London: Routledge, 2001), 29.

2. Lints helpfully notes that, though the language of imaging God is infrequent throughout the OT, the concept is present: "That to which the language of the *imago dei* points is most definitely present across the breadth of the canon though the particular language itself changes . . . at the point where the language of 'imaging' drops out, the language of idolatry becomes prominent." Richard Lints, "Imaging and Idolatry: The Sociality of Personhood in the Canon," in Lints, Horton, and Talbot, *Personal Identity*, 215.

3. Ryan Schellenberg and Timothy J. Geddert, "Phinehas and the Pharisees: Identity and Tolerance in Biblical Perspective," *Direction* 24 (Fall 2005): 171.

4. Christopher J. H. Wright, *The Mission of God: Unlocking the Bible's Grand Narrative* (Downers Grove, IL: InterVarsity, 2006), 164. For the generalization of the concept of idolatry to include (all) other sins, see Marcus, "Idolatry in the New Testament."

5. Harrington, *Holiness*, 16. Harrington works extensively with rabbinic sources on the topic of holiness.

6. Wright, *Mission of God*, 172.

7. Walter Brueggemann, *The Word That Redescribes the World: The Bible and Discipleship*, ed. Patrick D. Miller (Minneapolis: Fortress, 2006), 148.

8. Peter T. Vogt, "Social Justice and the Vision of Deuteronomy," *JETS* 51 (2008): 35–44.

9. For this discussion, see Gordon J. Wenham, *The Book of Leviticus* (Grand Rapids: Eerdmans, 1979), 18–25.

10. Peter T. Vogt, *Interpreting the Pentateuch: An Exegetical Guidebook* (Grand Rapids: Kregel, 2009), 83, where Vogt comments that "[t]he purity regulations are, at least in part, culturally appropriate object lessons intended to remind the Israelites of the order that exists in the world and their role in it."

11. See my discussion of this theme in the previous chapter in "Implications for Human Formation."

12. All the while remaining Gentiles, rather than converting to Judaism.

13. Robert W. Wall, "Reading Paul with Acts: The Canonical Shaping of a Holy Church," in *Holiness and Ecclesiology in the New Testament*, ed. Kent E. Brower and Andy Johnson (Grand Rapids: Eerdmans, 2007), 138.

14. Stephen C. Barton, "Dislocating and Relocating Holiness: A New Testament Study," in *Holiness Past and Present*, ed. Stephen C. Barton (New York: T&T Clark, 2003), 198.

15. With the focus being on God's presence in the tabernacle (Exodus 40) and then the temple (2 Kings 8; Ezekiel). Barton speaks of four spheres of Israel's life that were holy because of God's presence in and with them: the people, the land, the temple, and the Torah ("Dislocating and Relocating Holiness," 196).

16. NT writers also attribute this sanctifying work to God (1 Thess. 5:23) and to Jesus (Heb. 2:11). For God's sanctifying work in Israel, see Deut. 30:6.

17. We do not, however, have any unambiguous NT evidence that *Jewish believers* in Jesus disregarded Torah regulations in their own practices. Instead, the tension in such NT books as Galatians and Acts arises from pressure by Jewish believers in Jesus for Gentiles to convert to Judaism as they entered the church. The messages of Acts and Galatians affirm that Gentiles are not required to convert to Judaism to be full participants in the renewed people of God (cf. Acts 10–11, 15; Gal. 2:14–4:20).

18. Barton's term, in "Dislocating and Relocating Holiness," 208.

19. Michael J. Gorman, "'You Shall Be Cruciform for I Am Cruciform': Paul's Trinitarian Reconstruction for Holiness," in Brower and Johnson, *Holiness and Ecclesiology in the New Testament*, 155.

20. "Holiness refers to the primary relationship that God has initiated with his people." Paul S. Minear, "The Holy and the Sacred," *Theology Today* 47 (1990–91): 6.

21. Vogt, *Interpreting the Pentateuch*, 11–15.

22. Brueggemann, *The Word*, 151.

23. Schellenberg and Geddart, "Phinehas and the Pharisees," 175.

24. James K. Bruckner, "A Theological Description of Human Wholeness in Deuteronomy 6," *Ex Auditu* 21 (2005): 14.

25. Harrington, *Holiness*, 39. Douglas's work ties purity in the levitical system to wholeness and completeness, order and integrity. Mary Douglas, *Purity and Danger: An Analysis of Concept of Pollution and Taboo* (New York: Routledge, 2002), 63–71.

26. Schellenberg and Geddart, "Phinehas and the Pharisees," 175.

27. For an extended look at this Johannine theme, see Jeannine K. Brown, "Creation's Renewal in the Gospel of John," *CBQ* 72 (April, 2010): 275–90.

28. Given the prominence of Isaiah 42 here in Matthew, it is likely that an allusion to Isa. 42:1 can also be heard in God's commendation of Jesus at his baptism and transfiguration (3:17 and 17:5, respectively). See Jeannine K. Brown, "Matthew," in *Evangelical One-Volume Commentary on the Bible*. Rev. Ed. Edited by Andrew E. Hill and Gary M. Burge (Grand Rapids: Baker Academic, forthcoming).

29. The term translated "wholeheartedly" in these occurrences is *maleh*. In other occurrences this idea of wholeheartedness is communicated with the two words *kol* + *leb* ("whole" + "heart"; e.g., 1 Kings 8:23). As indicated earlier, there is no simple correspondence of language to concept when addressing the biblical notion of wholeness.

30. Hebrew: *yachad lebab*. Cf. Bruckner for the OT idea that a "healthy heart-mind is not divided" ("Human Wholeness," 6).

31. T. J. Geddert, "Peace," in *The Dictionary of Jesus and the Gospels* (Downers Grove, IL: InterVarsity, 1992), 604.

32. The rendering of *tsedaqah* as "well-being" in the TNIV indicates this relationship to the concept of *shalom* as wholeness.

33. Von Rad, *TDNT*, 2:403.

34. Nicholas Wolterstorff, *Until Justice and Peace Embrace* (Grand Rapids: Eerdmans, 1983), 70.

35. Bruckner broadly defines *shalom* as "well-being or health" ("Human Wholeness," 3). For a NT vision of communal wholeness, see Matthew's Beatitudes (5:3–10), which include blessings upon "peacemakers" (5:9) and "those who are persecuted because of [their commitment to] justice" (5:10; my translation). Mark Allan Powell, "Matthew's Beatitudes: Reversals and Rewards of the Kingdom," *CBQ* 58 (1996): 460–79.

36. As Bruckner notes, "The Shema encapsulated the whole-life relationship of Israel before the Creator" ("Human Wholeness," 4).

37. In James 1:4, *teleios* is defined by *holoklēros* and the phrase "not lacking anything."

38. William D. Mounce, ed., *Mounce's Complete Expository Dictionary of Old and New Testament Words* (Grand Rapids: Zondervan, 2006), 213. Mounce continues, "The notion of 'perfection' in contemporary English conveys the idea of 'sinlessness' but *teleios* refers to 'completion' without reference to fault or sin."

39. Bruckner describes the OT concept of blamelessness as "undivided loyalty" ("Human Wholeness," 9).

40. Wenham, *Book of Leviticus*, 22.

41. Brueggemann, *The Word*, 152.

Chapter 7 Reception and Integration of Offerings from Hermeneutics

1. Parker Palmer, *Let Your Life Speak* (San Francisco: Jossey Bass, 2000), 34.

2. Ezra Stotland, *The Psychology of Hope* (San Francisco: Jossey Bass, 1969), 15.

3. See, for example, C. R. Snyder, *The Psychology of Hope* (New York: Free Press, 1994).

4. Rose Mary Dougherty, *Group Spiritual Direction: Community for Discernment* (Mahwah, NJ: Paulist Press, 1995), 25.

5. I am using this word in a similar fashion to our earlier description that draws on the work of Geertz and Brueggemann (see chap. 1, n. 1).

6. Verhey, *Remembering Jesus*, 66–71. According to Verhey, reading Scripture becomes a moral practice when we pair three virtues in our reading: holiness and sanctification, fidelity and creativity, and discipline and discernment.

7. See the following select sources: Nancey Murphy, Brad Kallenberg, and Mark Thiessen Nation, eds., *Virtues and Practices in the Christian Tradition: Christian Ethics after MacIntyre* (Notre Dame, IN: University of Notre Dame Press, 1997); Samuel Wells, *Improvisation: The Drama of Christian Ethics* (Grand Rapids: Brazos, 2004); Stanley Hauerwas and Samuel Wells, eds., *The Blackwell Companion to Christian Ethics* (Malden, MA: Blackwell, 2004); and Stephen Fowl and L. Gregory Jones, *Reading in Communion: Scripture and Ethics in Christian Life* (Grand Rapids: Eerdmans, 1991).

8. There are degrees of discomfort in acknowledging how important discernment is in ethical reflection and action, especially in theological contexts where ethics is very rule driven and principle based. In these contexts what we should do is clear and no discernment is needed. It is one thing to claim a moral absolute or some kind of universal moral principle; it is quite another to know how to bring this moral claim to bear on complex problems and in diverse contexts. Discernment enables us to do this, to know not just what to do but *how* to do it in light of what is "fitting to the Gospel." See Verhey, *Remembering Jesus*, 20.

9. See Cynthia S. W. Crysdale, *Embracing Travail: Retrieving the Cross Today* (New York: Continuum, 1999), 121:

> A personal faith or a tradition that seeks to cling with certainty to its ideas about God, or to its prescriptions about how to know God, risks idolatry of the worst sort. Idolatry is, at its root, not worship of images, but taking what is tangible and finite and giving it ultimacy and transcendence. Even iconoclasm, which intends to root out idols, can become idolatrous by clinging with certitude to its path to God. The temptation to contain God in this way is ever present in Christian life. The only antidote for such a danger is to embrace the ambiguity and unpredictability of waiting for the insights that open the door to transformative decisions while trusting God's grace to bring them about.

Chapter 8 Being and Becoming: The Trinity and Our Formation (*Wyndy*)

1. Geertz, *Interpretation of Cultures*, 14.

2. Stanley J. Grenz, *Theology for the Community of God* (Grand Rapids: Eerdmans, 2000), 7.

3. See *The Documents of the Christian Church*, ed. Henry Bettenson, 2nd ed. (Oxford: Oxford University Press, 1964), 23–26, 51–52.

4. F. LeRon Shults, *Reforming Theological Anthropology: After the Philosophical Turn to Relationality* (Grand Rapids: Eerdmans, 2003).

5. The works are numerous, but my thinking has been particularly shaped by the following: Ray S. Anderson, *On Being Human: Essays in Theological Anthropology* (Grand Rapids: Eerdmans, 1982); Leonardo Boff, *Trinity and Society* (Maryknoll, NY: Orbis Books, 1988); Douglas Campbell, ed., *Gospel and Gender: A Trinitarian Engagement with Being Male and Female in Christ* (London: T&T Clark, 2003); David Cunningham, *These Three Are One:*

The Practice of Trinitarian Theology (Malden, MA: Blackwell, 1988); Stanley J. Grenz, *The Social God and the Relational Self: A Trinitarian Theology of the Imago Dei* (Louisville: Westminster John Knox Press, 2001); Michele A. Gonzalez, *Created in God's Image: An Introduction to Feminist Theological Anthropology* (Maryknoll, NY: Orbis Books, 2007); Catherine Mowry LaCugna, *God for Us: The Trinity and Christian Life* (New York: HarperSanFrancisco, 1991); Alistair L. McFadyen, *The Call to Personhood: A Christian Theory of the Individual in Social Relationships* (Cambridge, MA: Cambridge University Press, 1990); Shults, *Reforming Theological Anthropology*; Tom Smail, *Like Father, Like Son: The Trinity Imaged in Our Humanity* (Grand Rapids: Eerdmans, 2005); Miroslav Volf, *After Our Likeness: The Church as the Image of the Trinity* (Grand Rapids: Eerdmans, 1998); and Miroslav Volf and Michael Welker, eds., *God's Life in Trinity* (Minneapolis: Fortress Press, 2006).

6. Linda Woodhead, "God, Gender and Identity," in Campbell, *Gospel and Gender*, 95.

7. I refer to Reinhold Niebuhr's "Christian realism," and his articulation of sin as the desire to overcome our limitations and finitude because of anxiety about our creaturely existence, which produces various forms of pride. See Reinhold Niebuhr, *The Nature and Destiny of Man* (New York: Charles Scribner's Sons, 1943), 178–79. Even though Niebuhr also identified sensuality as sin (the underestimation of our value as image bearers), his work has received appropriate critiques from feminist theologians for an overemphasis on pride as the primary manifestation of sin, which may not be reflective of women's experiences. See the following: Judith Plaskow, *Sex, Sin and Grace: Women's Experiences in the Theologies of Reinhold Niebuhr and Paul Tillich* (Washington, DC: University Press of America, 1980); Beverly Wildung Harrison, "Keeping Faith in a Sexist Church," in *Making the Connections* (Boston: Beacon Press, 1985); Barbara Hilkert Andolsen, "Agape in Feminist Ethics," in *Feminist Theological Ethics* (Louisville: Westminster John Knox Press, 1994); and Carol Lakey Hess, *Caretakers of Our Common House: Women's Development in Communities of Faith* (Nashville: Abingdon Press, 1997).

8. See David Gushee, *Only Human: Christian Reflections on the Journey Toward Wholeness* (San Francisco: Jossey-Bass, 2005).

9. Paul J. Wadell, *Happiness and the Christian Life: An Introduction to Christian Ethics* (Lanham, MD: Rowman & Littlefield, 2008), 75.

10. Being schooled in bioethics is important for pastors in providing leadership and moral guidance to congregations because of the pervasive influence of medical technologies on our decisions about life. The following sources are important references for pastors: Lisa Sowle Cahill, *Theological Bioethics: Participation, Justice and Change* (Washington, DC: Georgetown University Press, 2005); Amy Laura Hall, *Conceiving Parenthood: American Protestantism and the Spirit of Reproduction* (Grand Rapids: Eerdmans, 2007); Gilbert Meilaender, *Bioethics: A Primer for Christians* (Grand Rapids: Eerdmans, 1996); C. Ben Mitchell, Edmund D. Pellegrino, Jean Bethke Elshtain, and John Frederic Kilner, eds., *Biotechnology and the Human Good* (Washington, DC: Georgetown University Press, 2007); and Allen Verhey, *Reading the Bible in the Strange World of Medicine* (Grand Rapids: Eerdmans, 2003).

11. See Volf, *After Our Likeness*.

12. See chap. 6, "Truly Human, Truly Divine," in William C. Placher, *A History of Christian Theology: An Introduction* (Louisville: Westminster John Knox Press, 1983), for a good historical overview and analysis of these debates.

13. This term refers to Constantine's "conversion" to Christianity in 313, resulting in the establishment of Christianity as the religion of the Roman Empire.

14. The main threats to Christology (and hence to Trinitarianism) were Arianism, Apollinarianism, Nestorianism, and Monophysitism, which were all condemned as heretical by church councils, solidified in the Fourth Ecumenical Council at Chalcedon in 451.

15. Kathryn Tanner, *Jesus, Humanity and the Trinity: A Brief Systematic Theology* (Minneapolis: Fortress Press, 1991), 40.

16. See Karen Baker-Fletcher, *Dancing with God: The Trinity from a Womanist Perspective* (St. Louis: Chalice Press, 2006).

17. LaCugna, *God for Us*, 270–71.

18. Alister E. McGrath, *Christian Theology: An Introduction*, 4th ed. (Malden, MA: Blackwell, 2007), 251.

19. LaCugna, *God for Us*, 273.

20. Volf, *After Our Likeness*, 211 (emphasis in original).

21. These implications are the subject of chap. 10.

22. Smail, *Like Father, Like Son*, 41.

23. Arthur J. Dyck, *Rethinking Rights and Responsibilities: The Moral Bonds of Community*, rev. ed. (Washington, DC: Georgetown University Press, 2005).

24. Ibid., 84.

25. I appreciate the recovery of communal language to describe God and our humanity and to ground our obligations to other persons. However, it is important to note that communities can also cause incredible harm to persons. This is an important critique made by feminists. Communities must also be porous and open enough to allow for internal moral critique and for other perspectives to be shared, respected, and appropriated. See Gloria Albrecht, *The Character of Our Communities* (Nashville: Abingdon Press, 1995).

26. See Volf, *Exclusion and Embrace*, 64–68. Volf expands on the idea of sin from Cornelius Plantinga Jr.'s book, *Not the Way It's Supposed to Be: A Breviary of Sin* (Grand Rapids: Eerdmans, 1995). Sin is the failure to bind and separate, which disrupts interdependent human relationships. The result is assimilation (the failure to separate) and sovereign independence (the failure to bind), which become the basis for exclusion, oppression, and injustice.

27. Woodhead, "God, Gender and Identity," 94.

28. Tanner, *Jesus, Humanity and the Trinity*, 82.

29. Smail, *Like Father, Like Son*, 145–46.

30. Richard Bondi, "The Elements of Character," *Journal of Religious Ethics* 12 (Fall 1984): 204.

31. See chap. 4, "The Social Formation of Persons," in McFayden, *Call to Personhood*.

32. See the important work by Mary Stewart Van Leeuwen, *Gender and Grace: Love, Work and Parenting in a Changing World* (Downers Grove, IL: InterVarsity, 1990).

33. I appreciate, with some reservations, the contributions of Carol Gilligan in *A Different Voice: Psychological Theory and Women's Development* (Cambridge, MA: Harvard University Press, 1993), and Nel Noddings in *Caring: A Feminine Approach to Ethics and Moral Education* (Berkeley: University of California Press, 1984). While they offer important criteria of care and responsibility as moral norms, I am concerned about the ways in which their proposals rely on an essentialist understanding of gender that assumes women, *because we are women*, are more inclined to care for and attend to the needs of others. This may exacerbate the expectations of self-sacrifice and self-giving of women *because* we are women. I do think care and responsibility are important moral norms for all *humans* because we exist, and become, fundamentally in relationships.

34. Miroslav Volf, "The Trinity and Gender Identity," in Campbell, *Gospel and Gender*, 170.

35. Even though Jesus was male, his life is normative for both women and men in Christian community. If we subject Jesus to these rigid gender ideologies, then we may have to concede that Jesus exhibits traits, such as weeping, care for the weak, teaching and nurturing children, nurturing disciples, and depending on God and others, that we often assign to women. It is also ironic that many typify and paradigmize David as the "man after God's own heart" and the icon of (male) Christian leadership when certain aspects of David's life—his adultery, premeditated murder, and other violence—fractured family relationships. All these characteristics are morally problematic, to say the least. How is David normative for maleness and Christian leadership given the iconic place he occupies?

36. Mary Catherine Hilkert, "Cry Beloved Image," in *In the Embrace of God: Feminist Approaches to Theological Anthropology*, ed. Ann O'Hara Graff (Maryknoll, NY: Orbis Books, 1995), 196.

37. Ibid., 199.

38. Ibid., 200.

39. Nicholas Wolterstorff, "Is There Justice in the Trinity?" in Volf and Welker, *God's Life in Trinity*, 187.

40. Tom Smail, *Like Father, Like Son*, 157–58.

41. Tanner, *Jesus, Humanity and the Trinity*, 64.

42. Ibid., 80.

Chapter 9 Wholeness and Holiness: Christian Moral Formation (*Wyndy*)

1. Paul Wadell, *Happiness and the Christian Moral Life: An Introduction to Christian Ethics* (Lanham, MD: Rowman & Littlefield, 2008), 3.

2. See the helpful definition of Christian practices offered by Craig Dykstra and Dorothy Bass as "things Christian people do together over time to address fundamental human needs in response to and in light of God's active presence for the life of the world," in "A Theological Understanding of Christian Practices," in *Practicing Theology: Beliefs and Practices in Christian Life*, ed. Miroslav Volf and Dorothy C. Bass (Grand Rapids: Eerdmans, 1998), 18.

3. See the discussion on the differences between a morality of obligation and a morality of happiness by William C. Mattison III, in *Introducing Moral Theology: True Happiness and the Virtues* (Grand Rapids: Brazos, 2008), 24–28.

4. The main purpose of my proposal is to offer elements of the Christian moral life that are often overlooked in theological debates about perceptions of God's sovereignty and how this may or may not limit human choice, or perceptions that we just need to let the Holy Spirit transform us. Of course, I assume God is active in the formation of our lives and actively involved in the world. My hope is to recover an element I find missing in much of Protestant ethics, that of our own humanity and the degrees of power we do have over the kinds of lives we choose to live.

5. Alasdair MacIntyre, *After Virtue* (Notre Dame, IN: Notre Dame University Press, 1984), 148.

6. John Kekes, *The Examined Life* (University Park: Pennsylvania State University Press, 1988), 162.

7. William Spohn suggests that perception is a function of moral character, indicative of our willingness to have our perceptions changed by conversion and seeing more rightly. See chap. 5, "Correcting Perception," in *Go and Do Likewise: Jesus and Ethics* (New York: Continuum, 2006).

8. Wadell, *Happiness and the Christian Moral Life*, 45–46.

9. Ibid., 37.

10. D. Stephen Long, *The Goodness of God: Theology, the Church, and Social Order* (Grand Rapids: Brazos, 2001), 22–23.

11. See the rich trinitarian description of Christian ethics provided by Dennis Hollinger in his book *Choosing the Good: Christian Ethics in a Complex World* (Grand Rapids: Baker Academic, 2002), 64–69.

12. Tanner, *Jesus, Humanity and the Trinity*, 71.

13. Matt 22:37. Mark O'Keefe, *Becoming Good, Becoming Holy: On the Relationship of Christian Ethics and Spirituality* (Mahwah, NJ: Paulist Press, 1995), 47 (emphasis mine).

14. Long, *Goodness of God*, 24 (emphasis mine). See also chap. 5, "Sanctification and the Ethics of Character," in Stanley Hauerwas, *Character and the Christian Life: A Study in Theological Ethics* (Notre Dame, IN: University of Notre Dame Press, 1994), for a helpful description of the relationships between justification, sanctification, and the formation of character.

15. See my analysis of Christian virtues in *Reviving Evangelical Ethics*, 120–23.

16. John Kekes, *Examined Life*, 162.

17. Corbin Reuschling, *Reviving Evangelical Ethics*, 22.

18. See Vigen Gurorian, *Incarnate Love: Essays in Orthodox Ethics* (Notre Dame, IN: University of Notre Dame Press, 1987), 13–17.

19. O'Keefe, *Becoming Good, Becoming Holy*, 63.

20. Ibid., 63.

21. Ibid., 64.

22. Samuel M. Powell, *A Theology of Christian Spirituality* (Nashville: Abingdon Press, 2005), 169.

23. Catherine LaCugna, "The Trinity," in *Freeing Theology: The Essentials of Theology in Feminist Perspective*, ed. Catherine LaCugna (New York: HarperCollins, 1993), 83–84.

24. Gorman, "'You Shall Be Cruciform.'"

25. Ibid., 161 (emphasis in original).

26. Ibid., 166.

27. Miroslav Volf, "Being as God Is: Trinity and Generosity," in Volf and Welker, *God's Life in Trinity*, 7. See also Miroslav Volf, *Free of Charge: Giving and Forgiving in a Culture Stripped of Grace* (Grand Rapids: Zondervan, 2005).

28. Volf, *Free of Charge*, 28.

29. Powell, *Theology of Christian Spirituality*, 172.

30. Dave Toycen, *The Power of Generosity: How to Transform Yourself and Your World* (Toronto: HarperCollins, 2004), 4.

31. Roberts, *Spiritual Emotions*, 139.

32. Volf, *Free of Charge*, 43.

33. Dykstra and Bass, "Theological Understanding of Christian Practices," 18.

34. Volf, *Free of Charge*, 68–69 (emphasis original).

35. According to William Mattison, generosity is a subvirtue of justice, which is one of the four cardinal virtues along with temperance, prudence, and fortitude. I do think generosity and justice are related, as are all the virtues necessary for becoming whole and holy. But unlike Mattison I do not see generosity as a subset, nor do I see the objects of virtues as "innerworldly activities." I see the virtues as social practices as well as intrinsic goods that are being formed as they form us. See *Introducing Moral Theology*, 65–66.

36. Corbin Reuschling, *Reviving Evangelical Ethics*, 132.

37. Walter J. Burghardt, "To Be Holy Is to Be Just," *Living Pulpit* 10 (July 2001): 4–5.

38. Jim Wallis, *The Soul of Politics* (Maryknoll, NY: Orbis Books, 1994), 73.
39. Burghardt, "To Be Holy Is to Be Just," 4.

Chapter 10 Reception and Integration of Offerings from Ethics

1. For example, Elihu's speech in Job 36:1–12.
2. Volf, *After Our Likeness*, 211.
3. Charles Horton Cooley, *Human Nature and the Social Order* (New York: Scribners, 1902).
4. Richard Perkins, *Looking Both Ways: Exploring the Interface Between Christianity and Society* (Grand Rapids: Baker, 987), 84n8.
5. Horton, "Image and Office," 181.
6. We will need to listen for similar or differing judgments rather than simply assuming that linguistic uniformity indicates conceptual uniformity; see chap. 1.
7. The connections are clear, although this text is "binitarian" (Hurtado's language) rather than trinitarian explicitly. Larry W. Hurtado, *Lord Jesus Christ: Devotion to Jesus in Earliest Christianity* (Grand Rapids: Eerdmans, 2003), 151–53.
8. Dan R. Stiver, *Theology after Ricoeur: New Directions in Hermeneutical Theology* (Louisville: Westminster John Knox Press, 2001), 175 (emphasis mine).

Chapter 11 Interface: An Integrative Conversation around Immigration

1. See chaps. 1 and 4 for discussions around the equal, though not identical, contributions of social science, ethics, and hermeneutics.
2. See chap. 1. The current chapter developed as a series of e-mail conversations on the topic of immigration, so we suggest it be read as such rather than as a script of a live conversation. As with any reading, genre expectations are important.
3. See two recent works on immigration that provide important resources for helping us think about this issue from the perspective of Christian faith: M. Daniel Carroll R., *Christians at the Border: Immigration, the Church, and the Bible* (Grand Rapids: Baker Academic, 2008), and Matthew Soerens and Jenny Hwang, *Welcoming the Stranger: Justice, Compassion and Truth in the Immigration Debate* (Downers Grove, IL: InterVarsity, 2009).
4. If we recount our own personal histories, we realize that many of us come from immigrant groups (Irish, Germans, Chinese, Japanese, Italians, etc.) who were treated with great hostility in the eighteenth and nineteenth centuries by those already here, since they were perceived as threats, different, even crass, and of lower classes.
5. It is important to remember that people emigrate or migrate ("to move from one country to another" and take up residence in lands to which they are not native) for a variety of reasons: job opportunities and employment, political or religious asylum, education, marriage, escape from oppressive regimes and countries that fail to sustain human well-being, natural disasters, and catastrophes. There is no one category that explains the myriad reasons why people immigrate, and there are laws that govern immigration and make provision for people to immigrate to this country for these various reasons. The typical focus in current U.S. discussions of immigration is on illegal or undocumented immigration. In these conversations the concerns can take on a decidedly racist tone since the ire is directed at people illegally immigrating from countries south of the United States.
6. What does this response say about our humanity, our sense of being and becoming? Are there more "whole and holy" ways of responding to the issue of immigration, as well as other issues, that are more integrative in our approach to Scripture, formation, and our moral capacities?

7. For descriptions of this process, see Lois Lindbloom, *Prayerful Listening: Cultivating Discernment in Community* (self-published, 2007); Dougherty, *Group Spiritual Direction*; and Killen and de Beer, *Art of Theological Reflection*.

8. Dougherty, *Group Spiritual Direction*, 21.

9. Killen and de Beer, *Art of Theological Reflection*, 51.

10. This is the often-cited phrase used by feminist theologian Nelle Morton, *The Journey Is Home* (Boston: Beacon Press, 1985), 204–5, for deep, attentive listening that enables the speaker to find a way to say what he or she had perhaps been unable to say or was unaware of needing to say.

11. Ana-Maria Rizzuto, Untitled Presentation to Marriage and Family Therapy students and faculty, Bethel University, April 16, 2010.

12. Lindbloom, *Prayerful Listening*.

13. Benny Tat Siong-Liew, "Acts," in *Global Bible Commentary*, ed. Daniel Patte (Nashville: Abingdon, 2004), 421.

14. Milton J. Bennett, "From Ethnocentrism to Ethnorelativism," in *Toward Multiculturalism: A Reader in Multicultural Education*, ed. J. S. Wurzel (Newton, MA: Intercultural Resource Corporation, 2004).

15. Kegan, *In Over Our Heads*, 232.

16. I think here of the poem "Patient Trust," by Teilhard de Chardin, which begins "Trust in the slow work of God," in *Hearts on Fire: Praying with Jesuits* (Chicago: Loyola Press, 2005).

17. William J. Goode, "Why Men Don't Resist," in *Rethinking the Family: Some Feminist Questions*, ed. Barrie Thorne and Marilyn Yalom (Boston: Northeastern University Press, 1992).

18. Nathan Hatch, *The Democratization of American Christianity* (New Haven, CT: Yale University Press, 1989).

19. When a group in an ethics class was presenting on Christian responses to immigration, we invited a student's colleague to attend who works with migrant workers in western Ohio. She is a United Methodist clergy originally from Mexico. The first insight she offered was the power of language, encouraging us to use the language of "undocumented workers" instead of "illegal immigrants." This shift in language is an important part of toning down the caustic rhetoric that often surrounds this issue.

20. Volf, *Exclusion and Embrace*, chap. 2.

21. Parker Palmer, *The Company of Strangers: Christians and the Renewal of America's Public Life* (New York: Crossroad, 1981), 68.

22. Ibid., 70.

23. Ibid.

INDEX

Made in the USA
Las Vegas, NV
18 January 2024

84542798R00132